Attracting the Heart

Topics in Contemporary Buddhism
GEORGE J. TANABE, JR., EDITOR

Establishing a Pure Land on Earth: The Foguang Buddhist Perspective on Modernization and Globalization
STUART CHANDLER

Buddhist Missionaries in the Era of Globalization
LINDA LEARMAN, EDITOR

Being Benevolence: The Social Ethics of Engaged Buddhism
SALLIE B. KING

Japanese Temple Buddhism: Worldliness in a Religion of Renunciation
STEPHEN G. COVELL

Zen in Brazil: Quest for Cosmopolitan Modernity
CRISTINA ROCHA

Land of Beautiful Vision: Making a Buddhist Sacred Place in New Zealand
SALLY MCARA

Attracting the Heart: Social Relations and the Aesthetics of Emotion in Sri Lankan Monastic Culture
JEFFREY SAMUELS

TOPICS IN
CONTEMPORARY
BUDDHISM

ATTRACTING THE HEART

Social Relations and the Aesthetics of Emotion in Sri Lankan Monastic Culture

JEFFREY SAMUELS

University of Hawai'i Press
Honolulu

Printed in the United States of America
15 14 13 12 11 10 6 5 4 3 2 1

Library of Congress Cataloging-in-Publication Data
Samuels, Jeffrey.
Attracting the heart : social relations and the aesthetics of emotion in Sri Lankan monastic culture / Jeffrey Samuels.
p. cm. — (Topics in contemporary Buddhism)
Includes bibliographical references and index.
ISBN 978-0-8248-3385-5 (hardcover : alk. paper)
1. Monastic and religious life (Buddhism)—Sri Lanka. 2. Buddhist sanghas—Social aspects—Sri Lanka. 3. Buddhist monks—Sri Lanka—Social life and customs. 4. Aesthetics—Religious aspects—Buddhism. 5. Emotions—Religious aspects—Buddhism. I. Title. II. Series: Topics in contemporary Buddhism.
BQ6160.S72S25 2010
294.3'657095493—dc22

2009052099

University of Hawai'i Press books are printed on acid-free paper and meet the guidelines for permanence and durability of the Council on Library Resources.

Designed by the University of Hawai'i Production Staff
Printed by Edwards Brothers, Inc.

I dedicate this book to Venerable Mangala, teacher and friend,
and
to my family: Benedicte, Claire, and Zach

Contents

Series Editor's Preface

An idealized and simple view of the lifestyle of a Buddhist monk might be described according to the doctrinal demand for emotional detachment and, ultimately, the cessation of all desire and yet monks must also practice compassion, a powerful emotion and equally lofty ideal, and live with every other human feeling—love, hate, jealousy, ambition—as they relate to other monks and the lay community. Drawing on extensive fieldwork in Sri Lanka, Jeffrey Samuels examines the intricate complexities of affective relations in the individual and communal lives of monks and their patrons and argues for an "aesthetics of emotion" in the rich social lives of monks and the emotional appeal of their monastic lives.

The books in this series have examined Buddhism in many places—Brazil, New Zealand, Japan, Taiwan—and in this volume, Samuels takes us to Sri Lanka and allows us to glimpse into spaces of the heart.

George J. Tanabe, Jr.
SERIES EDITOR

Acknowledgments

As I think about all the people who have helped me over the years and wonder how I could ever repay them, the concluding paragraph from Elizabeth Gilbert's *Eat, Pray, Love* (2007:334) comes to mind: "In the end, though, maybe we must all give up trying to pay back the people in this world who sustain our lives. In the end, maybe it's wiser to surrender before the miraculous scope of human generosity and to just keep saying thank you, forever and sincerely, for as long as we have voices." I have and will continue to say thank you, vocally, to all of those who have sustained me both intellectually and emotionally over the years. Here, however, I want to say it more formally, using paper and ink.

First, I would like to express thanks to my teachers, colleagues, and friends who have provided me with much encouragement while gently pressing me to think in new directions and with greater clarity: Glenn Benest, Stephen Berkwitz, Thomas Borchert, Kate Crosby, Charles Hallisey, Anne Hansen, Daniel Kent, Karen Lang, Hun Lye, Justin McDaniel, and Jonathan Walters. Sections of this book were presented at conferences and universities, and I appreciate the numerous comments and suggestions I received. I am also grateful to Selina Langford at the Interlibrary Loan office at Western Kentucky University, as well as the staff at the British Library, the National Archives in Colombo, the National Library in Colombo, Upali Newspapers Group, Lake House Printers, and the libraries at Peradeniya University, International Centre for Ethnic Studies, University of Cambridge, University of Colombo, and the School of Oriental and African Studies, for granting me access to their collections. I am especially grateful to the advice and support I received from my colleague and friend Anne M. Blackburn over the years. Her untiring commitment to learning, as well as her insights and wisdom, have been a tremendous inspiration to my own work and career.

During a year spent in England, I owe much to my uncles, aunts, and cousins, particularly Deborah Isaac, who read through the entire manuscript and offered helpful suggestions. Kate Crosby was also very generous with her time and ideas; I thank her for that as well as for arranging a research associate position for me at the School of Oriental and African Studies. I am also appreciative to the Faculty of Oriental Studies at the University of Cambridge for the one-year visiting scholar appointment.

Closer to home, I am grateful to my colleagues at Western Kentucky University for their support, especially my department head and friend, Eric Bain-Selbo, for reading through several chapters and always being open to sharing his insights. The support of Dean David Lee over the years has been unstinting, and I thank him for his kindness and assistance. Nathan Metcalf, a former student, helped with some of the research in Sri Lanka and remains very much on my mind. Finally, I would like to acknowledge the assistance I received from the Office of Sponsored Programs, particularly Phil Meyers and Pamela Napier.

At the University of Hawai'i Press, I thank Patricia Crosby and Professor Tanabe for their suggestions and encouragement. I also value the detailed comments of two external readers and appreciate the care with which they read through an earlier draft.

Research and writing would not have been possible without the generous support from a number of organizations and institutions. Western Kentucky University has provided numerous fellowships and grants to me over the years, and I remain forever indebted. I also received a generous two-year grant from Metanexus Institute, as well as funding and support from the Fulbright program. Completing the writing stage would not have been possible without the fellowship I received from the National Endowment for the Humanities.

Needless to say, this project would never have come to fruition without the support and love I received from my friends in Sri Lanka. I thank Thilak for his tireless work, as well as his family for taking care of me and sustaining me with their very tasty curries. I thank Kanthi for her help with collecting newspaper clippings over the years, Professor W. S. Karunatillake for teaching me Sinhala and being a model scholar, Professors Premasiri and Meegaskumbura at Peradeniya University, and the late Godwin Samaratna, who was both a teacher and friend. Of particular significance to this research project, however, are those who took the time to speak with me and teach me so much about Sri Lanka and Buddhism over the years. I remain forever grateful to the head monks who made their temples available to me, to monks and novices who shared with me so much about their lives, and to the parents of monks and novices who opened their families and hearts to me. May you all be well and happy!

Finally, I would like to thank my family: my parents for teaching me so much and for instilling in me a love for learning, my sisters for encouraging me, and my mother-in-law, who was always interested in the project. Most of all, though, I thank my immediate family: Claire for her humor and willingness to try new things as well as to experience new countries, Zachary for always bringing me back to reality, and Benedicte, who not only tolerated me during more stressful time but also supported me emotionally and intellectually throughout the research and writing phases.

Notes on Romanization and Naming Practices

To encumber the reader as little as possible, I have restricted the use of diacritic marks to certain Sinhala and Pali words, phrases, and sentences. I have also omitted the use of diacritics for the names of monks, villages, and temples for the same reason. When I do use diacritics, I have romanized Sinhala according to the system employed in Sōmapāla Jayawardhana's *Sinhala-English Dictionary*; Pali words and names follow the conventional system of romanization. Finally, when transliterating, I only note the language when it is Pali.

Although it is customary to use honorifics when referring to Buddhist monks and novices (e.g., Venerable Rahula or Reverend Rahula), I have chosen to use them only rarely. I feel their continued use would disrupt the flow of the text. I certainly mean no impertinence by my choice and respect them considerably.

As some of the content of this book deals with sensitive themes and issues, I have changed the names of all people, temples, and villages; I have not changed the names of major cities, districts, or provinces where the temples or villages are located. Finally, in Sri Lanka the names of monastics are comprised by a monk name that is preceded by their village name; to further guard their anonymity, I have only used their monk name.

Dramatis Personae

Ajit:	Boy from Ampāra whose interest in becoming a novice at Polgoda Vihara was sparked by a visit from his old neighbor, Venerable Santasiri.
Ven. Ananda:	Narada's senior student who comes from Ampāra in southeast Sri Lanka. While running his own temple outside of Kandy, Ananda has been overseeing the administration of the Ambana temple.
Ven. Anuruddha:	Venerable Narada's student who becomes the head monk of the Kumbukväva temple.
Ven. Candaratana:	A boy from Mahavela who became a novice through Venerable Sumedha's youth group.
Ven. Devamitta:	Venerable Narada's teacher. Until his death, he was the head monk of Ganegoda Vihara. Venerable Kassapa succeeded him as head monk.
Ven. Dhammadassi:	Novice from Huruluväva who was brought to Polgoda Vihara through Gunasena. Dhammadassi has continued to maintain very close ties with Gunasena after becoming a novice under Venerable Narada.
Ven. Dhammika:	Jayasundara's grandson who lived with his grandfather in a house that sat across the street from Venerable Ananda's parents' home. He is the first Ampāra villager to become a novice at Polgoda Vihara.
Mr. Gunasena:	Owns a house that shares a property line with the Madavala temple that Sumedha administered for some time. Mr. Gunasena has been a very strong advocate of Polgoda Vihara and brought a number of new recruits from the Huruluväva region to Venerable Narada's temple over the years.
Mr. Jayasekara:	Head of donor association in Kumbukväva.
Mr. Jayasundara:	Venerable Dhammika's grandfather who, after his grandson's became a novice, brought a number of other families and children from Ampāra to Polgoda Vihara.

Ven. Kassapa:	Narada's senior student who replaced Venerable Devamitta as the head monk of the Ganegoda temple.
Ven. Narada:	The head monk of Polgoda Vihara who established a large social service enterprise. Besides ordaining and educating numerous students, Narada is concerned with fulfilling the religious needs of Buddhists through establishing a number of branch temples.
Mr. Perera:	A principal lay donor of Polgoda Vihara who helped re-establish the Ambana temple outside of Mātalē.
Ven. Piyadassi:	Mr. and Mrs. Gunasena's first son who became a monk. He disrobed and left Polgoda Vihara after spending six years there as a novice.
Ven. Piyananda:	The second son of Mr. and Mrs. Gunasena who became a monk at Polgoda Vihara.
Ven. Piyaratana:	Deputy head monk of Polgoda Vihara.
Ven. Ratnasiri:	A monk who succeeded Venerable Suvata at the Ambana temple. After unsuccessfully running the temple, Ratnasiri disrobed and returned home.
Ven. Sarananda:	A nineteenth- to twentieth-century monastic who sought to improve the lives of poor, low-caste families by establishing a number of schools, temples, and monastic schools throughout Sri Lanka. He was also responsible for ordaining a number of low-caste children.
Sarat:	Boy from Huruluväva who was recruited through Venerable Sujata.
Ven. Silananda:	Boy from Huruluväva who became a novice through the *dharma* school that Sumedha established at the Madavala temple.
Ven. Sobhita:	A boy from Mahavela who became a novice through Venerable Sumedha's youth group.
Mr. Somaratna:	Sarat's father.
Ven. Sudhammananda:	Venerable Narada's preceptor who later administered two forest temples outside of Matara.
Ven. Sujata:	Novice from Huruluväva who was brought to Polgoda Vihara through Gunasena. Through him, a number of other boys from Huruluväva (like Sarat) became ordained at Narada's temple

Venerable Sumana:	Novice who succeeded Venerable Ratnasiri as the head monk of the Ambana temple.
Ven. Sumedha:	Narada's senior student who has been, over the years, a key recruiter for Narada. After running a temple in Madavala and another in Mahavela, Sumedha has become the chief monk of a temple in outside of Kandy.
Venerable Suvata:	A novice who ordained late in life under Venerable Narada. He was given the Ambana temple to run until the temple's patrons requested that he leave. He later disrobed.
Mr. Tilakaratana:	Principal donor and head of the village welfare society at Ambana.

Introduction

Buddhism and Social Relations in Contemporary Sri Lanka

One evening in late May 2004, I made yet another of countless ascents to Polgoda Vihara: a hilltop village temple in upcountry Sri Lanka. Because of some unforeseen car problems, it was already dark by the time I arrived. Leaving my car by the side of the driveway leading to the temple, I began a brief but tiring uphill walk. As I came around the bend in the road, the temple came dimly into view. To my left, I could see the shadows of about ten to fifteen young novices. They were sitting on the steps that lead up to the temple's large preaching hall. I could also make out the figure of Upali, one of the principal donors of the temple, seated with the group. As I approached them, I could see that several novices were holding Upali's arm, a mark of affection that one commonly sees among close friends of the same gender in South Asia. The conversation was light and jovial. They were laughing as Upali was sharing some of his personal stories.

I spent some time listening in on the conversation before continuing my rounds. I meandered around the temple's large living quarters and ran into another key donor chatting amiably with the temple's head monk, Venerable Narada. Although the atmosphere was relaxed and their conversation informal, their encounter was marked by a greater degree of deference than between Upali and the novices: Venerable Narada was seated on a chair, while the donor, Perera, was seated on a straw mat placed on the ground. Another frequent visitor to the temple—a mildly autistic teenage boy from the village—was next to Perera. He was massaging Narada's feet with some locally made Ayurvedic oil. Narada's legs had become quite swollen after a brief, but serious, bout of dengue fever.

After paying my respects to Narada and a quick exchange with Perera, I continued my rounds, this time with several young novices in tow. Similar to the young monastics clinging to Upali, these novices held on to my arm as we made our way through the main living quarters. Out back, a small fire was burning and a large covered pot sat on the makeshift hearth. Nearby, a few young novices were playing a game of marbles. A couple other monastics were there, including Suvata—an older man who became a novice a year earlier—and Piyaratana, the temple's deputy head monk, who was tending to the fire. As I approached the group, Suvata, not wanting to reveal the fact that he and the other novices at Polgoda Vihara[1] were about to break the sixth Buddhist precept—prohibiting the eating of solid food after midday—fidgetingly told me that they were boiling water for tea. One of the novices holding my arm quickly recanted, to the smiles and laughter of the other monks assembled there, "No we are not. We are cooking rice." After several long seconds of awkward silence, the deputy head monk reassuringly told Suvata "Don't worry. He knows us. He is close to us."

After spending another hour or so at the temple, I began to say my goodbyes. Before leaving I confirmed with Narada my intention of returning the following day to conduct interviews. He nodded and said, "No problem at all." I paid my respects to Narada as he wished me well.

It was such visits that caused me to pause and compelled me to reflect on the types of social bonds that exist among members of the Buddhist monastic community (Pali: *saṃgha*, hereafter *sangha*) as well as between monastics and laypeople. Although other more ritualized interactions between monastics and their patrons are colored by a greater degree of respect and what might be perceived as "emotional distance," the laughter and fatherly affection shared between Upali and the novices assembled on the steps to the preaching hall, the amiable and easygoing conversation between Perera and Venerable Narada, the loving behavior of the teenage boy as he massaged Narada's swollen feet, and the parent-like concern and compassion of the deputy head monk as he stooped over the hot fire and cooked rice for the temple's hungry novices were all examples of behaviors that are, I came to realize, reflective of complex bonds and affective ties that permeate Buddhist monastic life.

The purpose of this book is precisely to examine the types of affective bonds and shared aesthetic sensibilities that draw together groups of monastics and Buddhist laypeople. Turning to numerous conversations I had over the past ten years with head monks, novices, and laypeople associated with eight separate branch temples, as well as with recent recruits and their parents, I present a detailed, ethnographic study of one temple complex as it adapts itself to the needs of local and more distant lay patrons. Of particular importance to this book are the social processes associated with monastic culture in Sri Lanka, especially how monastics and laypeople relate to and affect one another in regard to recruitment, monastic training, and temple building. Focusing on the manner in which Buddhists describe their own histories, experiences, and encounters that relate to the formation and continuation of Buddhist monastic culture in contemporary Sri Lanka, I am specially interested in the role that affective states play in informing and shaping human relationships as well as the aesthetics of emotion: how emotions influence people's aesthetic sensibilities and how shared aesthetic standards make certain emotions and bonds possible.

I present four basic propositions throughout this book. The first one concerns how ideas about proper behavior, preferred monastic roles, and ideal appearance are formed. Although canonical norms have provided monastics and laypeople with a view of ideal monasticism, I maintain that images of good monks, ideal Buddhist temples, and appropriate monastic roles are sketched on people's minds and hearts through a variety of mediums. Viewing Buddhism, as Steven Collins (1998:57) does, not as a phenomenon deriving "from one or more ideal individuals from mythic antiquity but from actual, historical collectivities," I explore how concepts such as monastic, Buddhist temple, and pleasing appearance are shaped and determined by and within local communities of monastics and lay Buddhists. Although individuals from the past—especially the Buddha as depicted in texts, art, and architecture—inform modern-day images of an ideal monk, local social experiences and affective needs also shape the process of selection and interpretation as individual Buddhists develop a sense of what kind of monastic to have access to or what kind of monastic to become.

Closely related to the first proposition is the concept of decline and revival and its role in people's discourses about Buddhist monasticism. Notions of decline and revival are most commonly understood in terms of the ability of monastics to follow early Buddhist norms[2] or in regard to the processes of domestication and reform.[3] Although envisioning reform and revival in such a manner provides scholars and students of Buddhist monasticism with an interpretative framework through which to understand the monastic order and its ties to the state and society over the *longue durée*, such an understanding runs the risk of masking moments of profound changes in Lankan Buddhism (Blackburn 2001:9 and 76). Thus, instead of treating the notion of revival and reform as examples of Buddhism's continuity with the past, I consider the terms as important "strategies of legitimation."[4] Paying attention to conversations about decline and revival that I had with monastic leaders, monks, novices, lay Buddhists, and parents, I examine the innovative ways in which the concepts are used to validate distinct visions of the *sangha*, monastic vocation, and particular aesthetic standards.

The third proposition concerns the relationship between members of the *sangha* and their lay patrons. The bonds that draw lay Buddhists and monastics together are sometimes described in a utilitarian manner: using a model of generalized exchange, the lay-monastic relationship is sometimes portrayed as one in which the former provide the *sangha* with the four requisites (food, clothing, shelter, and medicine) in exchange for religious instruction, ritual performance, and the opportunity to make merit.[5] Although a close reading of the monastic disciplinary texts supports such a conclusion (e.g., the rules that pertain to food and accepting the laity's requests for preaching),[6] and even though there is ethnographic evidence to suggest that laypeople are driven to support Buddhist monastics out of their own ritual needs (Abeysekara 2002) and a desire for merit (Seneviratne 1999), I contend that conceiving the monk-patron relationship exclusively in this manner discounts other factors that hold together monastics and laypeople. In this book, I propose that, along with the *sangha*'s need for material support and the laity's desire for merit and ritual performance, the forces that bring and hold together groups of Buddhists—monastic and lay—include affective bonds that are, themselves, deepened by common histories, similar values, shared sentiments, and collectively held aesthetic standards.

The final proposition pertains to the topic of emotions. In examining the place and role of emotions in contemporary Sri Lanka, I must be very clear in my purpose. Despite the existence of Buddhist texts that portray certain emotions as problematic, stories of the Buddha that portray him as an embodiment of the quality of affective detachment,[7] and other facets of the tradition that suggest that emotions are antithetical to the Buddhist path,[8] it is difficult to uphold the view that emotions have no place in Buddhism. Thus, in examining how Buddhists perceive and express emotion in the contexts of recruitment, training, vocation, and patronage, my purpose is not to state the obvious: that Buddhists have or experience emotions. Instead, by considering the social aspects of emotions my aim is to assess how emotions, as cultural judgments of people and institutions, not only determine and influence people's social relationships and their aesthetic sensibilities but also function expressively and strategically in the contexts of building new Buddhist institutions and maintaining existing ones. Like Errol Bedford (1986:30), who contends that in "using emotion words we are able . . . to relate behavior to the complex background in which it is enacted, and so to make human actions intelligible," and similar to John Corrigan (2008:8), who states that "the study of religion and emotion provides a way to discuss religion as a human activity that is embedded in everyday life in the felt relations individuals experiences with other persons, nature, and the holy personages to whom they are devoted," I propose that examining the emotional and aesthetic responses that relate to and are articulated within the context of institution building and monastic vocation is central to a more complete understanding of the actions of monks and laypeople in regard to recruitment, training, and the formation and continuation of Buddhist communities.

ATTRACTING THE HEART AND THE FORMATION OF BUDDHIST COMMUNITIES

In exploring the role that shared emotions and aesthetic sensibilities play in shaping and determining the types of social bonds that are so essential to the formation and maintenance of Buddhist monastic culture in contemporary Sri Lanka, I turn to the Sinhalese expression "attracting the heart" that I heard on numerous occasions. The English phrase I translate as "attracting the heart" is from the Sinhala expression *hita ädaganīma* (literary Sinhala *leṅgatu*). The second term in the expression is the gerund form of the verb *ädagannavā,* which literally means "to draw, pull, attract, or absorb."[9] The term *hita* (or *sita*), which I translate as "heart" in this and subsequent chapters, however, is slightly more problematic as it—like *shin* in Chinese, *kokoro* in Japanese, and *citta* in Pali[10]—refers to one's cognitive, volitional, and emotional centers. Although such a definition might warrant translating *hita* as "heart-mind" in the pages that follow,[11] I have chosen to translate *hita* simply as "heart," partly because the mind is sometimes conceived as residing in the heart,[12] and partly for aesthetic reasons.

Throughout this book I turn to the phrase "attracting the heart" to identify and analyze patterns of action of Buddhist monastics and laypeople that relate to institution building and monastic vocation. Although this expression usually has very positive connotations,[13] I turn to a whole range of concomitant affective states—both positive (pleasure, joy, love, and affection) and negative (anger, disgust, sadness, distrust, jealousy, and shame)—to assess the role of emotional perception and expression in determining social relationships and the types of commitments that laypeople make in regard to their families, their communities, and the Buddhist monastic order.

In developing a methodological tool for interpreting the perception and expression of emotion, I turn to literature on the social construction of emotion.[14] In an introduction to an edited collection of articles on emotion in India and Hinduism, Owen Lynch (1990b:8f.) highlights six propositions related to the social construction of emotion: (1) emotions are basically appraisals of situations that are predicated upon particular cultural beliefs and values; (2) as appraisals, emotions are "constitutive for the individual and deeply involve, even move the self in its relationships to social others, things, or events"; (3) "emotions are learned or acquired in society rather than given naturally"; (4) they involve agent responsibility, that is action on the part of the person experiencing the emotion (even if that action is to do nothing at all); (5) they "involve moral judgments about prescribed or expected responses to social situations"; and, finally,

(6) emotions have certain functions, such as coloring and shaping how people relate to one another.

Indebted to Catherine Lutz's (1988) and Lynch's work, I am less interested, however, in engaging the debate concerning whether emotion or the emotional life is consistent across cultures or whether a universal situation would trigger the same emotion in different people.[15] Instead, drawn to the highly relational quality of apprehending and experiencing Buddhism in contemporary Sri Lanka, I am more concerned with emotional expression and the role that emotion plays in the social arena. Although I would agree with Charlotte Hardman (2000) and William Reddy (1997) that emotions are only partly constructed in culture, I remain interested in examining how particular emotions and aesthetic sensibilities originate through people's relationships with others and are shaped by people's shared histories, present needs, and future aspirations. Finally, intrigued by Lynch's (1990a), Stephen Berkwitz's (2003, 2001), Maria Heim's (2003, 2008), and Martha Nussbaum's (1990; 2001) work on the connection between emotion, cognition, and action, I consider how emotions—as sites of reason and judgment—function strategically in influencing and determining the types of bonds and commitments that people make to each other, to particular monastic institutions, and to the Buddhist religion.[16] I also explore the performative dimension of emotional expression, not in the sense of how phrases such as "I am ashamed" or "I am angry" actually make one ashamed or angry[17] but in regard to how emotional expression functions to legitimizes one's actions—past, present, and future.

This book contributes to a recent trend within the field of Buddhist studies examining local manifestations of Buddhist practice. Indeed, Gregory Schopen's critique of approaches to the study of Indian Buddhism (1991), Charles Hallisey's provocative article on the effects that interactions between Europeans and non-Europeans had on the study of Theravāda Buddhism (1995), and Philip Almond's account of the textualist approach of early British scholars of Buddhism (1988) have heralded a number of subsequent publications that have begun to assess the ways in which Buddhism has been previously approached. Although not all scholars have endorsed this trend of turning to other, nonclassical sources in the construction of Buddhism,[18] it has accelerated in the past ten to fifteen years, especially with the publication of such edited volumes as *Buddhism in Practice* (1995). Such a reorientation within the field, which by no means implies a complete abandoning of canonical sources, is perhaps best described in Donald Lopez's introductory text, *Buddhism*, where he writes (2001:14), "In the history of Buddhist scholarship, this is a period in which there is less interest in Buddhist philosophy and more emphasis on Buddhist practice, less interest in Buddhism as a global entity and more interest in its local manifestations, less interest in the practices of élites, especially monastics, and more interest in the practices of ordinary monks, nuns and laypeople. There is less interest in scholastic debates and more interest in social history. There is less interest in doctrine and more interest in ritual."[19] The present book—which focuses on the social histories, concerns, and practices of "ordinary" monks and laypeople as they seek out meaningful experiences and emotionally salient relationships in the face of economic and social challenges—examines the evaluations and negotiations that form an integral part to the social processes related to Buddhist institution building and the social construction of monastic vocation.

Chapter 1 provides the temporal and theoretical starting point for a discussion of recruitment, monastic training, and institution building. Discussing the life events of one monk, Venerable Narada, from his decision to become a monastic to his choice to remain in the *sangha* for life, I examine how social bonds influence the decisions that people—monastic and lay—make about their role in society and their commitment to the *sangha*. By assessing carefully the factors that contributed to Narada's decision to serve people's social and economic needs, I maintain that the model of generalized economic exchange that is sometimes used to describe Buddhist monasticism as a social institution limits our ability to understand and appreciate how groups of monastics and laypeople interact on a regular basis. Although it may correctly be asserted—as it has in a number of introductions to Buddhism (Gethin 1998; Wijayaratna 1990; Harvey 1990; Gombrich 2006) as well as in more focused studies (Southwold 1983; Abeysekara 2002; Seneviratne 1999)—that both monastics' material needs and the laity's ritual wants and their desire for merit are central factors that draw and hold together groups of monastics and laypeople, I posit in this and subsequent chapters that social ties based on shared emotions and collective histories play a central role in the formation and continuation of Buddhist monastic communities.

The two chapters that follow examine monastic recruitment, the first from the perspective of one monastic leader who has been very active in drawing newcomers to the *sangha*, and the second from the perspective of child monastics and their families. Building on the material presented in chapter 1, chapter 2 examines the roles that aesthetics and affective bonds play in influencing and determining the kinds of lifelong choices that people make toward the *sangha* and society. I posit that seeing and hearing have the potential to trigger particular religious responses, including the desire to become a full-fledged member of the Buddhist *sangha*. In addition to complementing existing scholarship that assesses why young children become novices, my effort in drawing attention to the language of emotion relating to monastic recruitment leads me to make two key theoretical points. First, I maintain that, far from being understood as blind surges of affect, emotions are part of a system of ethical reasoning (Nussbaum 2001:1; see also Lutz 1988; Abu-Lughod and Lutz 1990; Lynch 1990b; and Heim 2008:18f.). I further contend that affective states, as judgments of value about people and things in this world, have an instrumental function: emotions are not merely internal subjective states but also serve to inform and determine the types of lifestyle choices that families and young children make.

Chapter 3 builds on the previous one by focusing more specifically on the place of social networks in monastic recruitment. Examining the role that lay temple advocates and parents of Buddhist novices play in guiding potential recruits to certain temples, I posit that monastic recruitment should not be understood solely in terms of an individual's or family's desire for upward mobility. Instead, interpreting the manner in which parents and children describe the recruitment process (including the factors that shaped their own decisions) using several sociological theories of recruitment (Lofland and Stark 1965; Lofland and Skonovd 1981; Stark and Bainbridge 1985), I maintain that, along with the promise of a good education and greater financial security, monastic recruitment is driven by a range of aesthetic-affective-social factors that extend well beyond the needs and wants of a single individual or family. Finally, in exploring the social and emotive dimensions of monastic recruitment, I assess the degree to which people's articulated appraisal of monks and temples shape local conceptions of ideal Buddhist institutions and monastic leaders.

Chapter 4 considers the processes by which lay children become socialized as Buddhist novices. Along with examining the monastic curriculum that novices follow in the first five years of their studies, I investigate the role that relationships play monastic training. Returning to a point I raise in chapters 1 and 2—that conceptions of acceptable monastic behavior are influenced by local concerns and interest—I posit that more diffuse training methods such as completing temple duties, performing rituals, and using a specialized vocabulary are more attuned not only to the ways in which some young novices learn about proper deportment and behavior but also to local notions of aesthetics. Finally, I turn to one of Narada's senior students who, in 1999, became the head monk of another temple and consider how affective bonds that developed between him and his teacher, as well as between him and his patrons, influenced his own self-identity, his understanding of monastic vocation, and his levels of commitment and devotion to society and the *sangha*.

Finally, chapter 5 investigates the enterprise of temple building as a form of social service. Focusing on two temples that were reestablished in 2003 and 2004, I maintain that, far from being founded on a belief that any properly ordained monastic would suffice or on the laity's religious needs, temple building is driven by a desire for establishing close, affective bonds with monastics as well by the need to locate aesthetically pleasing experiences. I also posit that aesthetic sensibilities and ideas about ideal monastic deportment are the outcome of dynamic, emotional interactions that exist between monastics and laypeople. Sharing Ananda Abeysekara's and Yukio Hayashi's suggestion that we examine local contexts or "minute contingent conjunctures" within which ideas such as proper monks, ideal Buddhist institution, and pleasing demeanor and deportment are dynamically debated and formed,[20] I posit that the establishment of temples and their successful running are grounded in the experiences of the temple's patrons and monastics whose own religious values and social histories continue to shape their understandings of what constitutes an ideal Buddhist monastic and temple.

THE FIELD SETTING AND FIELD METHOD

As an ethnographic study, this book is largely derived from interviews conducted over a ten-year period with more than sixty novices and monks connected to Polgoda Vihara and eight of its fifteen branch institutions. It also relies on interviews with sixteen lay patrons along with twenty-two parents whose children are in robes. Although the majority of the material on which this book is based pertains largely to the Rāmañña Nikāya[21]—the smallest of three monastic fraternities in Sri Lanka—it also provides a larger perspective on Theravāda Buddhist society, particularly in relation to emotion, recruitment, monastic life, patronage, and institution building. Thus, apart from a close study of this temple network which now includes about 175 Buddhist monks and novices, I also include material collected from visits to more than a dozen other, non-Rāmañña Nikāya, temples as well as from conversations with their monastic leaders and residents. Finally, to situate the many voices presented in this study within wider discourses on Buddhism, monks, and monastic institutions, this study draws on a variety of written and visual sources, including Sinhalese and English newspaper articles, editorials, monastic histories, government reports, a Sinhalese historical novel, and a recently popular Sri Lankan film.

A large portion of the material contained in this book was collected using three principal field methods: closely observed accounts of monastic life, person-centered ethnography, and autodriven photo-elicited interviews. My decision to use a person-centered ethnographic approach is predicated on the belief that any understanding of Buddhist monastic culture and temple building must begin with specific, in-depth descriptions of human experiences and human subjectivity. Starting with the "individual's perspective on culture and experience rather than that of a collective system or external observer" (LeVine 1982:293), I believe that a person-centered ethnography is better suited to arriving at descriptions of "human behavior and subjective experience from the point of view of the acting, intending, and attentive subject, [as well as] to actively explore the emotional saliency and motivational force of cultural beliefs and symbols" (Hollan 1997:220).

While assessing the content and method of interviews carried out since 1999, in 2003 I began conducting *autodriven* photo-elicited interviews in 2003.[22] By allowing interviewees the opportunity to frame and photograph various aspects of their lives—e.g., a very important temple activity, an ideal Buddhist monastic, what is important to you as a monastic, and so on—I have found this particular research method to be an invaluable tool for providing monks and young novices the ability to illustrate and discuss their experiences of temple life in a way that is particularly meaningful to them. As I have discussed elsewhere (Samuels 2004a and 2007b; see also Collier 1957, as well as Collier and Collier 1986), the power of photographs to trigger rich, emotional responses from the interviewees has made this particular field method useful in collecting material that highlights, as much as possible, the affective, aesthetic, and social dimension of monastic life for ordinands, novices, and Buddhist monastics.

I understand that the manner in which laypeople speak about monastics or younger students speak about their teachers is highly idealized at times; I am also aware that people's accounts and descriptions may mask other concerns. Although I believe that conducting multiple interviews with many of my informants over a ten-year period, as well as using multiple field methods, would uncover a number of underlying agendas and interests, my approach to the material is not necessarily to interrogate what people say and how they describe their experiences. Instead, it is to examine how people's descriptions of their experiences and relationships—including their more stylized and sometimes inflated vocabulary—shape their social and emotional lives as well their understandings of and approach to religious praxis. Thus, throughout this book I have allowed the voices of my informants to come through as much as possible by evoking the categories and terms that ordinands, novices, monks, parents of monastics, and laypeople use as they speak about their experience of Buddhism.

1 Narada Thero

Affective Bonds and the Making of a Social Service Monk

During one afternoon in April 1999, I—along with Thilak, my research assistant—met Venerable Narada. Thilak and I received directions to Narada's temple from Thilak's wife, who had been working with Narada at the local high school at the time. After a journey that stretched well over two hours because of the heavy traffic that normally follows in the wake of the country's schools letting out each afternoon, we arrived at the foot of a narrow, steep driveway that, we were told, leads to the temple. Beside a concealed gateway *(torana)*, there was no sign of a temple from the road. The large street placard that now indicates the temple's name and address was not installed at the time.

We began our ascent. As we came to a small curve in the road, the temple came into view. The land around the temple, dotted with garbage and plastic bags, was somewhat large. The temple was not. To our right was a small Bodhi tree.[1] Several tattered Buddhist flags hung from its branches. To our left was the newest addition to the temple: a preaching hall that also functioned as a formal alms-giving hall *(dānasālāva)*. Opposite the preaching hall and immediately after the Bodhi tree was a run-down three-room residence building with a makeshift kitchen in the back. Several senior students, I quickly came to learn, lived in the small residence, and Narada and his many younger students slept on straw mats in the preaching hall. On a small hill next to the preaching hall was a small, damp image house *(pilimagē)*. Faded paintings that portrayed the Buddha's past lives, randomly culled from the *Jātaka* collection, covered the interior walls.[2] In the middle of the octagonally shaped room that symbolizes the Fourth Noble Truth—the eightfold path—was a four-foot-high tiled platform, with a small table to receive flowers and other offerings. Sitting on the center of the platform was a large, colorful sculpture of a Bodhi tree. At each of the four cardinal directions was a buddha statue, representing the most recent buddha—Gotama—and three of his predecessors.[3] At the time of that first visit, construction had only recently begun on what would become a four-story living quarters that would, in the course of the next ten years, be large enough to house more than seventy-five monks and novices.

On our arrival, the temple's deputy head monk welcomed us. He told us that Narada, who had just returned from his teaching duties at the village's high school, would see us shortly. After about a ten minute wait, we were offered tea and biscuits. As is customary, I had brought an offering to the temple: a box of milk powder to which I nervously clung as we waited to meet the temple's head monk.

Narada, who was forty-one at the time, arrived within twenty minutes or so. After sitting down on his chair, he warmly welcomed us to his temple. His clean-shaven head and face stood in marked contrast to the monks with whom I had previously interacted at the University of Peradeniya. I was struck by his vivacious demeanor and warm eyes. His bright, large smile immediately put me at ease. Although he was the temple's head monk (literally, big lord [*loku hāmuduruwo*]), he was quite unassuming; his maroon polyester-blend robes had several small holes which, I came to realize over the next week or so, were the result of his active participation in the temple's ongoing construction projects.

Thilak introduced me as an American student interested in studying the lives of Buddhist novices for my PhD. Luckily, Narada was quite familiar with the university system as well as with the process of thesis writing, because he was a university graduate and not at all suspicious of my wish to conduct research at his temple.[4] After some more small talk, Narada unhesitatingly opened his temple to us. The fact that Thilak's wife worked with Narada certainly helped.

After giving Narada a brief and somewhat imprecise description of what I hoped to research—namely, the phenomenon of Buddhist novices, their training, and education—Narada called all of his students to the residence hall. Apparently, he thought that we would be interviewing them all together at that very moment. When I explained to Narada that my research would entail much more than a single group interview, he understood. After dispersing his students, Narada provided us with a list of their names. He suggested that we use the adjacent preaching hall *(dharmaśālāva)* to conduct our interviews. He also said that we would be welcome to visit and even stay at his temple any time we wished.

Since that initial encounter, I have returned to Polgoda Vihara countless times: sometimes alone, sometimes with Thilak; sometimes for the day, sometimes for the weekend. In the process of visiting Polgoda Vihara (as well as a host of other Buddhist temples) and interviewing more than a hundred monks, novices, parents of monastics, and laity, my own ideas about Buddhist monasticism were challenged. Some were shattered, and the research I conducted over the years has pressed me to think about Buddhist monastic culture—ideas about social service, monastic behavior, the monastic disciplinary code *(Vinaya)*, monastic-lay relationships, and emotions—in many different ways.

In this chapter—which provides the background for the chapters that follow—I focus on Narada's life: from his decision to become a monastic, through the personal and social conflicts he experienced as he contemplated leaving the robes, to his decision to remain a monk and devote his time and resources to serving society. At the same time, however, this chapter is more than simply a biography of a contemporary monastic. In investigating the various influences that transformed Narada from a village monastic to a monk actively serving the needs of those living in more distant towns and villages, this chapter examines the complex social bonds and affective ties that bring and hold Buddhist communities together. By paying special attention to how monastics and laypeople relate to and affect one another in various circumstances, Narada's case study exemplifies how ideas about ideal monastic deportment and appearance come to be informed by the kinds of relationships that people have with particular monastics and by their own personal and collective experiences and histories.

Although I turn to several sources in this chapter, I have largely based Narada's biography on his own descriptions. Attentive to the fact that any account of past events is continually meditated by present concerns and experiences (Daniel 1996:4f.), I am less concerned with arriving at a neutral description of Narada's life or with uncovering the tension between what Narada says he believes and does from what he really believes and does.[5] Instead, influenced by Margaret Trawick (1990b:40), who, in studying a devotional poem to Shiva under the tutelage of her informant, Ayya, "came to see that Ayya's exegesis of the love poem was hooked into the everyday affairs of this [i.e., his] family," I am interested in how Narada's description of his own life story—the events and social relationships he chooses to discuss and emphasize—is intimately connected to the everyday affairs of being a monastic leader in present-day Sri Lanka. Consequently, in recounting Narada's biography, my concern is both to understand how Narada's story functions strategically to legitimize a particular view of monastic vocation as well as to explore what Narada's framing of his own story reveals about the centrality of emotion and affective bonds within the *sangha* itself.

VENERABLE NARADA: THE MAKING OF A SOCIAL SERVICE MONK

Narada grew up in the village of Nugaväla, located in the district of Harispattuva.[6] As a child he was raised in very modest circumstances with the family's income coming almost entirely from his father's agricultural work. Even though Narada's father did not pursue formal schooling past the primary level, he was an inspiration for Narada and would come to play a large part in shaping his son's views about the importance of studying.

Narada's father also played an indirect yet important role in forging a path to the *sangha* for the young boy. Besides spending much of his free time at the village temple, Narada's father would regularly attend and even sometimes participate in Buddhist rituals, particularly lay protection rituals *(gihi pirit piṅkama)* for other Buddhists.[7] Narada explained to me that his father's devotion toward Buddhism, his voracious appetite for things Buddhist, his thirst for knowledge, and his commitment to fulfilling the religious needs of others profoundly affected his own decision to become a monastic as a teenager. As we shall soon see, those same factors also influenced Narada's ideas about monastic vocation and his own interpretation of social service.

Unlike the majority of monastics who don saffron robes between the ages of eight and twelve, Narada contemplated joining the *sangha* when he was sixteen years old. What I found quite surprising, however, was that despite his father's religious sentiments, Narada was unable to secure his father's or mother's permission to become a member of the Buddhist *sangha*.[8] Apparently, Narada's father preferred to see his son follow in his own footsteps and earn his living as a farmer.

After pleading with his parents on an almost daily basis, Narada succeeded in wrestling the necessary consent from his parents. His new life as a Buddhist ordinand began. Although Narada intended to move to the temple in his native village, his father decided that it would be better to send his son for monastic training to Ganegoda Vihara, a temple that sits approximately ten kilometers from Nugaväla. The family's connection to Ganegoda Vihara, which was started by Venerable Devamitta and his brother-monk, Venerable Sudhammananda, in the 1940s,[9] went all the way back to Narada's father's school days, when he and the yet-to-be-ordained Devamitta were students in the same class. Narada's father felt assured that, by sending Narada to his friend's temple, his son would be treated as kindly as he would have at home.[10]

Narada arrived at Ganegoda Vihara on May 25, 1974. At the temple, Narada was placed under the tutelage of both Devamitta and Sudhammananda, the latter having recently returned to Ganegoda Vihara after spending almost fifteen years in Germany as a messenger of the *dharma (dhammadhūta/dharmadūta)*[11] for the German Dharmadūta Society.[12] Although Narada had pined for monastic robes for some time, he had a difficult time adjusting to life at Ganegoda Vihara. Narada returned home after spending several months at the temple. Why this sudden change of heart? Narada explained to me that his decision to return home was the result of the social and economic climate at the time. After characterizing the period in which he became an ordinand as not being the "golden period of

Sri Lankan history," Narada went on to discuss the period as one that was marked by high rates of unemployment and rising prices for necessary goods (such as oil, wheat, rice, and sugar).[13] Although it may be argued that monastics are, by and large, unaffected by the national unemployment rate or by the prevailing economy, reverberations from the economic problems and crises in relation to food production were, similar to earlier periods of social and economic upheaval, felt throughout Sri Lankan society, including the *sangha* itself.

It was the negative attitudes that some laypeople and monastics expressed toward the *sangha* (see Jiggins 1979) and, more so, the breakdown of affective bonds within the temple itself that drove Narada back home: "At that time, there were only older monks living at the temple. Many of them discussed leaving the temple. They had negative attitudes. Some of them told me that it is useless to live in a temple. Only one of them told me to stay. All the others felt negatively about the temple. No one seemed concerned about me. I felt isolated and felt compelled to return [home]." Once back in Nugaväla, however, Narada had a very difficult time reintegrating into village life because he was also unable to leave monastic life entirely behind him. While at home, Narada began attending the local Buddhist *dharma* school *(daham pāsäla)* once again. He also continued fostering his interest in *sangha* life by reading the very popular monastic handbook, the *Sāmaṇera Baṇadaham Pota*.[14] Describing his struggle at the time, Narada explained to me: "When I got home, I felt that I had made a wrong decision. Even after I was back at home, I kept reading the *Sāmaṇera Baṇadaham Pota*. I kept it all in my mind.... My mind was oscillating between the two places. I didn't feel like staying at home either. During that period, there were a lot of economic problems in the country. The same problems that forced me to leave the temple led me to leave home as well."

In May 1975, Narada returned to Ganegoda Vihara as an ordinand and became a novice on January 29 of the following year. His preceptor *(upajjhāya)* was Sudhammananda; his teacher *(ācariya)*, Devamitta.[15] Shortly following Narada's ordination, however, Sudhammananda left Ganegoda Vihara for the southern city of Matara to establish two meditation centers.[16] Although Sudhammananda would continue to make periodic visits to Ganegoda Vihara over the years and Narada would come to identify with him emotionally and intellectually, Narada largely remained under Devamitta's care.

Narada began his formal studies as a Buddhist novice at a local monastic school (*piriveṇa*, hereafter *pirivena*) in April 1976. In the middle of his first year of studies, Narada transferred to another *pirivena* as he found the educational standards at the first school too low. After completing his elementary *(mūlika piriveṇa)* studies, Narada transferred to the larger and more well-known Sarananda Pirivena.[17] At Sarananda, as at many other large monastic schools *(mahāpiriveṇa)*, students are able to choose between two different educational paths: one that culminates in a *paṇḍita* degree and is more focused on religious subjects and oriental languages, and one that leads, if one is successful on the advanced-level exams, to entrance into one of Sri Lanka's secular universities and includes both religious and secular subjects.[18]

As a student of Sarananda Pirivena, Narada studied both religious and secular subjects as, he believed, a monastic's education must keep up with the education that laypeople receive. During one conversation I had with Narada in 1999, he justified his chosen course of studies by arguing that, "due to the rapidly changing world and the present situation in Sri Lanka, only focusing on the religious path [i.e., a path leading to a *paṇḍita* degree] will not enable a monk to become that successful. Since new technology has developed and this country is developing, monks should learn how to preach religious things and serve the laity in modern ways. New technology must be combined with religious things. Thus, the monk must have a good knowledge of secular things."[19] Similar to Walpola Rahula and Yakkaduve Pragnarama, who, several decades earlier, spoke about the changes facing society to legitimate their own views about monastic education,[20] Narada made reference to certain changes, especially since the introduction of the free market economy in the late 1970s, as part of his own narrative of monastic vocation and of the *sangha*'s role in contemporary society.

While studying at Sarananda Pirivena, Narada was asked to take over the incumbency of Polgoda Vihara, a small temple located approximately four kilometers from Ganegoda Vihara. Polgoda Vihara, which had been left vacant for several years, was established in 1948 under the direction of and with partial funding from Narada's preceptor and teacher, Sudhammananda and Devamitta. To understand how the bonds that Narada would soon establish with the patrons of Polgoda Vihara would come to affect his own short- and long-term goals, we must look back several decades and examine the factors that led to the establishment of Polgoda Vihara.

As I have described elsewhere (Samuels 2007a), Polgoda Vihara was built by a group of laypeople living nearby. Although those lay donors were initially served by an already existing Siyam Nikāya temple (Sri Kirti Vihara) in the village, certain class- and caste-related problems compelled them to seek new avenues of monastic patronage.[21] Unlike the high-caste monastics living at Sri Kirti Vihara as well as some of the temple's high-caste patrons, the majority of the villagers responsible for building Polgoda Vihara hailed from the drummer *(beravā)* caste. As members of one of Sri Lanka's many service castes, they were sometimes treated quite poorly by key donors of Sri Kirti Vihara as well as by several of the temple's caste-conscious monastics. All of this was made apparent to me during a group interview I had with several laymen during a full moon *(poya)* holiday. When I asked the group from Polgoda Vihara to tell me the history of the temple, one of the men, Mr. Dharmadasa, replied, "This temple was built by our parents. We had faith in the Sri Kirti temple earlier. However, the head monk there was very arrogant [*ahaṅkāra*]." Shifting his position with an uncomfortable expression on his face, Dharmadasa promptly continued, "Is it all right if I tell you the truth? It was regarding the issue of caste [*kula*]. Look at this [Polgoda Vihara] temple. Anyone can come here, regardless of their caste." When I asked Dharmadasa what he meant by *ahaṅkāra* (arrogant), he continued by recounting the actual event that resulted in the establishment of Polgoda Vihara:

> That monk spoke with caste discrimination. [One day] there were some people sitting inside and outside of the preaching hall while observing the eight precepts. Some of them were from Pallekanda and some from our group. Some were from Godavela.[22] At that time, there was a problem inside of the preaching hall. The person who [usually] blew the conch had not come to the temple to perform his duties for two days.[23] However, he was there with the group [observing the precepts]. Then the monk came inside [the preaching hall] and, yelling at him, said "Hey you! Why didn't you come" [*äyi adhō tō āve nätte*]. He started yelling like that. The donor replied by saying something like "I couldn't come." Hearing that, the monk said, "You are all eating by using my temple land. Can all of you do that? You aren't doing your *rājakāriya* [duties] properly" [*tōpi mage pansalē iḍam allāganna kanavā. Tōpiṭa puluvanda ehema karannē. Rājakāriya karannē nä*].[24] It is said [*kiyenavālu*] that that guy answered back after which the monk said, "GET OUT! I won't eat a single grain of [your] rice brought [here]" [*pallehaṅ genena bat ulakvat mama kannē nä*].
>
> The monk had blamed that man in front of all the other patrons. At that time, the [high-caste] group from Godavela was looking at this other [low-caste] group and that group was looking back at them. That man felt really ashamed [*läjjāyi*]. The following day he and the others came and asked me whether there is a monk who can be brought here [to this village]. They told me what had happened there. I said to them, "I will tell you the way [to a temple]. If you want to go, I will tell you how to get there. . . ." They immediately agreed. We all went there. We met a monk

> who was from Hārispattuvē.[25] We met him and he asked, "What [would you like] son" [*putte mokadda*]? I told him that we are planning to get a good monk for our village from here. We told him that we were going to start a new temple.

To understand the ramifications of the encounter between the conch blower and the head monk on the members of the drummer caste, it is important to note that the Sinhala language, unlike English, has several words for the second-person pronoun and its accompanying verbal imperative.[26] Although there are many ways to view and interpret what ensued between the conch blower and the temple's head monk, from Dharmadasa's and the other donors' perspective,[27] the head monk's use of *tō* and *palayan*[28]—particularly when contrasted with how Venerable Devamitta addressed the group ("What son?" [*putte mokadda*])—was indicative of his own caste prejudices, particularly his low regard for Sri Lanka's service-caste members.

It has been suggested that the laity's greed for spiritual merit has often resulted in an "any monk would do" philosophy in contemporary Sri Lanka. According to H. L. Seneviratne and Ananda Abeysekara, moreover, most laypeople go about justifying their own support of bad monks by rationalizing that they are "worshipping the robe, not the wearer" (Seneviratne, 1999:278; Abeysekara 2002:56) or by claiming that their own rituals needs make them dependent on immoral monks (Abeysekara 2002:61). I too have heard some laypeople claim that they "worship the robe, not the wearer," and justify their support of certain monastics by noting that their ritual needs gives them little choice.[29] I have also found that not every lay Buddhist is content with adopting such a philosophy. Indeed, conversations with groups of laypeople associated with the founding of new temples or reestablishing vacated temples indicate that shared experiences (e.g., caste biases) and affective states (e.g., shame or anger) may function as powerful forces that drive Buddhist institution building as well as that emotions, by helping to create moral orientations (Parish 1994:199ff.), shape and determine local views about ideal monastic behavior and practice. For the laity involved in the establishment of Polgoda Vihara, for example, the shared *anger* they felt toward the monks from Sri Kirti Vihara and the *humiliation* they faced vis-à-vis the high-caste donors at Sri Kirti Vihara not only drew the new Buddhist community together but also guided and drove them in the temple-building process. Furthermore, although the group's aesthetic sensibilities will continue to be shaped by the types of bonds that they will come to form with their own monastic leader or community of monks,[30] their collective experiences and emotions (e.g., anger, disgust, hurt, shame, and praise) played a role in shaping their ideas about appropriate monastic behavior and deportment, particularly how a "good monastic" should talk and interact with his donors. Before I explore further the social relations and the aesthetics of emotion that permeate Sri Lankan monastic culture, however, we need to return to Narada's story and examine how he came to be the head monk of Polgoda Vihara.

Sudhammananda was the first incumbent of Polgoda Vihara. Prior to going to Berlin and assisting in the administration of the Sri Lankan temple there, Sudhammananda turned over the administration of Polgoda Vihara to Devamitta. Finding the task of administering two temples (Ganegoda Vihara and Polgoda Vihara) too arduous, Devamitta began handing over the administration of Polgoda Vihara to his own students. Unfortunately for the patrons of the new temple, there was no stable leadership: most of Devamitta's students remained at the temple for only short periods of time, though a few remained for several years. After the temple was left vacant for a four-year period, Narada was asked to take it over.

When Narada arrived at the temple, he was only a novice *(sāmaṇera)*. He had little more than two years of experience under his belt. Although most lay patrons prefer having a fully ordained *(upasampadā)* monk in charge of their temples, the patrons of Polgoda Vihara expressed an interest in Narada to Devamitta after Narada went there in March 1978 to conduct the *poya* temple activities. Even though it was Narada's first experience in giving sermons and conducting various other religious activities, the devotees were impressed, particularly with Narada's appearance and deportment, as well as with the way that he addressed the donors. After the full moon celebration, several lay patrons approached Devamitta and asked whether Narada could take over the temple's administration on a full-time basis. Devamitta discussed the matter with Narada, who agreed to take over the temple with one stipulation: that he be allowed to continue his course of studies at Sarananda Pirivena. Believing that "only through education can one have a better life" as well that the very survival of the *sangha* is intimately tied to having an educated group of monastics, Narada's predilection since becoming a novice had been "first educational activities, then religious activities" *(magē svabhāva, eka adhyāpana kaṭayuttu, deka āgamika kaṭayuttu)*.[31] Although some laypeople and monastics might interpret Narada's perspective on education—especially his predilection for secular studies—as indicative of a lack of commitment to the *sangha* or to a life in robes,[32] Devamitta and the patrons of Polgoda Vihara agreed to Narada's condition.

As the head monk *(vihārādhipati)* of Polgoda Vihara, Narada continued to progress in his studies. After doing very well on his advanced-level exams,[33]

Narada earned a highly coveted place in one of Sri Lanka's leading universities.[34] As a student at Peradeniya University, Narada pursued a bachelor of arts degree in Buddhism. Unlike many other university monks who choose to reside in one of the university's dormitories, Narada continued to live at Polgoda Vihara while completing his degree. Even though living on campus would have saved Narada the fourteen-kilometer roundtrip commute each day, he felt an obligation toward his patrons who had supported him over the past several years.

While pursuing his degree at Peradeniya, another tumultuous event occurred in Sri Lanka: the second uprising of the Marxist-oriented People's Liberation Front (Janata Vimukti Peramuna, hereafter JVP). Launched in 1987 and lasting two and a half years, this insurgency, which was far more reaching than the one in 1971, was less about instituting a Marxist agenda (as the 1971 insurgency was) than about nationalistic issues. Immediately following in the wake of the Indo-Lankan Peace Accord—which the Indian prime minister Rajiv Gandhi and the Sri Lankan ruling party (the United National Party [Eksat Jātika Pakṣaya] or UNP for short) signed in 1987—the JVP, along with other groups, vociferously began to express their opposition, claiming that by agreeing to a devolution of power, the UNP was capitulating to India and threatening Sri Lanka's sovereignty.[35] Although many of the other groups who protested the accord dissipated in the weeks after its signing, the JVP continued to voice strong opposition, including hostility toward the ruling UNP and their leader, J. R. Jayewardene. Within a very short time, the verbal conflict turned to physical violence, with targeted assassinations of sympathizers with the accord and with the UNP. Furthermore, by staging, on a massive scale, work and trade strikes (referred to as *hartals*), the JVP sought to bring down the UNP.

The power of the JVP was more strongly felt in southwest Sri Lanka. At the same time, the insurgency affected many areas throughout the island including Kandy and, on a more local scale, Narada and the patrons of Polgoda Vihara. Even though the fundamental ideology behind the 1987 insurgency failed to strike a cord with Narada,[36] and although Narada was able to maintain some distance from the political turmoil by not living at Peradeniya University (where monastics freely participated in numerous student-run political organizations and where the JVP drew many sympathizers), Narada's very status as a university student made him a suspect of the UNP.[37] When one of the temple's workers with alleged ties to the JVP was arrested and later killed by the police, the UNP began keeping a close watch on the temple and on Narada. Narada was frightened and sought the protection of the temple's devotees. His devotees, Narada explained, risked their own lives to shelter him: "I was taken by the devotees from place to place. They helped a lot to hide me. They placed me in various rooms and locked the doors."

It was near the end of this tumultuous period that Narada, with his bachelor's degree in hand, landed his first job: teaching Buddhist civilization to students at the local high school. Although the insurgency was starting to wind down at the time, Narada remained fearful. After assessing his own situation, he decided to return to lay life. Discussing with me that decision, Narada said,

> I wanted to disrobe. Sivali, the principal from the monastic school at Ganegoda Vihara, told me to leave. He said that he would look after the temple for me. He said that I should disrobe and escape. I informed my family about my situation. I got everything in order to leave the *sangha*.
>
> Then one day I reconsidered my options. I went to the university to meet a lecturer of mine. I told him that everything is arranged for me to disrobe. I told him that I had a teaching appointment. I asked him for his thoughts about what I should do. I already received my identification card.[38] He told me not to leave. I had a long chat with him.
>
> After that discussion I reconsidered once again about whether or not I should disrobe. I thought [to myself]: "I never killed anyone. I never did anything [wrong]. I did everything according to Lord Buddha's doctrine." I believed that since I had protected the *dharma*, the *dharma* would protect me. Whether due to the *dharma* or not, I was never taken in by the police. The insurgency ended.

Putting aside his almost daily experiences of death and terror, Narada resisted the general trend of disrobing among university monks.[39] For him, the *dharma* is not simply a body of teachings to be studied and transmitted; it is also something that is powerful and that, when protected, protects.[40]

Perhaps most influential to his decision not to disrobe (as well as to live in Polgoda Vihara rather than the university dormitories while pursuing his degree at Peradeniya University) were the bonds that developed between Narada and his supporters. Discussing the exchanges he had with his own donors and the close ties that grew out of those interactions, Narada said,

> At the beginning there was no regular alms food [*dāna*]. It was difficult [*duṣkarayi*]. Some of the donors [*dāyakas*] brought [food]. Some didn't. The people used to give me what they themselves ate as *dāna*.[41] I was very small. The people used to give me morning, noon, and evening meals.

> Those meals were very simple, such as coconut salad and rice. As they felt that it is not good to keep the young monk hungry, they used to send food at night.[42] *I developed sincere connections with the donors*. (Emphasis added)

The sincere connections, which were rooted in mutual feelings of respect, appreciation, and love—and further strengthened by common experiences (the JVP insurgency) and other emotions (fear)—compelled Narada to reevaluate his sense of commitment as well as own views of monastic service. Discussing with me some of the decisions he made after getting a job at the high school near the temple, Narada said, "I was compelled to think about doing something for society.... We have to serve society. If I did not remain a monk, I could have easily kept my job and looked after myself. But, it is not good to forget the society who helped me complete my studies.... I decided to do this myself because I understood my own situation. I asked myself: 'Who helped me to do my studies? Who should receive the benefit of my service?'"

As I intimated earlier, the close, affective bonds that continued to develop between Narada and his supporters also functioned to inform and shape the community's ideas about ideal monastic deportment and behavior. This can be seen most clearly with regard to the sixth Buddhist precept. All Buddhist monastics—novices and fully ordained monks—following the rules set down in the *Vinaya* are prohibited from eating solid food after midday.[43] Although it is widely recognized that many Sri Lankan monastics eat food in the evenings, most do so surreptitiously. What I found particularly surprising with Narada's case study is that during his first years as the chief incumbent of Polgoda Vihara he ate evening meals quite openly and that his own group of patrons had a hand in it.

Even though many lay donors of Polgoda Vihara discussed with me, on numerous occasions, the need for Buddhist monastics to abide by the "ten million rules of restraint" *(kōṭiyak saṁvara sīla)*, when it came to actual monastics they deal with on a regular bases—referred to as "our monks" *(apē hāmuduruwaru)*—affective states and social ties functioned to curb the extremes of an overly rigid orthopraxy. Ilana Silber (1995:92), in fact, makes reference to the role that social relationships play in influencing standards of purity when she writes, in reference to Thai village Buddhism, that

> Contemporary anthropological studies of traditional village settings would seem to indicate, however, that the virtuoso-layman relation is able to maintain a momentum of its own, not always dependent on the Sangha's actual conformity to the *Vinaya*. Obviously, laymen would not support

> monks who were blatantly unworthy, and the laity, as already suggested, may be seen as exerting continual normative control upon the monkhood, even if this control did not take as dramatic a form as the kings' "campaigns of purification." Nevertheless, standards of purity and adhesion to what was supposed to be a monk's role appear to be flexible or, more precisely, to comprise an interesting blend of ritualization and flexibility.

Silber and Narada's case study suggest that Buddhist monastic institutions are, as Steven Collins posits, a "cultural-ideological project of ongoing collectivities" (1998:57f.). Rather than derived from groups of monastics—real or mythic—depicted in the Pali canon, ideas about ideal monastic behavior and deportment are negotiated and determined through the kinds of affective bonds that people have with particular monastics and shaped, in turn, by a community's experiences and histories.

Ideas about acceptable monastic behavior, moreover, never remain static; changing circumstances and new experiences demand that such ideas are continually renegotiated by members of the community. For instance, even though the laity's acceptance of monastics eating after midday began with Narada's tenure there as a novice, Narada has felt the need to continue encouraging his closest patrons to see nothing wrong with his students eating outside of the prescribed times and, more recently, with the novices playing games such as cricket during evenings and weekends. By using the goodwill he has earned from particular groups of lay patrons as well as by encouraging his students to develop close ties with the temple's patrons,[44] Narada has been able to instill in his patrons shared understandings of ideal monastic behavior that does not necessarily correspond, in every detail, with the norms set forth in the monastic disciplinary code. Although I address this issue at greater length in chapter 5, discussing the relationship between emotions and aesthetics—particularly how affective bonds and shared emotions function to shape local conceptions of what is acceptable—helps us reconcile the patrons' demand that monastics follow the ten million rules of restraint with their own acceptance of Narada and his students breaking the rules.

Not all groups of monastics and laypeople always agree on what is appropriate or acceptable behavior. During one of my more recent visits to Sri Lanka, for example, I was informed by a lay donor that tensions had broken out between Narada and a small group of donors during the run up to one of the country's national elections. It turned out that one donor who had ties to the Sinhala Heritage (Sinhala Urumaya) Party had asked Narada to attend one of the party's political rallies.[45] Ardently believing that politicking is unsuitable for monastics,[46] Narada chose to skip out on the event. Even though it was unclear whether Narada explained his views directly to the patron prior to the rally, my conversations with other donors not supportive of the Sinhala Heritage Party disclosed that Narada's absence at the event was not taken lightly: after he failed to show up, the donor who had issued the invitation began a protest movement against him by arguing that, as a village leader, Narada had let the people down.[47] Many members from the dissenting group, I was told, also extended their critique of Narada to the temple itself, particularly its ongoing construction projects and its rapidly growing numbers of new recruits.

According to the accounts of several other donors who characterized the dissenters as a group of drunkards with no interest in Buddhism or temple life, those who had protested against Narada's behavior were eventually forced, perhaps on account of their own religious needs, to reconcile their differing views with Narada.[48] Regardless of the actual factors that brought the dissenting group back to Polgoda Vihara, the event illustrates, quite clearly, that consensus regarding what constitutes appropriate monastic behavior and roles are determined by contingent conjunctures among groups of laypeople as well as between groups of laypeople and monastics.[49] As ideas about communal standards of excellence develop and change over time and are influenced by groups of people, their experiences, and their inherited understandings of the past, however, the conjunctures must include more than simply minute, present-day moments.

COMPASSION FOR THE DOWNTRODDEN: ORDINATION AS SOCIAL SERVICE

Once Narada started his job at the local high school, he began investing all of his time and energy back into society, vowing not to forget "the society who helped" him. While catering to his patrons' religious and social needs, Narada also began focusing his social service enterprise on other targets: poor *(duppat)* and helpless *(asaraṇa)* children living in disadvantaged areas *(duṣkara paḷ̥āt)*. Explaining his vision of social service, Narada said,

> I felt that there are so many people living in society who are unable to do their studies; because of that [I thought] of bringing them and ordaining them. I don't take even a single cent from that group. I don't take money from their homes for robes and other monastic articles.[50] All expenses are borne by myself. I don't only support them through my [teaching] salary. I [also] get money [for them] through other means. For some sermons, I get

six hundred to seven hundred rupees. I use that money too for their education. The entire moneybag [that is passed around at the end of each ritual] is given, in its entirety, to their education. I provide them with everything they need to the best of my ability. They are not imprisoned. They are given mental and physical freedom.

Narada clearly sees his project of providing an education to those unable to pursue their studies as an important dimension of social service. Similar to his grand-teacher Udunuvara Sri Sarananda, who,[51] after intensely experiencing his country's ongoing social injustices (particularly as they related to caste),[52] sought to improve the lives of poor, lower-caste villagers,[53] Narada has focused his social service project on helpless children from disadvantaged areas. I might add that Narada's use of ordination as a way to effect social and economic change is quite different from other forms of social service proposed by Sri Lankan monastics over the past century.

One could argue, as Narada has, that the social service role of the *sangha* goes all the way back to the Buddha; nevertheless, H. L. Seneviratne's study of twentieth-century Sri Lankan Buddhism demonstrates how understandings of social service underwent a major conceptual shift in the late nineteenth and early twentieth centuries. With Anagārika Dharmapāla (1864–1933), social service was stripped of its religious and soteriological significance and took on, according to Seneviratne, both a pragmatic and ideological dimension. Seneviratne goes on to illustrate convincingly how Dharmapāla's comprehensive agenda of effecting economic change (pragmatic) and regenerating Sinhala culture (ideological) was separated into two distinct programs as it was adopted by monastics from Vidyodaya and Vidyālaṅkāra Pirivena. Seneviratne contends that, although a number of leading monks from the former institution (such as Venerables Pannasekhara, Dhammaloka, and Silaratana) adopted a more economic form of social service that was enacted through wide array rural development (*grāmasaṁvardhana*) projects,[54] several monks from Vidyālaṅkāra (e.g., Venerables Walpola Rahula and Yakkaduve Pragnarama) took up Dharmapāla's ideological dimension of social service. Through a number of their publications, especially Walpola Rahula's *Bhikṣuvagē Urumaya* (1946), Rahula and Pragnarama not only argued for the unity of the Sinhala language, the Buddhist religion, and the state, but also legitimated the place for monks in politics.

Even though Narada's social service enterprise is quite distinct from the types of rural developments projects administered by monastics such as Pannasekhara, Dhammaloka, and Sīlaratana, as well as from the political activism espoused by Rahula and Pragnarama, Narada has repeatedly maintained—like the monastics from Vidyodaya and Vidyālaṅkāra who turn to history, texts, and the Buddha to legitimate their particular social service agendas[55]—that his own use of ordination as a means to effect social and economic change is consistent with what the Buddha practiced. Making reference to the disciples of the Buddha, Narada explained,

> The *sangha* from the Buddha's period directed compassion to those who needed it, not to those who did not need it. So, we can say that the *sangha* is based on helpless [*asaraṇa*] people. The *sangha* should be founded on sympathy, compassion, and loving kindness. The Buddha is called "One with a heart cooled by compassion" and "The kind one for helpless people."
>
> ... When the Buddha was around, there were poor people such as Sunīta,[56] Sopāka,[57] Aṅgulimāla, and Upāli the barber. There were also rich people such as Rāhula, Ānanda, Anuruddha, and Moggallāna,[58] many of whom were Sākyas. Nowadays, it is the same—there are both rich and helpless people living in society. That being the case, *we have to consider helpless boys and give priority to them*. [Emphasis added]
>
> ... If we can raise street boys into a suitable person, why can't the others worship him? If people from a society where caste problems were prevalent worshipped people like Sopāka and Sunīta, then why can't people who live in a modern and interconnected world worship them [i.e., such people]. Loving kindness and compassion should be given to them. That must happen. Without that, there would be no humanity. Many monks select good boys to ordain: good boys who have nice appearances, good families, and who are healthy. They select them for ordination. No one considers boys who live on the street, who have snot coming out of their nose, and mucous oozing from their eyes. We would make a true difference if we can make those boys well and beautiful.

In pointing out the relationships that Venerable Narada draws between the life of the Buddha and his own social service enterprise, my goal is neither to argue that Buddhism has changed little over time nor to claim that *vox populi, vox Buddhae*.[59] Instead, my intention is to illustrate how stories of the Buddha and stories about one's own life (e.g., how the *sangha* enabled Narada to advance both socially and economically) are used to legitimate particular visions of monastic vocation and the *sangha*.[60] Indeed, by linking his own social service enterprise to that of the Buddha and by connecting notions of decline *(pirihenavā)* and revival *(diyuṇu venavā)* to his educational path,[61] Narada endeavored to defend and validate his own vision of what Buddhism is and what monks should try to do in contemporary society, a vision that, Narada believed, is largely being overlooked by monastic leaders in modern-day Sri Lanka,[62] including those from his own Rāmañña fraternity.[63]

In positing that the "*sangha* should be founded on sympathy [*anukampāva*], compassion [*karuṇāva*], and loving kindness [*mettā*]" Narada was not merely referring to the divine abidings that are to be cultivated through meditative exercises and expressed in an unbounded manner. Instead, he was referring to something much more tangible and visceral: providing helpless children with an atmosphere that they would *ideally* experience at home, namely, an atmosphere permeated with affection, love, and attachment.[64] Turning to examples of several of some his own students who were neglected (such as several parentless boys; motherless boys whose fathers have remarried;[65] boys who were sent to work as housemaids; and even one child whose own mother, in a fit of rage, attempted to kill him by throwing him in a well), Narada has repeatedly argued for the need to establish and develop affectionate bonds with his own students. Indeed, the kind gestures Narada shows to his students, the evening meals that he and others provide (and sometimes cook) for them, the manner in which he advises them in the evening, and the jokes he shares with them are all grounded in Narada's belief that the very success of his social service enterprise and his ability to hold together his own Buddhist monastic community are based upon establishing close, affective bonds between himself and his students, as well as between his own temple and his lay patrons.

Narada is certainly not alone in drawing a connection between affective bonds and the successful running of a monastic institution. In an editorial titled "Disrobing Is Not Because of [Romantic] Love" ("Sivuru Harinnē Prēmaya Nisā Novē") published in the Sinhala newspaper *Divayina*, the monk Daṅkäṭiyē Sumana (Sumana 2000) examines several factors that he believes are behind the declining number of monks and novices in contemporary Sri Lanka. Critical of what he regards as a widespread view that monastics tend to disrobe because of falling in love with women, Sumana turns to other reasons why young members of the Buddhist *sangha* leave the order. Along with mentioning more personal problems that sometimes force monks and novices to return to lay life (such as the need to take care of aging or infirm parents who cannot sufficiently care for themselves), Sumana argues that novices who lack affection from their teachers, as well as their own patrons, are more likely to disrobe. Speaking specifically about novices who disrobe within the first several years after entering the *sangha*, he writes,

> Normally, boys enter the *sangha* between the ages of eight and fifteen. That is the age that they really need love and affection. They are still getting it from their parents and siblings. Going to temple means that they have to change their environment completely, to move into a strange environment. In some of the temples, they don't receive the same [level of] affection that they received from home. They were really desirous [*āsāyi*] to become a monk; however, after that [ordination] they face a completely unexpected situation and environment. They live in fear in relationship to the head monk's role. [The head monks] don't talk to them while looking at their faces.... They have to wake up by 5:00 in the morning and work until 10:00 pm. They have to work according to a timetable. For those children who were sleeping in the embrace of their parents until dawn, waking up at 5:00 is something bizarre.

Even though several other points that Daṅkäṭiyē Sumana raised in his article on disrobing were challenged in a subsequent editorial (Dēvanārāyana 2000), his point about the need for novices to receive love and affection from their teachers and temple patrons seems to echo the very points that Narada has made in regard to the monastic community of Polgoda Vihara.

CONCLUSION

Prior to beginning research at Polgoda Vihara, my own conception of what binds groups of monastics and their lay supporters was based on a model of exchange in which laypeople receive religious instruction and the opportunity to earn merit in exchange for supporting those in robes with food, clothing, shelter, and medicine. I drew such an understanding from a variety of sources who spoke about "reciprocal generosity" and monastic-lay relationships that are founded upon mutual dependency and trust. In his introductory book on Theravāda Buddhism, for example, Richard Gombrich (2006:116) writes that "the Sangha gave the Dhamma, the laity gave material support, rather disparagingly termed 'raw fish.' Naturally the laity were conceived as having much the better of the bargain. In fact, since giving to the Sangha brought them merit, they were favoured by both halves of the transaction." This portrayal of economic and even spiritual exchange—in which the lay members supply monastics with their monastic requisites in exchange for the monk offering religious teachings and the opportunity to earn merit—is also elucidated in Rupert Gethin's (1998:94) *Foundations of Buddhism*. Focusing on the monastic rules that make the laity and the *sangha* dependent on each other (such as the rules that prevent monks from growing their own food and thus require them to turn to the laity on a daily basis), Gethin writes that "the lifestyle of the Buddhist monk is thus founded on a relationship of trust between himself and his supporters. By accepting lay support in the form of robes, food, and lodgings, the monk enters into a kind of social contract; it becomes his responsibility to live in a certain way, namely to live the holy or spiritual life *(brahmacarya)* to the best of his ability" (see also Harvey 1990:240–243 and Carrithers 1983:51).

This way of envisioning monastic-lay relationships is certainly not incorrect and, as Gombrich, Gethin, and Wijayaratna (1990) point out, is supported by a number of canonical texts. Still, conversations I had with Narada and his patrons have enabled me, over the years, to acquire a more nuanced appreciation of this relationship: while ritual needs and the desire to make merit bring laypeople and monastics together at certain times and for certain occasions, Buddhist institutions are held together by bonds that are, themselves, shaped and sustained by shared experiences and emotions. When discussing his early years at the temple, Narada mentioned on numerous occasions how his donors treated him with love and affection. The affective bonds that Narada developed with his own patrons was further deepened by their shared experiences during the second JVP insurgency when, risking the safety of their own lives, they hid Narada in their homes. Thus, more than simply a social contract founded on a system of economic exchange, trust, or reciprocal generosity, the social bonds between Narada and his donors were and continue to be informed and determined by a whole host of emotions, positive (love, praise, affection) and negative (fear, anger, distrust).

A careful consideration of the webs of social relations that existed at Polgoda Vihara also reveal how affective bonds and shared sentiments influence the very commitments that laypeople and Buddhist monastics make to the *sangha*, their own local communities, and even Sri Lankan society as a whole. Narada's choice to remain in the *sangha* and his decision to adopt a more social service vocation were largely the outcome of the relationships he forged with his patrons and teachers. In the same manner, the patrons' dedication to continue supporting Narada while he attended Sarananda Pirivena and Peradeniya University and their long-term support of the temple as it was transformed into an institution large enough to house and sustain seventy-five residents were, by and large, the result of their affective ties with Narada, whom they proudly referred to as "our lord" [*apē hāmuduruwo*].

Finally, questioning the tendency of some laypeople (such as members of the Vinaya Vardhana Society)[66] or monastics (such as those who were part of the ascetic or *tāpasa* movement or the forest tradition) to base notions of ideal monastic behavior solely on the *Vinaya*, I have contended that social bonds may function, at times, to mold people's—monastic and lay—aesthetic sensibilities, especially in regard to who constitutes a "good" *(honda)* and "upright" *(yahapat)* monastic in contemporary Sri Lanka. Although the monastic disciplinary code still informs people's ideas about appropriate behavior and demeanor, the connection that is sometimes made between following the monastic rules and becoming a potent field of merit that, in turn, attracts lay Buddhists may be somewhat overstated.[67] Many lay patrons spoke to me about morality and the need to locate upright monastics; at the same time, our conversations about Polgoda Vihara and its history suggest that their own sensibilities concerning who constitutes a good monastic and who is an appropriate recipient are dynamically determined and redetermined as a result of their shared histories and current experiences.

2 Aesthetics of Emotions and Affective Bonds

Monastic Recruitment in Two Sri Lankan Villages

Unquestionably, one of the most popular Sinhalese films in 2004 was *Sūriya Araṇa* (English title: *Fire Fighters*) by the renowned director Somaratne Dissanayake. The film tells the tale of a hunter and his ten-year-old son as they lay sole claim to the bordering jungle's bounty by frightening others with conjured up stories of the forest's many wandering ghosts.

Problems for the hunter and his son crop up when an old monk and his young novice student set up their monastic residence in one of the jungle's small caves. Besides threatening the hunter's career by being spiritual exemplars, the two monastics—portrayed as sincere, peaceful, and humble—encroach upon the hunter's exclusive claim to the jungle when they begin attracting many villagers to their jungle retreat. In seeking to reassert his own claim on the jungle, the threatened hunter tries his hand at several surreptitious tricks. Not only does the hunter fail, but he is also forced into a close, personal relationship with his nemesis after losing a limb to one of his animal traps. Perhaps the most touching subplot within the film is the burgeoning relationship between the hunter's son and the young novice *(sāmaṇera)*, a friendship that was encouraged by the *sāmaṇera*'s teacher. Although the hunter's son colludes at first with his father's schemes for ridding the jungle of the two monastic "pests," the young boy succumbs to the novice's innocence and friendship. As the two boys begin spending more and more time together—including playing and bathing together at the nearby stream—the hunter's son comes to love the very animals that he and his father had previously sought for their livelihood. As the relationship between the two boys intensifies, the young hunter is also impressed by the beauty of monastic life. The film concludes when the boy, seemingly awed by the young novice's life in robes, decides to leave his father and become a novice himself. His father consents.

Sūriya Araṇa is a work of fiction, but the manner in which the film depicts what draws young children to the *sangha* is not. Specifically, the film implicitly challenges (perhaps "complexifies" is a better term) certain economic models used to understand monastic recruitment by poignantly showing that although the *sangha* plays a role in providing boys and their families with opportunities that would not otherwise be available to them, monastic recruitment is, in many cases, also dependent on a variety of factors.

Drawing heavily on the voices of one of Reverend Narada's senior students, Venerable Sumedha, as well as several novices Sumedha recruited when he was a head monk of two different temples, this chapter examines how bonds forged between monastics, children, and families of potential recruits affect the lifelong choices that people make toward the *sangha*. By also focusing on aesthetics of monastic deportment, this chapter presents a more holistic vision of monastic recruitment. Before closely examining Sumedha's method of monastic recruitment, it may be helpful to consider a brief biographical sketch of his early life as it clearly shaped his ideas about how to draw newcomers to the Buddhist *sangha*.

RECRUITING THROUGH THE HEART: VENERABLE SUMEDHA

I first met Sumedha in 1999. He was thirty-four years old at the time. I found Sumedha to be serious and intense, unlike his teacher. Although his forthright demeanor and attitude led me, at first, to characterize him as a business-oriented monastic, I have come to conclude—after speaking with his students and observing the manner in which he interacts with his patrons, his students, and his own teacher—that similar to Narada, Sumedha is a warm-hearted monastic who cares very much about the welfare of those around him. The time and energy he devotes to developing his temple, training his students, and serving his patrons and Sri Lankan society as a whole are indicative of his religious and social commitments.

Many of my first interviews with Sumedha focused on monastic training and the *sangha*'s role in contemporary society. Although I only interviewed Sumedha on occasion from 1998–2000, I began spending more time at his temple during my subsequent visits in 2003, 2004, 2005, and 2006. It was during those visits that I came to realize that Sumedha has, over the years, played a fundamental role in the dramatic rise in the number of novices at Polgoda Vihara and his own temple, Hinagoda Vihara. As I will suggest below, Sumedha's skill in recruiting newcomers to the *sangha* is anchored in his sensitivity to the economic requirements, aesthetic sensibilities, and emotional needs of local Buddhists, as well as in his ability to forge close bonds with Buddhist laypeople and potential recruits.

Born in 1965, Sumedha grew up in close contact with Buddhist monks and Buddhist temples. As a young boy, Sumedha lived in close proximity to Ganegoda Vihara, Devamitta's temple where Narada was first sent by his own father to live, train, and eventually ordain as a Buddhist monastic. Sumedha's connection to the temple began with his grandfather, who was not only a generous donor of

Ganegoda Vihara, but also Devamitta's relative. Given his family's economic and personal ties to the temple, it is not surprising to find that Sumedha was always treated well at the temple. It is also worthwhile to note, as Sumedha explained to me, that the close bonds that formed between Devamitta and Sumedha were very influential to the young boy:

> The Ganegoda temple was build on my grandfather's [land]. The entire land [where the temple sits] is not my grandfather's, just a section. Not all of our land was given to the temple. We kept a section ourselves. During my childhood, I used to go back and forth to the land [we kept]. Whenever I went [there], I also used to stop by at the temple. My family members were patrons [*dāyakas*] of that temple.... Because of that, the head monk was very close to me. My grandfather was Devamitta's brother. [Devamitta] was very affectionate with me.... He requested that I ordain. My grandmother told me: "When you were young, they wanted you to ordain." She told me that. That would have remained in my heart. I was very small at the time.

Another important force drove Sumedha to the *sangha:* seeing one of Devamitta's monk-friends waiting for a bus on the side of the road. Describing the encounter and the effects that it had on his desire to become a monk, Sumedha said,

> There was a monk waiting by the Bodhi tree at the one mile post. He was waiting to catch a bus. He had a palmyra-leaf umbrella.[1] That monk must have been about thirty-five years old at that time. Siddhartha became the Buddha when he was thirty-five, right? We cannot compare him [to the Buddha]. We cannot do that, right? However, that monk was very beautiful [*lassaṇayi*]. I was thrilled to see him, like Lord Buddha, holding a palmyra-leaf umbrella. I was very small at the time. That monk was the monk who was living in the Madavala temple in Anurādhapura. That monk died recently. Seeing him, I felt a longing [*āsāva*] toward monks.

Rather than being driven, as some scholars claim, by a desire "to get a free education and economic security to put them through school and college" (Obeyesekere 1981:41), Sumedha's interest in joining the *sangha* was generated, partially at least, by the types of bonds that formed between him and other monastics (especially Devamitta), as well as by certain aesthetic experiences (such as seeing a well-dressed, beautiful monk holding a palmyra-leaf umbrella). As we shall see below, these experiences, which clearly stuck out in Sumedha's mind, would come to play a future role in the methods that Sumedha would use to draw potential recruits—particularly poor children living in disadvantaged areas—to the *sangha*.

Before continuing with Sumedha's story, I should note that the manner in which Venerable Devamitta recruited Sumedha to the *sangha* is quite typical. Indeed, many head monks *(vihārādhipati)* within the largest of the three monastic fraternities in Sri Lanka, the Siyam Nikāya,[2] often recruit their own relatives—most commonly their nephews—with the expectation that they will take over their temple some day.[3] Although people familiar with this type of pupillary succession might find Venerable Narada's and Sumedha's active recruiting of poor children from disadvantaged areas to be anomalous or even bizarre, it is important to consider their ideas about the *sangha* and Sumedha's method of recruitment for several reasons.

The first reason concerns cultural attitudes about monastic ordination. Certain monastic fraternities and monastic leaders tend to restrict ordination to particular groups such as high-caste members and children from good families. Although this tendency may be quite pervasive, it remains, as I discussed in the previous chapter and will discuss in chapter 5, quite contentious. In that regard, taking into account how others—particularly nonélites from less commonly studied fraternities—think about monastic vocation, the *sangha*, and ordination is important to acquiring a greater understanding of Buddhism in contemporary Sri Lanka.

Second, while Narada's and Sumedha's ideas about actively recruiting poor children to the *sangha* are somewhat uncharacteristic,[4] the very methods by which Sumedha goes about drawing newcomers to the *sangha* are, as we shall shortly see, not that unique. Just as Sumedha seeks to bring others to the *sangha* by establishing and cultivating affective bonds with them as well as by providing them with a certain aesthetic experience, so too does recruitment within the Siyam Nikāya—even those who are recruited from a monastic's own family—contain some affective and aesthetic dimensions.

Finally, even though this chapter focuses on a specific monastic's views about and practices in relation to monastic recruitment, it illustrates how the distant past may sometimes be used to legitimate one's actions in the present.[5] It also points to a dialogical process that exists between the present and the past: how the past shapes one's present actions (i.e., how the factors that drove one to the *sangha* might shape how one recruits others) as well as how one's present experiences (e.g., the successes and failures in monastic recruitment) may be used to frame the past.

Sumedha ardently wanted to become a monastic; his father, however, refused to grant his son permission to ordain. His opposition to the idea, moreover, was even unshaken after Devamitta personally asked him to allow his son to ordain during a politically sponsored ordination event.[6] Sumedha's father had other plans for the boy after realizing that his son showed a lot of promise in regard to his education; indeed, in 1980 Sumedha was one of two boys from his high school to do extremely well on his ordinary-level exams. Unable to procure his father's consent, Sumedha began to devote more and more of his time and energy toward studying for the upcoming advanced-level exams.

Sumedha's future prospects looked extremely bright. Suddenly, however, his dream of being accepted at a university was shattered by an unfortunate turn of events:

> I got someone from the village to help me for my advanced levels. He filled out my application form. He signed me up for commerce. I didn't know anything about commerce! My strength was in the arts. With the application completed, I had no choice but to do commerce. I went to [private tuition] commerce classes. I did nothing on Sinhala or Buddhism. Because of that [extra time I had to devote to studying], I stopped going to the temple.... During that period, I began gradually to forget about it [i.e., ordaining]. That was my situation. I had trouble with my advanced levels. I was fed up.
>
> One day I went to the lake in Kandy and walked around and around [it] alone. Why? Because I was fed up! From there, I went straightaway to Polgoda Vihara. I told Narada: "I want to become a novice. I can't stay [at home]." That was how I came to be a monk. That is how I got the opportunity to ordain. I did not ordain when I was small.

While the hope of gaining admission into university was still strong, Sumedha's vision of himself as a monastic remained dim. It was only when his frustrations flared and his dream faded that Sumedha began to feel a particular attraction to the robes once again. Meeting Venerable Narada at Polgoda Vihara was the final catalyst that drove Sumedha toward a life in saffron robes: "Narada cut my hair, Devamitta tied the belt.[7] That is how it happened.... I was a student of both of them. Nonetheless, it was Narada who made me feel a greater longing to ordain. When seeing Narada Thero's discipline, restraint, as well as behavior and deportment [*ākalpa*],[8] everyone feels longing [*āsāva*]. That was what happened [to me]. He helped me get rid of the darkness during that period of my life." Similar to the buddha-like monk waiting on the side of the road, Narada's appearance and demeanor not only helped to incline Sumedha toward a life in robes but also would come to shape the techniques that he would soon use to draw other potential recruits to the *sangha*.

It is very common for students to remain by their teacher's side until they take higher ordination or are put in charge of their own temple or are sent by their preceptor to live at a monastic school. Sumedha, however, believed that monks who remain in or close by their native villages are less likely to succeed.[9] Thus, shortly after ordaining, Sumedha decided to leave his teachers and move to Anurādhapura. After spending several months at Nikkaväva Pirivena, Sumedha decided to take a short trip out to the village of Madavala and call on one of Devamitta's friends: the monk whom Sumedha, as a young boy, saw by the side of the road. Impressed by Sumedha's determination, the monk invited Sumedha to stay with him at his Madavala temple. Preferring life at a small village temple over the bustle of a large monastic college, Sumedha immediately accepted.

After several months of living together at Madavala, Devamitta's friend was asked to administer another temple. He agreed and, before leaving, handed the Madavala temple over to Sumedha. For the next three years (1989–1992) Sumedha remained permanently at the temple, running its daily affairs single-handedly at first.[10] Besides fulfilling the religious needs of the temple's immediate patrons (e.g., accepting alms on a daily basis,[11] attending alms-giving rituals at his patrons' homes, and performing *bodhipūjā*, protection, and funeral rituals), Sumedha would sometimes also assist monks living in neighboring temples. It was during the time of his incumbency of the Madavala temple that Sumedha began actively recruiting the village's children to the *sangha*. Because Sumedha's success in drawing newcomers to the *sangha* is inherently tied into his sensitivity to the backgrounds and needs of local Buddhists, it is helpful to give a brief description of Madavala and its surrounding villages.

Madavala is one of many villages that are part of the Huruluväva colonization scheme that was established in the 1950s as part of Prime Minister D. S. Senanayake's post–World War II agrarian revolution (Jayawardene 1973).[12] Because the area is part of Sri Lanka's dry zone (a zone that comprises roughly two thirds of the country), its residents depend quite heavily upon the Huruluväva reservoir that had, before Senanayake's revolution, fallen into disrepair. With the reservoir restored, new settlers—the majority of whom were Sinhalese[13]—were encouraged to settle there through enticing government giveaways such as free cultivatable land, housing, and other public amenities.

Huruluväva (whose residents largely hail from Mātalē, Kurunägala, and Kandy) consists of 6,447 acres of irrigated land and has a total population of approximately 40,000. It is the third-largest colonization scheme in terms of irrigated land in Anurādhapura (Abeysinghe 1983:5). Although Huruluväva and other new colonies were packaged to potential settlers and other backers as playing an important part in Sri Lanka's bright future, the situation on the ground soon took a turn for the worse. Indeed, quite unlike the early, almost fairytale, descriptions of the colonies that mentioned "thousands of flourishing homesteads, mile upon mile of lush paddy fields, . . . extensive cattle farms, neat and efficient agricultural stations, [and] schools with healthy and smiling children," ("Profiles: The Prime Minister" 1950), descriptions of the colony by today's residents are very different. The majority of Huruluväva residents—because of limited resources, reduced subsidies, scarcity of available land, and the area's harsher climate—fall well below the poverty line, have poor educational facilities,[14] experience abysmally low food and nutrition standards, and face deplorable living conditions with only meager basic amenities (see Abeysinghe 1983:58). Moreover, with the colonies' government schools barely able to keep up with the national norm,[15] high rates of underemployment, rampant alcoholism,[16] substantial dropout rates for school-going children, and few opportunities for the villages' children (Abeysinghe 1983:30), it is no wonder that Madavala and many of its surrounding villages are often referred to as a difficult or disadvantaged area *(duṣkara paḷāta)* by its residents and those familiar with the area.

Sumedha began carrying out Narada's social service enterprise after coming to understand the background and plight of the children from the area. Believing that children are truly incapable of grasping the concept of poverty,[17] Sumedha sought to recruit newcomers to the *sangha* by focusing on the same factors that drew him, as a young boy, to the monastic community: embodying a particular monastic aesthetic and cultivating affectionate bonds with potential recruits.

Several of my conversations with Sumedha that touched upon the place of appearance in the recruitment process focused on the uniqueness of his own monastic fraternity, the Rāmañña Nikāya. Well aware of the positive impressions that the Rāmañña Nikāya has made historically,[18] Sumedha has sought to capitalize on the somewhat pervasive view that monks from the Rāmañña Nikāya tend to be less worldly and more monklike.[19] Distinguishing the dress of his own fraternity from the predominant and more widely criticized Siyam Nikāya,[20] Sumedha discussed the effects that his own appearance and demeanor had on the people living in and around Madavala:

> There is a tendency that one becomes pleased seeing us [Rāmañña monks] more than seeing other monks. I never use an umbrella. I use a palmyra-leaf umbrella. I have never grown my hair, even to the shortest of lengths.... In Anurādhapura, there was a [Siyam Nikāya] monk who always fought with people. That was the type of situation there. The people who felt disgusted about those types of things would have been pleased to see us. By seeing us, people would think "These are the monks who have good qualities."... They would have also thought: *"This is a real monk. Our son should also become like this."*
>
> ... The area around Madavala is surrounded by Siyam Nikāya temples.[21] Those [monks] wear their robe covering one shoulder. We wear our robes covering both shoulders.... These are differences that pertain to restraint [*saṅvaraya*]. It is not about morality [*sīla*]. It has nothing to do with whether *sīla* is there or not. The people are simply [*nikaṅ*] pleased [*satuṭa*] seeing [our] external appearance.... The people gathered around me because [I had] that external appearance.
>
> ... There are differences [in acceptable behavior] from place to place.... When I was in Anurādhapura, I used to travel by tractor, bicycle, and truck. Here [in Kandy] I don't travel in that manner. It is not acceptable.... *We have to know how to live according to the area's requirements.* [Emphases added]

From Sumedha's perspective, saffron robes and other accoutrements are not merely signs of Buddhist monastic life. They are aesthetic objects. Robes that cover both shoulders and a cleanly shaven head and face symbolize the "good qualities" of monastics and, as such, have the potential to draw people toward the temple and, in turn, toward a life in robes.

Although one might expect, from reading stories about Gotama while he was still a prince, that the decision to ordain should be prompted by an acute awareness of suffering and the possibilities available to those who choose the religious life, it is worthwhile to point out that the power that a monastic's appearance and demeanor have in driving people toward a life in robes has a long history within the Buddhist tradition. In his *Buddhist Monastic Life*, for instance, Mohan Wijayaratna (1990:6f.; see also Gokhale 1965) discusses the powerful effect that the Buddha's own appearance and demeanor had on the people around him: "According to the canonical texts, the Buddha had a very powerful personality. He was graceful, gentle, always in good spirits, full of energy and ever smiling.... Some more examples will illustrate the spell cast by the Buddha's physical appearance on certain people. Sujātā . . . happened to see the Buddha on her way home from a carnival. She was so impressed by his gentle and friendly air that she decided there and then to join the Community. . . . Sundara-Samudda, the son of a merchant family in Rājagaha, also decided to become a monk because he was delighted by the Buddha's appearance."[22]

What is perhaps most interesting about Sumedha's explanation is how his distinction between morality *(sīla)* and restraint *(saṁvaraya)* implicitly challenges the tendency to judge monastic behavior solely against the standards set forth in the disciplinary code *(Vinaya)*. Indeed, quite unlike a number of monastic and lay movements that have sought to align contemporary monastic behavior with canonical norms—for example, the Vinaya Vardhana Society (Kemper 1978), the ascetic *(tāpasa)* movement (Carrithers 1979; Gombrich and Obeyesekere 1988), and the forest movement (Carrithers 1983)[23]—Sumedha's comment points to other factors—such as people's collective aesthetic sensibilities that are more often than not, determined by time, region, and context—that influence and even determine people's conception of monastic purity.

In his article "Jainism and Buddhism as Enduring Historical Streams," Michael Carrithers similarly argues for a more complex understanding of monastic restraint and purity. Suggesting that ideas of self-restraint are quite indeterminate, Carrithers goes on to distinguish, as Sumedha has, what is aesthetically pleasing—which Carrithers refers to as an "aesthetic standard"—from morality as determined by the monastic disciplinary code. Although it may be correctly suggested that the contours of the aesthetic standard are formed from, or informed by, the monastic disciplinary code—especially the rules of decorum or etiquette *(sekhiya)*—Carrithers (1990:158) proposes that the aesthetic standard is something more: "The aesthetic standard so understood is different from a morality or rules in that it is partly embodied, that is, it exists partly as a quality of bodily movement, or as a physical posture, or as a propensity in speech and action. In that respect, the aesthetic standard is essentially fuzzy and indeterminate, since it does not fully prescribe actions, but only a quality of actions."

Similar to Carrithers (1990:159) and Silber (1995:92), who have drawn attention to the role that social relationship play in shaping people's standards of purity, Sumedha has maintained that ideas regarding what constitutes ideal monastic deportment and appearance are influenced by the affective relationships that form between monastics and their lay patrons. In that regard, aesthetics and emotions are closely linked. Emotions such as anger, disgust, pleasure, and awe are essentially appraisals that inform people's ideas about what is pleasing; certain aesthetic responses, in turn, may trigger affective states that subsequently shape or color a subsequent judgment or response. To understand more fully the aesthetics of emotion in Sri Lankan monastic culture, I need to turn to the second component of Sumedha's enterprise of temple recruitment: establishing close, affective bonds with potential recruits and their family members.

Reflecting back on the close bonds that he had formed with Devamitta and the effects that those bonds had on the desire to ordain, Sumedha realized that he needed to find a way to connect—on a personal, affective level—with the young children living in and around Madavala. Within several months Sumedha decided to establish a Buddhist *dharma* school *(daham pāsäla)* at his temple which, he believed, would quickly draw the area's children by his side.[24] Describing his *dharma* school and how it impacted his ability to recruit, Sumedha said,

> Normally *dharma* schools are only on Sundays. The one there [in Madavala] was daily.... The name of the *dharma* school was Sangha Bodhi Daham Pāsäla. In that school, I often made up songs for the students to sing. I wrote poems too. One song was: "We, who decorate the country and nation, are the students of Sangha Bodhi Daham Pāsäla in Madavala Rajamahavihāra which bathes itself in the cool [waters] of Huruluväva."[25] The temple there was an ancient royal temple [i.e., *rajamahavihāraya*]. That was the song of the Sangha Bodhi Daham Pāsäla. I remember that song even now. It may have been the case that children came to the *dharma* school simply because they longed to sing those songs. Through that [school], they became close to me. They often came to the temple.
>
> ...Children here [in Kandy] have a lot of playthings and toys. It is less for those living there [in Madavala]. They need freedom and entertainment. Sometimes, parents leave their children at home and go to their garden plots or paddy fields. As a result, [the children left at home alone] are happy to see a monk. Monks are compassionate, right? They long for the compassion of a monk. Because of that, they become closer and closer to the temple. Temples do religious rituals. There are *dharma* schools. There are youth groups. They recite poems and songs. Because of that, the children long to come.

Buddhist *dharma* schools—originally affiliated with the Buddhist Theosophical Society, which was created by Colonel Olcott during his first visit to Sri Lanka—were established to compete with Christian Sunday schools by communicating and instilling in children Buddhist doctrine and mores.[26] For Sumedha, however, Sangha Bodhi Daham Pāsäla (whose members met every day rather than only on Sundays) functioned as a conduit to the *sangha* and the means through which Sumedha could begin forming bonds with the area's children. By offering the children an alternative to staying home unsupervised, as well as the children's parents a safe place where their children could play freely, Sumedha naturally began drawing children around him. He also became a surrogate parent or caretaker for children whose own biological mothers and fathers were busy with agricultural duties. By showing the school's participants an almost "parent-like" compassion and by repeatedly asking them to ordain, Sumedha sought to cultivate a sense of longing *(āsāva)* within each child that, he hoped, would eventually drive him to the *sangha*.

There was another element to Sumedha's ability to recruit through the *dharma* school. Recalling how appealing Buddhist rituals and singing songs were to him as a child,[27] Sumedha believed that offering the children the chance to learn and recite poetry, the opportunity to compose and sing songs, and the occasion to organize and participate in a number of alluring Buddhist rituals (such as *bodhipūjā* and *kavi baṇa*)[28] would appeal to the children's aesthetic sensibilities. Just as the aesthetic dimension of older all-night preaching rituals functioned to draw crowds to the event,[29] Sumedha felt that illustrating a certain aesthetic of monastic life as well as involving children in rituals and activities that most find beautiful and appealing would be another way to draw others around him and attract their hearts to a life in the *sangha*.

Conversations with a number of novices associated with the temple's *daham pāsäla* suggest that the *dharma* school was an effective recruiting tool and that Sumedha had correctly surmised the role that aesthetics and affective bonds would come to play in the recruitment process. Indeed, one novice who ordained in 1992, near the end of Sumedha's tenure at the Madavala temple, was Silananda. Born in 1984, Silananda was nine years old when he decided, after visiting Sumedha's temple on an almost daily basis, to become a monastic. During one of my interviews with him in 1999, Silananda divulged what drew him, as a young boy, to the *sangha:*

> Whenever I used to go to the *daham pāsäla,* the head monk used to tell me to come and become a monastic. While patting me on the head, he frequently asked me to become a monastic. I used to go to *dharma* school regardless of what was going on at home. . . . I became very close to the temple. I was very desirous to see monks. I always used to go to the *dharma* school. That was the main cause. The head monk had a lot of affection for me. He told me to become a monastic. He was affectionate to me like a

> mother. He was very beautiful. The way he wore his robes was very beautiful.... When I went to the temple, he spoke affectionately to me saying "You should become a monk." When monks talk like this, one becomes close. That monk was very close to many children. Along with being connected to the children, he was also close to our families. That is why there was a connection.... That is why I became one with them [*ekatu venavā*].

Silananda was well aware of his family's economic plight; at the same time, there were other factors than a desire for a better education that drew him to the *sangha*. Sumedha's affection (e.g., patting the boy on the head as a parent might their own child and speaking affectionately to him)[30] and the ties that he developed with Silananda's family contributed to the young boy's decision to ordain. Moreover, the boy's and his mother's comment that they came to learn about what is a good monastic through their relationship with Sumedha suggest, among other things, that their own emotive bonds not only triggered a particular response toward the *sangha*, but also shaped their own aesthetic sensibilities in regard to the qualities of a good, upright monastic.

In 1992 Sumedha began residing at the Madavala temple on a temporary basis; two years later, he left the temple for good.[31] Even with Sumedha's physical absence from the village since 1994, the images of monastic restraint that he embodied, as well as the personal bonds that he established, remained imprinted on most villagers' minds for some time. Throughout the next twelve years, the effects of Sumedha's five-year tenure at the Madavala temple—which were sustained by his and Venerable Narada's intermittent visits to the area as well as by their incessant contact with many of the area's resident—not only ensured a continuous flow of new recruits from the area to Polgoda Vihara, but also permitted Narada to fulfill, approximately ten years later, a different type of social service agenda in Anurādhapura and throughout Sri Lanka: building numerous branch temples.[32]

SUMEDHA'S MAHAVELA INCUMBENCY

The second temple that Sumedha administered was located in the village of Mahavela. Situated in Mātalē District (Pallepola District Secretary division), Mahavela is a village of approximately 500 households. Unlike Madavala, Mātalē and Pallepola would not normally be considered a "disadvantaged area." Nonetheless, census data, personal observation, and conversations with Sumedha and several novices from the area indicate that a number of villages throughout Pallepola have, like their Huruluväva counterparts, poor educational facilities (including above average teacher absenteeism) and high rates of alcoholism. Statistics also indicate that the area's residents tend to have lower educational achievements than those living in the city of Mātalē or in the so-called educational anchor that stretches along the west coast and from Colombo to Kandy.[33]

The boys in Madavala were easily drawn to the temple through Sumedha's *dharma* school. Sumedha had to work much harder in Mahavela to build a conduit from the village to the temple. One reason for this, according to Sumedha, is that whereas people living in Madavala are inclined "to direct or send [their] children [to the temple]," those from Mahavela, having had several uncomfortable experiences with long-haired, belligerent monastics living nearby, have preferred to maintain a greater distance from the temple and its residents.

In light of the very different environment at Mahavela, particularly what Sumedha described as the people's more secular orientation, Sumedha sensed that a *dharma* school would not effectively attract the village's children to the temple. In its place Sumedha decided to establish a youth group *(lamā samājaya)* that met on a daily basis. Although the youth group members, as their *dharma* school counterparts in Madavala, would come to be involved in the everyday workings of the temple (including planning and performing various Buddhist rituals, ceremonies, and temple dramas), the group itself had, Sumedha admitted, an even greater secular focus: "When I went there, the people in the village had no religious sense [*āgamika dänuma*]. All the boys came for the youth group. There were children in the temple every evening. My purpose for it was to educate the boys. I have to tell the truth, I didn't think about enlightenment at all."

Unlike many Huruluväva colony residents who have continued to maintain contact with relatives and friends living in other villages and towns throughout Sri Lanka, the residents of Mahavela—whose roots go back to a group of Salāgama caste members who settled there long before Sri Lanka's independence—have tended, according to Sumedha, to live much more isolated lives.[34] It was the children's insular lives that Sumedha sought to transform through his youth group:

> From [the youth group] they had the chance to immerse themselves in the wider society. They were isolated within the village. They were like frogs trapped in a well. At the beginning, they were imprisoned in the village. Through me, they were able to build connections with the society around them. I took them on trips. I took them to the Peradeniya Botanical Gardens, to Kandy, and so on. From that, they began to understand that there is a whole world outside [of Mahavela]. . . . On the 17th of January, 1993, there was a big ceremony at Ganegoda Vihara to celebrate the 75th

> anniversary of the head monk [Devamitta], who died recently. I brought them for that ceremony. They began to understand "There is a world which we have not seen here."

By providing the youth group members with the opportunity to broaden their horizons, Sumedha hoped that they would come to see and understand the limitations inherent in life in Mahavela and the opportunities available to monastics.

There were other ways that Sumedha encouraged the children to question their future in Mahavela; singing the group's theme songs and reciting poems that Sumedha composed for the children were two such methods. Openly discussing with me the role that such "expedient" means or tricks *(upāya)* played in the recruitment process, Sumedha said, "Madavala did not have a dark period. Mahavela had one.[35] The name of the youth group was Śrī Narada Youth Group. There was a theme song for the group [that I wrote]. The song included the following phrase: 'The heart of Mahavela is Śrī Siri Narada youth group. Ending the dark era of Mahavela where we were born, let's keep walking toward the sun and the moon.'[36] From that, a sense of longing [to ordain] arose in the boys." Although the theme song did not elaborate on the nature of the darkness, Sumedha was quite clear about what he meant: rampant alcoholism and soaring school dropout rates.[37] In place of the dim shadows of village life, Sumedha sought to enlighten their lives by turning them toward a life in robes. He did this not only by telling the children captivating stories about famous monks (such as Variyapola Sumangala, the monk who was reputed for pulling down the English flag on March 2, 1815, shortly after the signing of the Kandyan convention), but also by performing as many Buddhist rituals as possible. Sumedha, however, did not merely perform Buddhist rituals; in the hopes of attracting the children's hearts, he also involved the youth group's members in their organization and performance. Explaining the effects that the youth-group sponsored and youth-group organized rituals had in "attracting the heart," Sumedha said,

> I organized a procession. One day I brought the head monk [of Polgoda Vihara] from the junction [of the Matale-Anurādhapura road] to the temple in a big procession.... We had a big celebration. Up until that time, there was no similar type of celebration ever.... For the procession, the children from the youth group sang: "The great *sangha* is coming to Mahavela, with golden flowers in hand, with the gods and a happy heart. All male and female lay devotees thirsty for the *dharma,* will listen to the sermon preached by the great Narada." All the children sang it beauti-

> fully. . . . I did that with the members of the youth group. It was completely organized by the youth group. I did that to incline them further toward the religion. In 1992, for the first time, I organized *kaṭhina* and protection [*pirit*] rituals [*piṅkama*] in the village.[38] That too was organized by the youth group.

Slowly, several members of the youth group began expressing an interest in the *sangha*. Sumedha, however, felt that he needed something more, some type of catalyst that would transform their interest into action. Recalling the effects that watching an ordination ceremony had on his own path to the *sangha*,[39] Sumedha decided to hold an ordination ritual at the Mahavela temple:

> [The boys from Mahavela] didn't know anything about the monkhood [*pävidikama*]. I used a trick [*upāya*] there to attract their hearts. I brought a boy from Madavala who wanted to be a monk and ordained him at Mahavela. I brought him from Madavala and ordained him in Mahavela.[40] Regarding the ordination ritual, all the members of the [Mahavela] youth group were involved in it. They saw it. From that, they started to feel a longing [*āsāva*] to ordain. So did their parents.

Saying that the boys started to feel a longing to ordain truly understates the full impact that the ritual had on the villagers and youth group members. Indeed, within six months following that ordination ritual, five boys from the youth group became novices; several more from Mahavela's outlying villages also joined the *sangha* the following year. To understand more fully the effects that Sumedha's strategies *(upāya)* had on the youth group's members, I will briefly turn to personal narratives of two novices who entered the *sangha* during the months following the ordination ritual held at the temple.

Candaratana grew up in what he referred to as a comfortable environment. Despite the family having few (if any) financial problems, Candaratana was often put in charge of tending his family's herd of water buffalo, a responsibility that sometimes forced him away from school. On days that he did attend school, he was not allowed to spend time with his friends after school let out. Besides the burden of household agricultural chores, Candaratana's father believed that his son hanging around the village would negatively affect the boy.

It is no wonder, in light of his father's strictness and the school-to-home-to-chore routine that normally punctuated his life, that Candaratana found instant respite in Sumedha's youth group. Although his father was somewhat suspicious at first about Sumedha, he soon allowed Candaratana to join the group, realizing that Sumedha was not like the previous monks he encountered in and around Mahavela and that the temple itself would be a safe environment. Candaratana joined the group and soon became an avid member, attending the group approximately twenty-five times a month.

During our conversations, Candaratana explained to me how his membership in the temple's youth group impelled him toward a life in robes: "I came to become a monk through Sumedha's youth group. When he came to establish the temple, he founded a youth group. We knew him through that. He always dealt and spoke affectionately with us. As a result, we developed a relationship with him. Since this [youth group] was a new thing, I happily joined it." As Candaratana's connection with Sumedha developed and Candaratana became close to other youth group members as well as several of the novices living at the temple at the time, so too did his interest in ordaining. Explaining further what led him to ordain, Candaratana said: "The reason I became a monastic was because of the connection I had with the [village] temple. While the other children generally went outside to play, I used to go to temple to play. I went to the temple immediately after returning home. I was close friends with the young novices living in the temple. They used to play with me. I became a monk because of the association I had with the temple. My time was mostly spent in the temple."

Whereas Sumedha spoke and sang songs about the village's shortcomings to the youth group's members, it was, in part, Candaratana's more positive encounters at the temple—seeing the beauty of monastic life and enjoying his friendship with others—that, in the end, drove him toward monastic life: "In that temple, there was no cruelty. We were treated and looked after like children. They talked to us kindly, while rubbing our heads. Therefore, we liked to work in that society. I was never hit when I played in the temple.... The young novices have good qualities. Temple society is good. When compared to the village society, temple society has [a sense of] unity, affection, pleasantness, and compassion. They speak [to one another] with smiles." Subsequent interviews with Candaratana further revealed the role that compassion the novices and Sumedha showered on each other as well as on the members of the youth group, the concern and attention that the monastics exhibited toward the lay children from the village, the affection and sense of unity exhibited in monastic life, and the pleasing manner in which monastics spoke to others played in his assessment of his own life as a village boy and in his commitment to becoming a monastic.

Sobhita, the second case study, is another boy from Mahavela who became a novice after regularly attending Sumedha's youth group. Similar to Candaratana, Sobhita ordained in 1993, shortly after the ordination ritual that Sumedha organized at the Mahavela temple. Similar to Candaratana, Sobhita came from a family with sufficient financial resources: his father is a professional dancer and dance instructor, and his elder brother works as a computer consultant in Colombo. Village life for Sobhita was, in his words, pleasant *(satuṭak)*.

Similar to Candaratana's father, Sobhita's father did not allow his son to play with the other boys in the village after school, believing that village youth culture would negatively influence his son. With an equally tight leash around him, it is not surprising that Sobhita was quite keen to join Sumedha's youth group after the boy's father agreed. Sobhita explained: "If father saw us play [in the village], we were hit.... He didn't allow us to play with the boys along the road. Even though my father was strict, I had a chance to go to the village temple. The youth group was held every day at five o'clock. I used to go there early because I was able to play there. I didn't go to the youth group to learn. I wanted to play. Even Candaratana came from that group. The young novices living there were closer to me than other boys. Because of that friendship, I felt longing [to ordain]."

As it was the case for Candaratana, the close friendships that Sobhita began to form with Sumedha and, even more so, with the novices living at the village temple provided Sobhita with the chance to reflect on the differences between lay life and life within the *sangha*. Thinking back with a current awareness of why Sumedha established the youth group there, Sobhita said,

> That youth group was established primarily to grab boys for the *sangha*. That means, [we came to see that] the young novices are good. The monkhood is good. How beautiful is the life of that group [*ē gōla koccara lasaṇaṭa innavā da*]? You know, village boys don't button their shirts.... Young novices live much more cleanly in their robes. They made us feel delighted to go [in] that direction.
>
> When I saw the novices living in the village temple, I felt that they were somehow better than us. They dressed beautifully. They had more opportunities. Whereas there were problems with the environment around our village, the novices didn't have any problems. They were so calm.... You know our village. It is not that great. We are not that rich. When we begin thinking about it, we realize that [the young novices] have everything.... They have freedom. They can study. That's not how it is for us at all.
>
> ...As I became closer to them, they began telling me their secrets. Then I did not feel that there was anything between them and me.

The desire to go in the "same direction" as the other novices was, among other factors, the result of aesthetic-affective causes that included experiencing firsthand how monastics lived cleanly, had beautiful lives, dressed well, had more opportunities, were calm, and had everything they needed. Speaking specifically of the affective bonds that he perceived to be inherent in *sangha* life, Sobhita added,

> More affection was shown toward them, even by our own parents. It is strange. I can't explain it in words. When people come to the temple, the villagers show affection [*ādaraya*] to the young novices. Everyone is affectionate to them. I also felt to become like that [*Maṭat hitunā ē vāgē venḍa*]. [I thought,] "Once I become like that, the people would be affectionate toward me." You know, the situation in the village was not like that. Not like [lay] boys, young novices get a lot of affection. . . . We were hit by others. They were never hit. . . . That never happened to the novices. You can't hit them. We felt that instantly.

Sumedha's youth group provided Candaratana and Sobhita with the chance to open their eyes to a life that was quite different from the village culture with which they were familiar. Even though Sumedha and the other young novices living in the temple discussed the benefits of monastic life with Candaratana and Sobhita, reducing their interest in the *sangha* to such benefits neglects the complex set of factors that are, more often than not, part of the recruitment process. Indeed, conversations with both Candaratana and Sobhita suggest that affective ties and the recognition of the beauty inherent in monastic life were attractive features of temple life that, when combined with an experience in which their own peers became novices, were powerful enough to draw them to the *sangha*. As Candaratana explained, "Even though the young novices living in the temple told me that I could do my education as a novice, I wasn't interested in that. I simply liked the group living there and I knew that they liked me too. We were happy when we were together. Though I was happy at home too, I felt happier when I was in the temple."

SERVING RELIGION, SERVING SOCIETY: THE PULPIT AS A TOOL IN MONASTIC RECRUITMENT

In 2000 Sumedha moved, at the behest of Venerable Narada, to his current temple in the village of Uduvela, located approximately 40 kilometers from Mahavela and 130 kilometers from Madavala. Since moving there, Sumedha has not devoted as much of his time to recruiting boys to the *sangha* as he had previously. Instead, Sumedha began to focus his attention on other matters: developing the Uduvela temple and, more recently, establishing new temples throughout Sri Lanka. Saying that Sumedha shifted his attention to other tasks, however, does not mean that he has relinquished his role as monastic recruiter. In fact, since leaving Mahavela Sumedha brought approximately two dozen children to his Uduvela temple and to Narada's Polgoda Vihara. He did this mostly through sermons he preached to lay audiences and families of existing monastics.

One example of Sumedha's use of the pulpit as apparatus for recruiting was the well-attended death-anniversary alms-giving *(dāna)* ritual that took place at the home of Sumanamangala, one of Sumedha's students. The event, located in a village near the commercial center of Dambulla and attended by well more than a hundred villagers, was identical in structure to other alms-giving rituals I attended in Sri Lanka. In addition to extolling the merit that results from giving to the *sangha*, Sumedha conducted a water-pouring ceremony to transfer the merit to the deceased (i.e., Sumanamangala's father).[41]

As in most alms-giving rituals, the officiant (in this case Sumedha) gave a short sermon in which he praised the deceased and his family. The speech he gave following the eulogy was more atypical. Addressing the large crowd, Sumedha declared,[42]

> Oh meritorious ones [*pinvatuni*]! This is your opportunity to perform a great wholesome action. You have entered your beloved son, your beloved grandson, prince Udaya Bandara Kahawatta into the great religion [*sāsana*]. He was given the name Nahinivela Sumanamangala. He was ordained in Harispattuva, at the temple in Uduvela.
>
> . . . Meritorious ones! There are about fifteen novices in our temple. . . . The monks who are ordained with us are the sons of parents who come from various parts of the country. They are clever. They are disciplined and obedient to their teachers. I would like to mention here that they all work to win the donors' hearts [*hita dināganna*].
>
> The young reverend Sumanamangala [lit. Sumanamangala *poḍi hāmuduruwo*] can preach the *dharma*. He also can perform *bodhipūjā* rituals very beautifully. He can even perform *Buddhapūjā* [rituals]. Our young novice can recite, from memory, some of the discourses from the blessed book of protection [or *piruvānā potvahansē*]. I would like to mention here that he works to win the hearts of all the monks and devotees of our temple in Uduvela, our new temple in Uturu Kondadeniya, our forest temple—Kapparagala Arañña—and our head temple, Polgoda Vihara.

> ...Oh meritorious ones! This is the kingdom of Gotama Buddha. The door of that kingdom is open for you. You have the opportunity to enter your sons into the religion [*sāsana*] of Gautama Buddha's kingdom.[43] I have to remind you that it would be a great amount [of merit] for you.[44]
>
> This is not the occasion to speak for a long time. [You] all should be very happy. We were born here as humans and we should be happy thinking that we have done a great meritorious activity [*piṅkama*] which will cause us to have a comfortable life, cause us to have happiness in this world, and if remembered when we die, will cause us to be successful in the next life.
>
> ...Oh meritorious ones! It is very rare that parents get such an opportunity. Many parents do not get the chance to enter a son into the religion [*sāsana*]. Therefore you should come forward and give your sons to the religion of the perfectly enlightened Buddha [*sammāsambuddhu sāsana*]. Monks are necessary to maintain the *sāsana* for a long time.
>
> We know that the monk in this village is very old. His temple is closed, although religious activities are sometimes performed there. There is a scarcity of monks in Lanka. We must protect the *sāsana*. Therefore, I would like to make a request, invitation, and plea during this occasion. Hand over your sons to us! Enter them into the *sāsana!*

Sumedha's sermon—his choice of words, his tone, his use of pregnant pauses, his fluctuating voice, his calm demeanor, and his idyllic appearance—was impressive. The mass of heads continually nodding up and down as well as the frequent, approving cries of "*sādhu, sādhu, sā*" ("it is good, it is good, it is good") suggests that Sumedha more than succeeded in attracting his audience's hearts. Moreover, by colorfully depicting his students' accomplishments (especially Sumanamangala, whom Sumedha implicitly likened to the Buddha by referring to the young novice as a prince), Sumedha was able to trigger specific emotional responses: pride *(āḍambaraya)* for Sumanamangala's family members and longing *(āsāva)* or even envy or jealousy *(īrṣyāva)* for outsiders who do not *yet* have a buddha-like son or relative in the *sangha*. Finally, by discussing Buddhism's decline on the island in general,[45] and the recent closing of the village's temple in particular, Sumedha was able to conjure up such affective states as dismay, sadness, and feelings of loss and, in the process, legitimate his request for new recruits.

As I later reflected on his speech and spoke to Sumedha more privately about the event, it became quite clear to me that Sumedha sought to use those emotions instilled through the pulpit as well as through Sumanamangala's pleasing appearance strategically.[46] Just as other instances when "Buddhist preaching can be seen as a composite of 'strategies' for converting the hearts of ordinary people and for transforming their personalities by persuading them to engage in good works" (Deegalle 2006:16), the range of emotions that Sumedha inculcated through the pulpit (e.g., pride, fear, jealousy, and anger) played an important role in determining people's future actions. Discussing with me the relationship that he saw between emotion, cognition, and volition, Sumedha said,

> That was an opportunity to please the people's heart. By seeing the young monastics, the children would have also been happy and would have felt a longing [thinking], "I also should ordain." At the same time, parents also would have felt like sending their children to the temple. I specifically mentioned that it was a special opportunity to enter the boys in the *sangha* because it was an occasion when the children and their parents were happy about ordination.... To sustain the *sāsana,* it is necessary to please people.... It includes behavior, the way that one talks, the way that one walks, the way that one does things.[47]

Stephen Berkwitz (2003:582) has pointed out that certain emotions instilled through reading Buddhist historical narratives condition devotional acts of present-day Buddhists by "structuring the ways people think, feel, and act with respect to what happened previously" (ibid. 586; see also Heim 2003:551). In the same manner, it could be suggested that through his sermon Sumedha triggered certain shared emotions (e.g., pride, envy, sadness, and dismay) that influenced people's thoughts about the future of Buddhism on the island and, in turn, conditioned their future actions in safeguarding Buddhism with respect to present perceptions of decline.

CONCLUSION

I began this chapter by briefly recounting the recent Sinhala film *Sūriya Araṇa*, particularly how the young hunter's interest in the *sangha* was sparked by his growing sense of awe toward a life in robes and the close friendship he developed with the young novice. Analogous to the monk and novice depicted in the film, Sumedha's recruitment methods center on embodying a particular Buddhist aesthetic as well as on forging affective bonds with potential recruits. Through the creation of close-knit, emotionally supportive communities, Sumedha was able to appeal to the children's longing for relief *(sahanaya)*, compassion *(karuṇāva)*, love, and affection *(ādaraya)* and, thus, was able to succeed as a temple recruiter in both Madavala and Mahavela.

In examining monastic recruitment in contemporary Sri Lanka, I also posited the need for taking into account more local conceptions of ideal monastic behavior and deportment. As I have also suggested in the previous chapter in regard to the sixth Buddhist precept, ideas about ideal or even appropriate monastic behavior and demeanor are not only derived from some codified norm; local social experiences and affective needs shape the process of selection and interpretation as individual Buddhists (both lay and monastic) develop a sense of what kind of monk to have access to or to become. By becoming aware of each area's "fuzzy and indeterminate" aesthetic sensibilities and molding his own behavior, dress, and appearance accordingly, Sumedha was able to trigger certain emotional states (longing, adoration, and even awe) in the minds and hearts of others that, he believed, would naturally drive people to assess not only monastic life more positively, but also their own lives and social worlds more critically.

In highlighting the role that aesthetics and emotions play in monastic recruitment, I posited that the two, in fact, cannot be separated. By using Sumedha's incumbencies as case studies, I suggested that people's ideas about what attracts the heart is also affected by the emotional bonds that people form with monastics. Although it is quite true that people's ideas of ideal monastic behavior are not solely dependent upon the bonds that people form with monastics, the case studies reveal the degree to which people's ideas regarding what constitutes appropriate or even acceptable behavior is determined or influenced by the types of relationships that they form with monastics. I would argue that not taking into account how people relate to and affect each other in this regard may lead one to overlook the very dynamic nature of Buddhism as a continually evolving social institution.

Finally, in looking at the aesthetics of emotion, I have posited a close relationship between emotion and action. Emotions are not merely subjective, partial states of mind; they lie, in the words of Robert Solomon (1995:257), at the very heart of "experience, determining our focus, influencing our interests, defining the dimensions of our world." As judgments of value that lie at the heart of ethics, emotions demand agent responsibility; the attraction that one feels toward the robe, the jealousy that one feels toward families with buddha-like children in the *sangha*, and the fear and anguish that one feels toward temples that are permanently closing their doors requires action. In view of the interrelatedness between affect and ethics—particularly the role that emotion plays in determining people's values and visions—it becomes necessary to consider emotion and the emotive language that people use in order to make their actions intelligible.

3 Aesthetic-Affective Social Networks and Monastic Recruitment

Venerable Sumedha, who was so instrumental in drawing new recruits to Polgoda Vihara, left the Madavala temple in Anurādhapura in 1994. Since that time, however, Polgoda Vihara has enjoyed a continuous flow of new recruits from the area, with every subsequent year bringing more and more ordinands to Narada's temple. When I asked Venerable Narada in 2003 to explain to me why new recruits continue to come to Polgoda Vihara from the Huruluväva-Madavala area, he mentioned that it had much to do with village social dynamics. Along with noting how he stays in contact with families from the area by traveling there and fulfilling those families' religious and ritual needs on occasion, Narada discussed with me the role that local social networks—what John Lofland and Rodney Stark have called "*preexisting* friendship pairs or nets" (1965:871)—play in communicating information about the temple to local residents.

Perhaps most relevant to our conversation about monastic recruitment, though, is the role of local advocates who actively search for potential recruits.[1] Speaking about such a person from the Huruluväva-Madavala area, Narada explained, "First we inform the crowd [of monastics] here. We discuss with some of them that on such and such a day we are going to hold an ordination ritual. Some of these monks send letters home.... Sometimes I ask [the novice] Piyananda to send his father [Mr. Gunasena] a letter to inform him about it. Gunasena is someone who is well traveled in those villages. He has connections. Because of those connections, people tell him [about potential recruits]."

This chapter examines the role that local social networks and temple advocates play in monastic recruitment by turning to two separate case studies: one in Madavala and one in Ampāra. Focusing on numerous conversations I had with a number of parents, ordinands, and novices, I seek to provide a further nuanced and more holistic understanding of monastic recruitment. I highlight, for example, the complex array of relationships and social ties that are often a part of the process itself, thus implicitly challenging the tendency to interpret recruitment as a single household's or a single family's desire for upward mobility.[2] Finally, in complexifying the social-economic deprivation model that is sometimes used to account for temple recruitment in South and Southeast Asia, I posit that, along with financial concerns and the desire to provide children with certain educational opportunities, monastic recruitment is driven by aesthetic-affective factors, particularly the parents' and children's desire to find caring, beautiful, and socially harmonious environments, where children will learn while being treated with a parent-like and sibling-like affection.

MR. GUNASENA AND THE MADAVALA-HURULUVÄVA SOCIAL NETWORK

Echoing Venerable Narada's assessment of the role that temple advocates play in locating potential ordinands, many parents I spoke with from the Madavala-Huruluväva area mentioned Gunasena. An educated man in his late forties, Gunasena is, as Narada pointed out, quite well known and well traveled throughout Madavala and Huruluväva. He and his wife reside in one of the largest homes in the area. The economic prosperity that the family once enjoyed ended during the early 1990s. As a result, the family was forced to sell their rice-crushing mill and two tractors. In spite of those changes and having recently been accused by several "jealous" families from the area of taking money set aside for the development of the Madavala temple, Gunasena remains largely well regarded in the area. As the village "big man," Gunasena is regularly consulted on a wide range of village and even more personal issues.

The Gunasenas are parents to five sons and three daughters. Three of their sons became monastics at Polgoda Vihara, although the first one to ordain disrobed after spending six years in the *sangha.* Along with directing his own sons to Polgoda Vihara, Gunasena has had a personal hand in bringing eighteen other boys from the Madavala-Huruluväva area to Venerable Narada's temple over a period of several years. His choice of Polgoda Vihara was because of the close bonds that he and his family forged with Venerable Sumedha while he administered the Madavala temple from 1989 to 1994.[3] Gunasena was and continues to be very impressed with Sumedha, particularly his demeanor, appearance, and the sense of commitment he exhibited as a Buddhist monastic of the Rāmañña Nikāya. It was through Sumedha that Gunasena came to know and trust Venerable Narada.

Gunasena decided to ordain his eldest son, Piyadassi, while Sumedha was still the head monk *(vihārādhipati)* of the Madavala temple. Even though Gunasena had intended for Piyadassi to remain at Sumedha's side, the boy was sent off to Polgoda Vihara for his ordination and training after living two months at the Madavala temple. After the move Gunasena made frequent visits to the Kandyan temple and became close to Venerable Narada. Gunasena noted on several occasions that he was quite impressed with Polgoda Vihara and even more taken by Narada; he was particularly captivated by the manner in which Narada treated his students and conducted himself as a monastic. He also described, on several occasions, Narada's manner of speech, noting particularly that Narada had the power to attract anyone through his speech.

Gunasena largely shares Narada's vision regarding the *sangha*'s role in providing assistance to poor boys from disadvantaged areas. Even though his particular view of the *sangha*'s role in contemporary society has had an effect on the types of boys that Gunasena recruited throughout the years,[4] his decision to ordain his eldest son was based on other factors.[5] Gunasena explained, "Each family should ordain one of their sons.... I too wanted to ordain one of my sons. I have five boys in the family. I had that idea from the beginning. That is why I ordained the eldest one. In our families, there is no one who is ordained. I have many brothers in my family. None of their sons are ordained. No one on... [Mrs. Gunasena's side] is ordained. Because the *sāsana* is declining, one must ordain one son from each family. It is a great merit. [Nowadays] they ordain, stay five days, and disrobe." Even though Gunasena—an ex-lay *pirivena* student who completed his *pirivena* primary studies *(mūlika piriveṇa avasāna)* at a monastic college—recognizes the educational opportunities available at monastic colleges,[6] his decision to ordain his own son was triggered less by such opportunities and more by the responsibility he felt toward protecting the religion *(sāsana)*. His direct experiences of temples permanently closing their doors and the shortfall of monastics in the area functioned as poignant reminders of the responsibility he has as a lay Buddhist to protect the religion.

Piyadassi was well aware of his father's views regarding the high rate of disrobing that currently plagues the *sangha*.[7] Nevertheless, Piyadassi left the *sangha* after spending six years at Polgoda Vihara. The decision to disrobe came as a shock to Gunasena, who at first refused to accept his son back home.[8] Although he later came to terms with—"accepted" might be an overstatement—his son's decision, he, feeling a sense of shame *(läjjāyi)*, insisted that the boy no longer reside in Madavala.[9] After consulting his wife (who was much more accepting of her son than her husband), Mr. Gunasena decided that Piyadassi should go to live with Mrs. Gunasena's distant relatives in Colombo. There, Piyadassi soon found work as a laborer in factory that makes canopies.

Five years after Piyadassi left the *sangha*, one of Gunasena's other sons, Piyananda, became a novice at Narada's temple. His ordination in 2000 was followed, two years later, by the ordination of Piyananda's younger brother, Vimalasiri. Piyananda's ordination, I soon learned, had little to do with the responsibility that Gunasena felt toward protecting Buddhism. Instead, Gunasena's decision to ordain him was prompted by a desire to circumvent the harmful path down which Piyananda was heading.

In Sri Lanka, every fifth-grade student is expected to sit for a national scholarship exam.[10] Passing the exam provides young children from poorer families with new educational opportunities. The scholarship offers families with little financial resources the chance to send their children to one of the more popular schools that sit alongside the so-called educational anchor (i.e., along the southwest coast from Colombo to Matara and along the road from Colombo to Kandy) and so is one of the only ways for poorer families living in educationally disadvantaged areas to ensure a better education for their children.[11]

Failing to pass this very stressful exam carries no repercussions; however, narrowly missing the pass mark sometimes has psychological effects, for both the child and his or her family.[12] This was certainly the case for Piyananda, who was always at the top of his class. Despite everyone's certainty that he would pass the scholarship exam, Piyananda narrowly missed passing. The results stunned Piyananda, who in time coped with his marks by diverting his attention to other interests. His father dealt with his son's "deteriorating" situation by threatening his son and by severely limiting his ability to socialize.

It was within this context that the boy became a novice at Narada's temple. Two years after Piyananda's exam, Gunasena was informed about Narada's plan to hold a large ordination ceremony on January 1, 2000. Concerned about his son's future, Gunasena felt that ordaining his son would be the right thing to do "[When] he sat for the fifth-grade exam, he failed by a margin of five or seven points. From that day he started losing his interest [in his studies]. His class percentile became lower and lower. The only things that caught his interest were cricket matches, television programs, and playing outside. I thought that if he were to remain at home, he would take a bad turn and end up in a terrible situation. That is why I made the decision to send him to the [Polgoda] temple. . . . I was concerned about his education, that is why I ordained him." Although Gunasena hoped, at the time, that Piyananda would not emulate Piyadassi by disrobing but focus, instead, on "saving the religion" after his studies, Gunasena admitted that his initial decision to ordain his son had little to do with protecting Buddhism.

Gunasena broached the idea with his son and the boy agreed to go to Narada's temple. When I asked Piyananda shortly after his ordination why he chose to enter the *sangha*, he succinctly replied, "To beautify my life" [*jivitaya sundara karaganna*]. Corroborating his father's account, he added,

> In my family, my father and I were the only ones who were educated.... Father told me that if I stayed at home, I would become a wretch [*kālakaṇṇiyā venavā*]. I was told "Go there and become a monk." My elder brother who disrobed also said "Go there. It's good [at Polgoda Vihara]." That is how I came to become a monk.... A friend of mine who was better at studies and more popular than I became a wretch. Think about what would have happened to me! When I look at village society, no one there [in Madavala] reached grade ten. They sat for their ordinary level exams and failed. No one ever passed. If I stayed there for two more years, I would have surely become like that.

Piyananda's description of the area's second- or third-rate schools, high dropout rate, and limited opportunities certainly lends support to the view that "many boys join as novices to get a free education and economic security to put them through school and college" (Obeyesekere 1981:41); at the same time, however, reducing recruitment only to a desire for economic and social well-being detracts from the role that social bonds, emotions, and aesthetics also play in the process.

There were a number of other options that were available to Piyananda at the time, including attending Nikkaväva Pirivena as a lay student. This would have, in fact, seemed an obvious choice, especially given the fact that Gunasena himself followed this exact route. Instead of choosing this larger and more prestigious college for his son, Gunasena chose a temple that was associated with a smaller, less prominent college. I asked Piyananda how he ended up at Polgoda Vihara rather than at another temple or *pirivena*. He replied, "When my father comes to this temple, Venerable Dhammadassi used to treat him well. The other reason is that those young novices who are in [the Polgoda] temple always visited us during the new year and [school] vacation[s]. They brought sarongs and gifts for my father. Father also treated them well when he had the means to do so.... My father looked after Dhammadassi like his own child when Dhammadassi used to come to our home for the new year.... Dhammadassi used to bring clothes to father. Father likes Dhammadassi. We too like him." Along with the opportunity to study, the close and mutually sustaining relationships that were forged and sustained between Piyananda's family and the monastics of Polgoda Vihara—visiting one another, caring for each other well, and treating one another with gifts and other forms of hospitality—were central to Gunasena's decision to ordain his son.

What about Piyananda? Why did he agree to go to Polgoda Vihara when his father first suggested it? Why didn't he choose a different temple or, well aware of the greater educational prospects available in *pirivenas*, choose to study at a *pirivena* as a lay student? Reflecting on the path he took to Polgoda Vihara, Piyananda explained, "I associated with monks in the [Madavala] temple to a great extent [*bohō duraṭa*]. They helped us to learn. They gave us books and such when we went there. We were treated well. They were affectionate to us. They used to call us 'younger brother.' When I went to the [temple's] *dharma* school, I wasn't really interested in learning. I went there waiting for the young novices to come. They were really affectionate to me. They liked me very much.... Even the head monk [Sumedha] kept a plate of rice for me when I returned from school." Such replies suggest to me that for Piyananda, as for the novices mentioned in the previous chapter, emotional connections he had formed with Sumedha and the other novices were essential factors to accepting his father's suggestion that he ordain at Polgoda Vihara.

BEYOND GUNASENA'S CHILDREN: THE BIRTH OF A TEMPLE ADVOCATE

One key study noted in sociologists Rodney Stark and William Bainbridge's (1985:308f.) article on the effects of interpersonal bonds on recruitment is of American members of the Korean sect of Reverend Sun Myung Moon. They posit that the study convincingly shows that recruitment tends to move through preexisting social networks. They explained, for instance, that when the group moved from its early home in Eugene, Oregon, to San Francisco, California, the group was unable to grow for some time as they lacked social ties to local communities there. Recruitment began again only when members of the group "found ways to connect with other newcomers to San Francisco and develop serious relations with them" (p. 309; see also Lofland and Stark [1965] as well as Lofland and Skonovd [1981]).

Their findings are helpful to our own understanding of why Polgoda Vihara has continued to receive an influx of new recruits from the Huruluväva-Madavala area throughout the years. Just as the bonds that the Gunasenas forged with Sumedha played a role in Gunasena's decision to ordain Piyadassi and Piyananda, so too were Gunasena's preexisting social ties to the area's villages and residents a key factor behind the influx of new recruits to Polgoda Vihara from the area after Sumedha left. For most children and parents from the area, the path from their homes to the Kandyan temple went through the Gunasenas.

Two important distinctions, however, need to be drawn between Stark and Bainbridge's, as well as Lofland and Stark's, studies and the Huruluväva-Madavala case study. First, even though Gunasena was connected to Polgoda Vihara, he was not a so-called insider. As a layman with social ties to the temple, Gunasena only facilitated contact between potential recruits and Venerable Narada.

Furthermore, as an "outsider," Gunasena was never concerned with getting a particular child or family to accept a particular group's message or ideology (see Stark and Bainbridge 1985:311). Although his concern about the survival of the religion compelled Gunasena to ordain his first son, his role as a temple advocate were driven by neither religious ideology nor Buddhist chauvinism. As Gunasena explained, his role in Madavala was simply making people aware of Polgoda Vihara, as well as acting as a bridge between families living in Madavala and Venerable Narada: "We say good things. 'The monks are good. The temple is good. The head monk is good.' Many know the head monk [Narada] as well as Sumedha. The neighboring [village] people know Narada. Everybody likes him.... Of all the temples we know, Polgoda Vihara is the best. That is why I directed many boys there.... There are many people here who have a connection with that temple. Their hearts are attracted to the temple."

Other parents, like Gunasena, were clearly interested in the educational opportunities that life in the *sangha* provides. At the same time, though, what struck me about my conversations with a number of parents in which they discussed the decision to ordain their children is how important Gunasena's descriptions of Narada's qualities were to them. While they wanted their children to learn, they were not looking for a top monastic school. They were concerned with finding a head monk who would treat their children with love and respect, as well as a temple environment that was nurturing. As the mother of a twelve-year-old novice brought through Gunasena explained in response to my question concerning why she chose Polgoda Vihara: "We expect a head monk who is compassionate.... Compassion should be the same as a mother or father for a child. He should be taken care of when he is sick and looked after in regard to his educational activities. That is what is called compassion. When these things are there, we become happy. We feel as if the boy is still living close to us.... *We got to know from everyone the meaning of 'good' as it relates to this head monk. That is why he was brought here*" (emphasis added). For her, the good qualities of a monk are not necessarily defined and grasped through reading accounts of certain "ideal individuals from mythic antiquity" (Collins 1998:57); rather, the ability to distinguish good monks from bad occurred through present-day conversations about (and encounters with) certain monastics who are themselves recognized and praised by others.

Along with advocating Polgoda Vihara to a number of parents, Gunasena sought to attract the hearts and minds of some children with descriptions of

Narada and his temple. One young novice who attributed his own presence at Polgoda Vihara to Gunasena is Sujata. I first met him in 2003,[13] when he was fourteen years old. As a young boy growing up in Huruluväva, Sujata was first drawn toward a life in saffron robes after paying several visits to a temple in Kurunägala, his father's native town. During one of the first interviews I conducted with him, Sujata discussed with me the impact that those visits had on him:

> I had been to the Kurunägala temple two or three times. When I saw the young novices living there, I felt a longing [*āsāva*]. Unlike us, they recited books in the morning in a much better manner than we at home.... At the temple, I saw the novices doing their lessons. They were reading stories. The novices also worshipped the Buddha [*buddhapūjā*] in the image house.... They did *buddhapūjā*, preached, and recited [other] verses.
>
> When thinking about our school, I found the lessons to be unpleasant. We were hit a lot. I felt a sense of unpleasantness. The monks in the temple were not hit like us. [I felt that as a monastic], I would be able to do my lessons freely. I thought: "It would be great if I became a novice."
>
> They did their lessons beautifully. When listening [to them recite verses], I felt longing because of their voice and the way that they read. When they did their lessons, they used different words.[14] When lay boys study, they read and chat. These novices were alone. They had a calm and isolated life, unlike us at home where we face a lot of problems. It wasn't like that. Unlike back at home, the novices in the temple lived like brothers. I felt a longing.

Sujata was very clear in distinguishing studying in a temple and studying at his village school, and his remarks clearly point to the importance that studying and learning have for him. Taken as a whole, however, they also suggest that it was not merely the opportunity to study that was appealing to him; Sujata's interest in ordaining was also piqued by other facets of Buddhist monastic culture, including the social bonds related to temple life (living calmly together like brothers) as well as the aesthetics of studying (the students' attentiveness, their voices, and the words they used) and performing Buddhist rituals (such as worshipping the Buddha and preaching).

In spite of his attraction to a life in robes, Sujata's wish to ordain went unmet. As for Narada and Sumedha, Sujata's parents refused to grant their son the needed parental permission to ordain. Seeking to redirect their son's interests, Sujata's parents and uncles—in collusion with several disrobed monks from Huruluväva—

began to paint less than ideal pictures of monastic life; Sujata explained, "Some of them said 'Temples are not good. It is impossible to study.' When I thought about that, I began to have unpleasant [*apriya*] feelings about temples. Many of them [who spoke to me] were disrobed. They said dirty things [*jarā deval*].[15] They said, 'They don't provide you with anything for home.[16] They hit. We came back because of those things. We came because it was unpleasant for us. The robe is a burden. There is no freedom. You can't be as you want. Stay at home. Don't go.'" Such unpleasant images clearly left an impression on the young boy.

Several years after Sujata gave up on his wish to become a monastic, Gunasena came to learn about the boy's initial interest in monastic life from Sujata's neighbors. Gunasena decided to intervene by speaking directly to Sujata about Polgoda Vihara. Gunasena's brief descriptions of Polgoda Vihara and Narada was enough to rekindle a desire for temple life in Sujata.[17] With the dirty images still fresh in his mind, however, Sujata promised himself that, were he to move to a temple like Polgoda Vihara, he would not be ordained. Staying at a temple as a lay boarder would provide Sujata with the chance to return home unstigmatized when temple life becomes too unbearable.

Gunasena heard about Sujata's parents' reluctance about sending their son to a temple. Although the family's financial problems certainly contributed to their eventual decision to allow their son to go to Polgoda Vihara,[18] it was, according to Sujata's mother, the meeting that Gunasena arranged between them and Venerable Narada that made them receptive to the idea. Discussing their change of heart with me, Sujata's mother said,

> Gunasena brother[19] came to our house and asked us "Sister, would you like to send your boy to Polgoda Vihara?" I said: "I have to discuss it with my husband." He was working in the back of the house at that time. I went there and spoke to him. He agreed to speak with Gunasena. He told Gunasena "I have to go look at the temple first." Gunasena brother replied: "Brother, there is nothing to see. It is a good place. In a couple of days the head monk [of Polgoda Vihara] will be coming here. If you are interested, you can send the boy on that day."
>
> ... When we met the head monk our heart was relieved. When we saw him we could just feel his principles [*pratipatti*]. I thought "If we could send my son with this monk [literally, *hāmuduruwo*], there wouldn't be any problems for him." That is what I thought at that time. By just seeing [him], I felt that way. He is very simple and humble, isn't he? We can tell the qualities of monks by just looking at them. I felt that he has very

> good qualities, not like the monks who are living here. The head monk's qualities are very different from the head monks living here.... The way he talks and the way that he walks are so different from our monks.

Sending their son to Polgoda Vihara provided Sujata's parents with a way to attend to their son's educational needs that did not place a further strain on the family's resources. At the same time, monastic recruitment for them was not simply a financial matter; it was also a matter of the heart. In the end it was Sujata's parents' meeting with Narada and verifying, for themselves, Gunasena's descriptions of Narada's principles and qualities—his humility, simplicity, way of speaking, and physical demeanor—that led them to agree to their son's request.

Sujata came to Polgoda Vihara in 2002. Although he originally intended to reside at the temple as a lay boarder, he quickly decided to ordain. Just as Sujata's parents' attitudes toward temple life were transformed after seeing Narada's qualities and principles, so too were Sujata's feelings toward a life in robes transformed after seeing and interacting with the temple's many monastic residents. The close ties he began to forge with a number of other novices and monks—which he regarded to be similar to an ideal "brother-brother relationship"—were central to his change of heart:

> When I was here for about a week, the thought of ordaining came again after seeing the group [of novices] living happily here, particularly [seeing] their behavior and conduct.... They live well here. They live here looking after each other. They speak in a way that attracts everyone's heart. As they treat others like their own younger brothers, we feel like treating them back as if they are our older brothers. [In the same way], when we treat others similarly, they feel more longing toward becoming a monastic.

Since his ordination in 2002, Sujata has immersed himself in his new role as a Buddhist monastic. Besides excelling in his *pirivena* studies, Sujata began taking on more and more temple responsibilities, particularly ritual duties that are commonly shouldered by more seasoned novices. Within a year after his ordination, Sujata began performing numerous *buddhapūjā*, *bodhipūjā*, and *paritta* rituals; he also began preaching several sermons to the lay patrons of Polgoda Vihara.

EXPANDING SOCIAL NETWORKS

The social networks that are so central to the recruitment process are constantly changing as new monastics, new families, and new villages are incorporated and other ties are reduced or eliminated. As new networks that include different "friendship pairs and nets" are formed, new temple advocates are born and with them, new or slightly different aesthetic sensibilities regarding what constitutes an ideal Buddhist institution and head monk.

When I returned to Polgoda Vihara in May 2004 there was an influx of recently recruited boys. All of them were waiting for the ordination ceremony scheduled to be held that October. As I began speaking with them, particularly about how they came to be connected to the temple, Sujata's name came up repeatedly. When I mentioned it to Sujata, he retorted, "There is a big group living in this temple from that [Huruluväva] area. When we go home, the people there receive news from us. We get together with our old friends. As friends, we get together as we were earlier, [as lay children]. They come here because of that."

Many of my subsequent interviews with Sujata and the boys who attributed their presence at Polgoda Vihara to him suggest more of a natural method of monastic recruitment, much like between the young novice and the hunter's son as portrayed in the film *Sūriya Araṇa* described in the previous chapter. Quite unlike Sumedha, who drew newcomers to Polgoda Vihara through very calculated methods (see chapter 2), and Gunasena, who actively intervened in people's lives with stories of Narada and by arranging visits to Polgoda Vihara, Sujata's style of recruitment was largely effortless. Although many novices from Polgoda Vihara, including Sujata, behaved like Buddhist monastics during certain religious events held in and around the Huruluväva area, it was their more relaxed demeanor outside of these more formal events that led their peers to contemplate a life in the *sangha*.

One boy who attributed his presence at Polgoda Vihara to Sujata is Sarat, a twelve-year-old boy who comes from a very economically disadvantaged background. Already being barely able to make ends meet, the family's economic problems worsened further when the boy's mother left him and her husband, Mr. Somaratna, for good. To put food on the table, Somaratna was compelled to take on a variety of odd jobs, which, though helping the family financially, directly impinged upon Sarat's schooling.

In the hopes of easing some of the family's woes, Somaratna—under pressure from his own parents and siblings—remarried. Although having an additional live-in caretaker was a boon for Somaratna and Sarat, that change was short lived. Indeed, several months after their wedding, Somaratna's new wife decided to accept a job as a housemaid in the Middle East.[20] When she left, Sarat was sent to live with his paternal grandmother in another village. That move adversely affected Sarat's schooling even further; by the time of his arrival at Polgoda Vihara in April 2004, the twelve-year-old was still unable to read well.

In April 2004 Sarat returned to his native village to spend the Sinhala new year holidays with his father. It was during his stay there that Sarat began demanding that he be brought to Polgoda Vihara. Explaining the situation there to me, Sarat said, "When I saw our young novice [Sujata],[21] I felt like ordaining. When our novice came home [for new year], I went back with him." Further detailing the process of how he came to Narada's temple, Sarat added,

> [Sujata] came home and told me, "Let's ordain." On the first day I told him "I can't" [ordain]. The second day, I said "Yes" and came with him. . . . I was in school in the village [of Huruluväva]. Then I left that school to go to another village [where my paternal grandmother lived]. I felt like I couldn't go to school there. I came here [to Huruluväva] for the holidays. I came to our novice's house. I was there [in Huruluväva] when our novice came [home on holiday]. Sujata came and said, "Let's go." We went. . . .
>
> [Sujata] told me, "During the December break I will give you kites to play with." He told me, "The well where we wash is near a rocky area." I asked him whether I would be hit [there]. He said, "No, they will not hit you."
>
> . . . [Sujata] is very good. If I tell him that I don't have a pen, he gives me money to buy a pen or pencil. My heart is attracted to him.

Like Gunasena, Sujata briefly described to Sarat what life at Polgoda Vihara would be like. Unlike Gunasena's descriptions of Narada's qualities and principles, however, Sujata's account focused on aspects of monastic life that would attract the heart of a young child: playing with kites, the physical setting of the temple's well, and so on. Perhaps most relevant, though, were the close bonds that existed between Sarat and Sujata. Similar to the hunter's son and the young novice depicted in the film *Sūriya Araṇa*, Sarat and Sujata played in the village like old friends as well as bathed together at the local reservoir *(väva)*. Their time together stirred up pleasing memories in Sarat which, when contrasted with the unpleasant experiences of attending school at his grandmother's village, were enough to draw him toward Polgoda Vihara.[22]

I first met Sarat's father—Somaratna—at Polgoda Vihara in August 2004, two months prior to Sarat's ordination. During our interview, I came to understand that Somaratna was, like so many other parents, at first very reluctant to send his son to Venerable Narada's Kandyan temple. Similar to Sujata's parents, Somaratna tried to convince Sarat otherwise, by telling him that he would be hit in the temple, both as an ordinand and after his ordination.

Sujata was well aware of Somaratna's attitude. During one of his baths with Sarat at the Huruluväva reservoir, Sujata suggested that they go to Somaratna together and plead their case. When they did, Sujata approached Somaratna and first informed him of his own progress since becoming a novice at Polgoda Vihara. Sujata then suggested to Somaratna that all of them go to Polgoda Vihara together so that he and his son could see for themselves what life at the temple would be like. The three of them traveled to Polgoda Vihara on April 23, 2004. One night was all Somaratna needed to make up his mind. He returned home the following evening, alone.

When I asked Somaratna why he decided to leave his son at Polgoda Vihara, he explained, "When I saw this temple and met the head monk, I felt that both the temple and the head monk are good. From that point, I began to fix in my heart that this temple would be good for him to do his studies. The head monk has good qualities. There are enough young novices for him. At home there are a lot of difficulties. Here all things are given to them for their studies.... I thought that by going to the temple, he would have a good future. That is what I thought.... Sujata told me about all that. Since Sujata is [at Polgoda Vihara], I have nothing to fear. Sujata's family also comes." Somaratna was clearly aware of the educational opportunities available to monastics; nonetheless, it would be misleading to reduce the recruitment process solely to such opportunities. From his account, it was also the large social networks at the temple and Venerable Narada's personal qualities that contributed to his decision to leave his son at Polgoda Vihara. Continuing his discussion about why he allowed his son to come to Polgoda Vihara, Somaratna explained,

> I have been to several temples there [in Huruluväva]. Those head monks are not like [Narada]. [Narada] speaks well. He is very kind.... The monks living in those [Huruluväva] temples sometimes address children with [bad] words [such as] "*tō*," "*umba*," and "*palayan*."[23] Children don't like it. I have spoken with [Narada] several times. I noticed that he is not like that. He addresses everyone with proper manners. I have found four boys who are willing to come to this temple. I told them, "Actually, it is a good temple. If you wish, go and take a look for yourself. The climate is good. The temple is good. There are enough young novices for playing."... There are no problems for the boys. There are many novices here. Our Dhammadassi is also here.[24] We are really happy. Sujata is also here. When I spoke with him, he mentioned how much he changed after coming here. When I hear that, I am also really happy. He even told Sarat:

> "Look at me. I have reached a good position. You also can do the same if you stay here."

Since leaving his son at Polgoda Vihara, Somaratna has become an advocate for the temple. Although Somaratna has not been as active as Gunasena in drawing new recruits to Polgoda Vihara, he has in fact, within a very short period of time, brought several boys to Polgoda Vihara from Huruluväva, and this point should not be overlooked. Indeed, by sharing his own experiences at Narada's temple with Huruluväva parents and children, Somaratna has become one more link in an ever expanding web of people advocating Polgoda Vihara to people living 130 kilometers away.

AMPĀRA: FURTHER CASE STUDIES

The novices and ordinands from the Huruluväva area comprise the largest group of monastics at Polgoda Vihara. Another sizeable number of novices and ordinands at the temple comes from villages within Ampāra District, in eastern Sri Lanka. The Ampāra villages from where many come are—as their Huruluväva counterpart—agricultural settlements. Many of the residents have ties to the area that go back to the 1950s and 1960s, a period that witnessed a huge population boom due to enticing government giveaways that were part of the Gal Oya colonization scheme (Uphoff 1996:28; see also Wanigaratne 1975:14).

Similar to the villages that surround Huruluväva, many villages that are part of the Gal Oya agricultural scheme have taken a turn for the worse in more recent times, including the three villages from where the majority of Ampāra novices and ordinands living at Polgoda Vihara come. Despite huge tracts of land being offered to settlers, the overall quality of life has precipitously declined in the region, particularly since the 1970s. Explaining some of the reasons for the decay, P. H. Sugathadasa (1985:6) has suggested that

> the rapid increase of population in the district has resulted in many social and economic problems. These problems have restricted the employment opportunities for the new generation—thus limited economic expansion. At the inception of the Gal Oya Colonization, the unit of alienation was 7 acres and this unit has now been reduced to 1½ acres. Job opportunities were limited as new major development projects were inoperative except for a few minor projects.... The extent of cultivated land had not increased comensurately [*sic*] with the increase in population. It was therefore inevitable that the family income dropped resulting in serious social and

> economic problems such as education, housing, health, and unemployment.... More than 50% of the people are below the poverty line. There had been a break-down in good family relationship to a certain extent.[25]

It was, in part, the economic and social problems, especially the "breakdown in good family relationship," that contributed to the ordination of Venerable Dhammika, the first boy from Ampāra to become a monastic at Polgoda Vihara. Dhammika's father committed suicide when the boy was two and a half years old. Having no other place to turn, the boy, his sister (who subsequently died from a high fever) and his mother went to live with Dhammika's paternal grandfather, Jayasundara. Although Jayasundara treated Dhammika and his mother well, the boy's paternal uncles and cousins did not. Many of them blamed the boy and his mother for Dhammika's father's death and regularly fought with the boy and his mother; on a number of occasions Dhammika's uncles and cousins physically beat the boy and his mother. Unfortunately, Dhammika's family's economic plight left them with no other options than to remain in what Dhammika referred to as "that troubling situation." Luckily, a new opportunity arose when the boy turned ten.

Jayasundara's house sits across the street from the home of one of Reverend Narada's senior students, Venerable Ananda. During an alms-giving ritual that was held at Ananda's parents' house, Ananda's mother informed her son and Narada about Dhammika's situation. After the ritual, Ananda encouraged the boy to come back to Kandy with them. The boy immediately agreed. Dhammika's mother, who was looking for a better life for her son, did not protest. Although Dhammika's story is a fascinating one, it is Jayasundara's role in the current growing number of new recruits from the Ampāra area that is of greater importance to our understanding of monastic recruitment in contemporary Sri Lanka.

As with so many other ordination rituals, Dhammika's ordination was attended by many of his relatives, including his mother, paternal grandmother, and paternal grandfather. After Dhammika became a novice, Jayasundara continued to visit his grandson from time to time. During some of those later, though not frequent, visits to Polgoda Vihara, Jayasundara brought other relatives along with him. With news of the temple slowly spreading throughout the nearby villages in Ampāra, other boys started making their way to Venerable Narada's temple. Some were Dhammika's relatives. Others were not. Explaining the impact that Dhammika's ordination had on the other residents in Ampāra, Ananda said,

> After I brought Dhammika here, his grandfather began visiting the temple. Then [Dhammika's grandfather's] niece started visiting too. She

> is Dhammasiri's mother.[26] Santasiri is a relative from the same village. Their parents came to my house to get information about this temple. That is how the news spread. When Dhammika's grandfather came to this temple for Dhammasiri's ordination, he brought several relatives and friends with him. From that, they got to learn about this temple. When they went back home, they continued talking about the temple. Both Sumanasiri and Santasiri are connected to this temple in that way.[27] There was also another boy who is a relative of Dhammika who ordained here. He disrobed. From one family, several members ordained. Their family is spread out. Also, people who are not related to them, yet who live close to them, started coming here [to Polgoda Vihara]. In that way, a lot of people came to know about this temple. The system [of recruitment] is through relatives and friends.

I was fortunate enough to observe firsthand the role that social networks and interpersonal bonds play in temple recruitment when I visited Ampāra, in 2003, with Narada, Ananda, and two young Ampāra novices that Ananda mentioned by name: Santasiri and Dhammasiri. The purpose of the trip was partly religious (to take part in an alms-giving ritual at Ananda's parents' house) and partly mundane (to collect two large wooden doors that Ananda's elder brother had made for the temple).

We arrived at the city of Ampāra at approximately six o'clock in the morning. After making a short stop at a bakery where Narada bought cakes and short eats—a Sri Lankan version of fast finger-food—we continued to Ananda's native village, stopping on the way at the village's temple to bathe and eat a morning meal. Prior to arriving at Ananda's house, we dropped Santasiri off at his house. Before leaving Santasiri by the path leading to his mother's house, Narada gave the young novice one of the several cakes purchased in Ampāra and advised the young novice, "Give this to your family. Don't be naughty. Don't forget to be dropped off before one o'clock at Ananda's house."[28] Our next stop was a brief one at Ananda's house. We then proceeded further to Dhammasiri's village, approximately five kilometers away. Dhammasiri also took a cake home with him. Within a minute or so after leaving us, Dhammasiri's father came out to greet us. He assured us that he would bring his son to Ananda's house by one o'clock.

We returned to Ananda's house and within a short time participated in the alms-giving ceremony. The ritual lasted about one hour, after which Ananda's brother and his friends began loading the wooden doors into the truck. It was at that time that Santasiri and Dhammasiri arrived, along with many of their relatives and family members. Santasiri was also accompanied by an old school friend. After spending about thirty more minutes at Ananda's house, we left for Kandy.

One or two weeks after our return to Kandy, I stopped by Polgoda Vihara to conduct follow-up interviews with some of the novices. While there, a woman and her small boy showed up, seemingly unannounced. Although I did not recognize the boy, Thilak, my research assistant, pointed out to me that he was the young boy who accompanied Santasiri and his father to the Ananda's house. Although my attempts at interviewing the boy, Ajit, were largely unsuccessful, the boy's mother (who was in Colombo during our visit to Ampāra) explained what led her and her boy to Polgoda Vihara.

During our visit to Ampāra, Santasiri and Ajit played quite a lot together. Soon after Santasiri left for Kandy, Ajit began nagging his mother to take him to Polgoda Vihara so that he could see his brother *(ayyā)*.[29] Ajit's mother explained, "He said that he wanted to go to the temple with [little older brother]. I didn't take him seriously. However, he stopped [going to] school.... When the young novice came home, [Ajit] went there [to his house]. After that he started saying 'I want to go with *ayyā*.'"

Her arrival at the temple on June 19 was not the first time that Ajit's mother came to Polgoda Vihara. When I asked her how she came to learn about Polgoda Vihara, she explained,

> There is a person in our village who knows the head monk well. That is uncle Jayasundara.[30] You visited his place when you came, right? I came with him and Santasiri to this temple. Often Santasiri used to stay with me at my house. He was very affectionate to me when he was with me at home.
>
> When I was small I used to visit uncle [Jayasundara's] home. That aunty and uncle are like my parents. My father died when I was small. I used to go to that uncle's house when I was small. They are very affectionate to me. I met them frequently.
>
> When my younger sister's son [Santasiri] informed them that he wanted to become a monk, they didn't take it seriously.[31] Then the son kept telling me, "Aunty, I want to go to a temple." I spoke to uncle [Jayasundara] and came to this temple [with him]. Only after visiting the temple did [Santasiri's] parents agree. I came to know about the temple that way....

> We understood that the head monk is very good. We are able to think for ourselves, aren't we? Others there also felt the same way.

Through a connection to the temple that was forged through Jayasundara—the Ampāra advocate for Polgoda Vihara—Ajit's mother came to know about the Kandyan temple. By playing a role in the ordination of her own nephew, Ajit's mother unknowingly planted the seeds of her own son's future wish to become a novice at Polgoda Vihara.

Similar to many of the parents living in Madavala, Ajit's mother referred to Polgoda Vihara as a "good" temple. When I asked her what she meant by "good," she explained,

> The way that the head monk speaks is not like the other monks. When I see the head monk I feel a sense of calm. When I went home, I told them, "The head monk is not like the monks in Ampāra." Many people say the same thing. When he talks, even we are able to understand. When he speaks, we see that he is virtuous. We can't say that monks from Ampāra are as good. From childhood, [Ajit] was raised with Santasiri and his brother. I felt that there are good monks in this temple. Santasiri *ayyā* is also here now. I felt that it is better to bring the boy here for ordination as his brother [actually cousin] is here and as the monks are good....
>
> After they ordain, they are raised with love. They say that there is a lot of love [in this temple]. The head monk is not that strict. Only after hearing those things did I bring him here.

Ajit's mother's economic problems and her job at a garment factory in Colombo inclined her to comply with her son's wish to be taken to Polgoda Vihara, a point she actually briefly raised in our conversation. Along with certain financial strains, her willingness to allow her son to ordain and choice of temple was predicated on a complex set of aesthetic and affective experiences: the disgust and disappointment she felt toward the monks living in Ampāra,[32] and the pleasure and attraction she felt toward Narada and the other novices at Polgoda Vihara. Although Ajit's mother mentioned that her son would be able to complete his studies at Polgoda Vihara, she also mentioned the compassion and love her son would receive, the aesthetic standard that Narada embodies, and the affective bonds that exist between Ajit and his cousin. Thus, rather than simply being a decision of one child or set of parents seeking an avenue for upward mobility, for her temple recruitment was driven by matrices of relationships that extended far beyond her own family or home. Indeed, Santasiri's and Ajit's presence at Polgoda Vihara was based on social bonds that include Ajit's mother, Dhammika's grandfather, Ananda's mother, and Santasiri's parents.

CONCLUSION

In this chapter I made several references to an article by Stark and Bainbridge titled "Networks of Faith: Interpersonal Bonds and Recruitment," maintaining that it provides us with an important vantage point from which to view and interpret monastic recruitment in contemporary Sri Lanka. Their model, I asserted, not only shows how recruitment extends well beyond the walls of a single home or household, but also illustrates the role that aesthetic-affective social networks play in the process. It also provides us with a lens through which we could interpret and understand what happened to Mahavela.

To recall, prior to moving to his current temple in Uduvela, Sumedha resided in two temples: one in Madavala and one in Mahavela. By establishing *dharma* schools and youth groups at those temples, by embodying an aesthetic standard, and by cultivating close ties with the villages' children, Sumedha was able to recruit a number of boys from those areas to Polgoda Vihara. Since permanently leaving his first administrative post in Madavala in 1994, Polgoda Vihara has continued to enjoy an influx of new recruits from the Madavala area. In contrast to that region, no new recruits have made their way from Mahavela to Polgoda Vihara or any of its branch temples since Sumedha permanently left the area in 2000. The reason the flow of new recruits from Mahavela to Polgoda Vihara ceased with Sumedha's tenure there is because the social networks that are so essential to the formation and continuation of Buddhist monastic culture in contemporary Sri Lanka had completely broken down. While Narada traveled semi-frequently (approximately four times a year) to Madavala and less frequently (once or twice a year, access permitting) to Ampāra, I never once saw or heard about his visits to Mahavela. Moreover, unlike the residents from Ampāra and Madavala who sometimes requested help from the monastics of Polgoda Vihara to fulfill their own religious needs, no such calls came from Mahavela.[33] This almost complete breakdown of what Stark and Bainbridge have called "preexisting social networks" (1985:309) and "interpersonal bonds" (1985:308) has, it seems, adversely affected temple recruitment from the area.

Besides illustrating the role that interpersonal bonds also play in recruitment, the Mahavela case study points to certain limitations regarding the belief that economic and social deprivations are the central forces that drive monastic recruitment throughout South and Southeast Asia. Economic factors and social problems certainly contribute to some families' decision to send their son to the *sangha*. Nonetheless, reducing recruitment solely to a desire for upward mobility obscures the multiplicity of causes that go into monastic recruitment. It also fails to account for why, out of the many boys who are economically and socially deprived (including the ones still living in Mahavela), only a few become monastics. It is to this problem, in fact, that Stark and Bainbridge allude when they write that "deprivation and ideological compatibility seem unable to serve as more than very general contributory conditions in any satisfactory theory of recruitment. Although they do limit the pool of persons available for recruitment, they do not limit it very much in comparison to the very small numbers of such persons who actually join. Many people are deprived and are ideologically predisposed to accept a cult's message. But in explaining why so few of them actually do join, it is necessary to examine a number of situational variables" (1985:323). By examining aesthetic and emotional concerns and interests that parents of potential ordinands and ordinands themselves have in locating a suitable temple and teacher—a humble teacher who attracts the heart, a loving and caring environment, a place where one can play, a temple where one could easily develop affective bonds with others, and an environment that is conducive to studying—this chapter has considered several additional situational variables.

4 Learning to Be Novices

Monastic Education and the Construction of Vocation*

> Everyone needs love and affection. If I am affectionate with you, wouldn't you like it?...I too am happy when you care for me and are concerned about my well-being. Love and affection is needed by all people in the world—young children, middle-aged people, and the elderly. Societies exist because of love and affection. Therefore, we [as older monastics] need to look after and care for the other [young] ones.
> —Venerable Narada, personal communication

> Here it is no problem to address [the temple's donors] by the terms brother, mother, and father. People do not like to accept monks who are apart from society. Laypeople want to accept monks as people who are always connected to society. That is why people call us "Our Reverend Sir" [*apē hāmuduruwo*].
> —Venerable Piyaratana, personal communication

Drawing children to the *sangha* is only one dimension of Narada's social service enterprise. The second one is educating them as Buddhist monastics in the hope of sending them out, as well-trained novices and fully ordained monastics, to the temple's ever growing number of branch temples. In examining Buddhist monastic education and training in this chapter, my concern is the very processes through which lay children become Buddhist monastics. Although the formal monastic curriculum that novices follow in the first five years of their schooling (including the texts that they read and memorize) is important to the learning process, I suggest—by drawing on conversations I had with novices and monastic leaders (such as the two monks quoted above)—that social bonds that newly ordained novices form with other monastics, their preceptor, and the temple's lay patrons also play a fundamental role in their socialization as members of the Buddhist *sangha*. Also, building on one point raised in chapters 1 and 2—that conceptions about acceptable monastic behavior as well as the aesthetic standard are more indeterminate—I posit that any understanding and embodiment of such conceptions must come through more diffuse pedagogical methods. In that regard, this chapter explores ritual performance as a form of socialization, particularly how the participation of novices in so-called communities of practice instills in them ideas about ideal deportment and appearance that are sensitive to local concerns and needs. Finally, I consider how affective bonds that develop further between monastics, their teachers, and the laity impact the monastics' self-identity, their understanding of monastic vocation, and their levels of commitment and devotion to society and the *sangha*.

PREORDINATION TRAINING: COMMUNITY, EMOTION, AND SOCIAL BONDS

As I began thinking about the training and socialization of newcomers to the *sangha* during fieldwork I conducted in 1999, I had a more limited image of monastic education: ordinands and novices learning texts and monastic handbooks in the more formal setting of a monastic classroom *(pirivena)* and during less formal nightly advice *(avavāda)* gatherings with their preceptor. Although *pirivena* studies and *avavāda* sessions are essential, I came to realize after speaking to ordinands, recently ordained novices, older monks, and monastic leaders that a significant amount of learning and training occurs as a result of the bonds that newcomers to the *sangha* form with other novices, with older monks, with their preceptor, and with the temple's laity.

When I spoke to Narada about how he goes about training newcomers to his temple, for example, he made reference to a preordination education that was largely informal and spontaneous. Making the case that young children learn more from their peers than from those who are considerably older, Narada explained,

> It is not my own advice that is important. The thing I do here is put them into the group. For example, take a trained group of hunting dogs. If you put another dog among them, the newcomer will be trained automatically. The newcomer doesn't know what to do but by being in a group, he automatically learns. I cannot approach the ordinands so easily because I am older than they are. They have their own age groups so I cannot be with them. They do it [among] themselves. The method I am using here is like that. It is more important than the teachings I give them. My teaching is secondary.

By placing potential candidates in the same dormitory rooms as novices of similar ages from identical regions or villages, close bonds naturally begin to form.

As newcomers tag along with their new monastic-friend(s) and start imitating their friend(s) behavior and deportment throughout the many temple activities and duties that punctuate their days, the newly recruited boys naturally become adjusted to and learn about monastic life.

Narada's "hands-off" approach to monastic training, however, does not last long; several months after the arrival of most ordinands to his temple, Narada begins building relationships with them, believing that close bonds between him and his students are essential to his own ability to shape and correct their behavior. Discussing this aspect of training shortly after an ordination ceremony held in 2003, Narada said,

> When they are ill, I look after them well. From that they begin to think, "[Narada] is the only one who can look after me." When they receive my compassion and affection, they never think of going home. It is from that environment that I can begin to shape [*hadanavā*] them. They trust me because I take them on outings, give them the chance to play, and give them all the facilities [they need] to do their studies. They naturally become close to me. Only then can I tell them: "Don't do this. Act in this manner. This is a temple, not a home." They really listen to me.

Expressing compassion to his students (e.g., patting them on the head as well as speaking softly and endearingly to them), making sure that they have enough to eat (even during the evening), and ensuring that they have ample time to play in the afternoon and weekend were all, I would argue, grounded in Narada's belief that monastic training and the successful running of a temple are based upon the establishment and maintenance of close, affective bonds between himself and his students, as well as between his more senior students and those who just arrived or recently ordained. As I will also discuss below, such bonds—as well as the students' recognition of the care and love that Narada has given them over the years—also influence their ideas about monastic vocation and role performance.

Finally, Narada also encourages his students, including those who were newly recruited, to become familiar with and close to the temple's patrons. During a number of his nightly advice sessions that followed several different ordinations I attended over the years, Narada repeatedly exhorted his students to speak with the temple's patrons, to smile at them, and to approach them when they visit the temple. By also praising the temple's donors during the nightly advice session, by communicating the devotees' admiration of certain novices in front of all of his students, and by encouraging his students to address the temple's patrons with kinship terms (e.g., "father," "mother," "grandfather," "grandmother," and so on), Narada sought to create lasting ties between his patrons and students, thus implicitly challenging the very notion of ordination *(pabbajjā)* as going forth from lay society.[1]

Narada believes that by encouraging his students to use kinship terms, they will come to see the temple's patrons as their own surrogate parents.[2] Such a perspective, he maintains, is essential not only to the novices' early training—as they are more likely to accept criticism from those who are close to them—but also to their long-term goals and ideas about vocation. By reminding his student about the patrons' unceasing support, including their parent-like love and affection, Narada is able to impress on his students—in a more emotionally tangible way—the need to act appropriately or, in his words, to be qualified enough to receive the patrons' respect. During one advice period, for instance, Narada explained to his recently ordained students,

> Before, you were wearing shirts and pants. Now you are wearing a robe. Earlier, no one worshipped you. Now everyone worships you. People now feel affectionate toward you. As monks, we are living on the help of others. Thus, we have to serve them and make them happy. We have to live according to their satisfaction. Life in this temple is very good and the devotees bring so many things for you all, like rose-apple fruits. They bring those fruits for us not because they have no children to take care of but because you are monks. Thus, you should do a good job for them. You have to live and behave as monks. You should now think and understand that you are a monk and be concerned about your behavior.

Although one might argue, from a utilitarian point of view, that the wish to establish harmonious ties with the temple's patrons is based on the monastics' need to ensure continuous support from the village, such a perspective, when taken exclusively, neglects to account for the role that such relationships play in ensuring the monastics' commitment to the *sangha* and service to society.[3]

During the nightly advice session in which the newcomers to the *sangha* were encouraged to begin thinking like monastics, Narada did not go into detail regarding what behaving like a monastic actually means. In many of his following nightly advice sessions, however, Narada provided more detail about how his students might serve and please their own constituency. Narada's advice was further reinforced by the other dimensions of monastic training in which his students were immersed. Through a more formal system of education at a monastic school, and through more diffuse pedagogical methods, novices came to learn about and eventually embody correct behavior and an aesthetic standard.

FORMAL EDUCATION: THE ELEMENTARY MONASTIC COLLEGE CURRICULUM

When I first began studying the lives of child monastics in 1999, I expected their actual ordination to be preceded by a long probationary period during which they and others would assess whether a life in the *sangha* is a suitable choice for the ordinand. As I began to inquire about the preordination training that newcomers receive, however, a number of senior Sri Lankan monks told me that, although such a probationary period was quite common several decades ago, things have changed.[4] Although the length of the preordination training period is ultimately left in the hands of individual temple leaders, most newcomers to the *sangha* begin a more formal course of study at a *pirivena* within several months of becoming a Buddhist novice *(sāmaṇera)*.

In each of the five years of their elementary *(mūlika)* education, novices take courses in six areas of study: Sinhala, Pali, Sanskrit, Buddhism *(Tripiṭaka Dharmaya)*, English, and math; students in grades three, four, and five take at least two additional courses from a list of electives that includes history, geography, sociology, general science (including basic anatomy and physiology), health science, Tamil, and Hindi. Even though there is usually a choice of electives, the range of available courses is largely determined by each *pirivena*'s resources.

On numerous occasions, Narada spoke to me about the need for monastics to pursue a very broad course of study, including classes in computer science;[5] at the same time, he has also maintained that the study of Buddhism, referred to as *Tripiṭaka Dharmaya* within the *pirivena* curriculum, remains the most important component of a novice's education. To convey, as clearly as possible, the content of this important subject, I have divided it into six separate topic areas that are covered in the textbooks issued by the government's Educational Publication Department.[6]

A key dimension of a novice's Buddhist education is learning about the Buddha and his activities. In the first three years of their elementary studies, novices are taught, in a somewhat detailed manner, about his life: from the time of his descent from Tusita heaven at the urging of the god Śakra (Indra), through his youth and enlightenment, through the establishment of the fourfold Buddhist community (monks, nuns, laymen, and laywomen), to his death and final enlightenment *(parinirvāṇa)* at the age of eighty.

Along with learning about the major acts of the Buddha *(Buddha caritaya)* in the first three grades, novices are taught, in their fourth year of studies, about the Buddha's special qualities, particularly the nine qualities *(navaguṇa)* that are elaborated upon in the often-recited *itipi so* formula.[7] In their fifth and final year, novices are taught about the Buddha's social service enterprise: helping the helpless, taming the untamed, providing relief to the sick, and guiding others with an attitude of equanimity and religious tolerance.

Novices also learn about the lives of several key Buddhist figures in the form of stories *(carita kathā)*.[8] In their first year, novices are taught about two important monastics—Rāhula (the Buddha's son, who becomes a monastic while only a child)[9] and Mahāpajāpatī Gotamī (the Buddha's maternal aunt responsible for the establishment of the order of nuns)—as well as two important lay Buddhists—Anāthapiṇḍaka (a lay supporter of the Buddha unparalleled for his generosity) and Visākhā (the chief among the female supporters of the Buddha). In the following four years, novices study the lives of several eminent monks (Mahākassapa, Sāriputta, Moggallāna, and Ānanda), nuns (Khemā), and novices (Nigrodha-sāmaṇera). They also learn about the deeds of paradigmatic Buddhist kings such as Asoka of Magadha (who is responsible for spreading Buddhism within and beyond India) and Duṭṭhagāmaṇī-Abhaya (the Sri Lankan hero-king praised for the war he waged against the Tamil king, Eḷāra). Novices also study about the monk (Mahinda) and nun (Sanghamittā) responsible for bringing Buddhism to Sri Lanka as well as two other more recent Sri Lankan figures: Välivita Saraṇaṃkara (the monk responsible for the reintroduction of the higher ordination lineage in 1753) and Anagārika Dharmapāla (the famous lay-renouncer who fought for the reestablishment of Buddhism in Sri Lanka). Finally, novices are taught about the history of Buddhism *(śāsana itihāsaya)* through examining the first four Buddhist councils, as well as the social, economic, geographic, and religious environment of India during the Buddha's time.

The third component of the elementary monastic curriculum falls under the general category of what I would label as "ideas and doctrine." This component is taught through three overlapping approaches: reading stories about the Buddha's previous lives *(Jātaka)*, reading a selection of discourses (*sūtra dharma* [including selections from the *Dhammapada*]), and learning directly about the various facets of basic Buddhist doctrine *(mūlika igänvīm)*. In the final three years, students also read selections from the Abhidharma Piṭaka.

In the first three years of their elementary *pirivena* studies, novices read nine *Jātaka* stories. With the exception of the *Sāma Jātaka*, all of the *Jātaka* stories—*Tittira Jātaka*, *Haṃsa Jātaka*, *Culla-Seṭṭhi Jātaka*, *Tila-muṭṭhi Jātaka*, *Mahā Dhammapāla Jātaka*, *Dīghitikosala Jātaka*, *Khantivādi Jātaka*, and the *Vaṭṭaka Jātaka*—are quite short in length, making them easily accessible to young students. As part of the *pirivena* curriculum, the *Jātaka* stories fulfill two important purposes. Along with instilling, in the minds of the young novices, various contours of the Buddha's previous lives, the stories—which often form the foundation for sermons *(baṇa)* and even poetic sermons *(kavi baṇa)*—provide the students with a small "preaching arsenal." The major themes of the *Jātakas*—which are relevant not only to lay life, but also to contemporary Sri Lankan society—are about the importance of treating one's elders with respect; the need to look after one's parents; the importance of doing good deeds and being virtuous; the benefits of being prudent and honest; the problems with greed, desire, and anger; the benefits of honoring one's teachers; the advantages that result in living a virtuous and righteous life (including having a long life); the importance of doing good deeds and speaking honestly; the benefits of keeping good friends and the disadvantages of bad friends; and the advantages of cultivating patience and forgiveness.

Whereas *Jātaka* stories are taught in the first several years of a novice's education, reading Buddhist discourses *(suttas)* is tackled in the last three grades. There, novices study twelve Buddhist discourses, all but one of them—the *Sigālovādasutta*—being quite short in length. As with the *Jātaka* stories, the *suttas* provide the novices with a basic background to the Buddhist worldview. The majority of themes covered in these texts remain quite relevant to the concerns of contemporary society and, thus, provide novices with a certain amount of preaching material: the heavenly rewards for practicing generosity *(Ādittasutta)*; the six factors that are conducive to amiability *(Sārāṇiyasutta)*;[10] the benefits of mental cultivation, particularly cultivating the four divine abidings *(brahma vihāra)* and practicing the four foundations of mindfulness *(Saṅkhittasutta)*;[11] the four conditions that lead to happiness and well-being *(Vyagghapajjasutta)*;[12] the importance of testing and ascertaining truth for oneself rather than blindly believing what others say *(Kālāmasutta)*; the ten factors that contribute to one's downfall *(Parābhavasutta)*;[13] how to live the good life as a layperson and householder *(Sigālovādasutta)*;[14] the preciousness of human life *(Pathamāyusutta)*; the seven qualities that makes one a good friend *(Mittasutta)*;[15] and rebirth *(Udayasutta)*. Novices also study two other discourses—the *Bahudhītisutta* and the *Hirigāravasutta*—that pertain to their own lives as Buddhist monastics. Finally, novices are also taught and made to memorize the first ten sections (145 verses, or one third) of the popular Buddhist text, the *Dhammapada*.[16]

In the later grades, students are also taught several key Buddhist doctrines. In years 3–5 for example, novices learn about the four noble truths (suffering, origin of suffering, eradication of suffering, and the path to the eradication of suffering), the doctrine of cause and effect *(karma)*, the three qualities of existence (impermanence, suffering, and selflessness), the five mental hindrances (i.e., lust, ill will, sloth and torpor, restlessness and worry, and skeptical doubt), the concept of rebirth, and the doctrine of enlightenment.[17]

Novices are also taught several key meditation practices: recollecting the Buddha *(buddhānussati)*, meditation on the foulness or impurity of the body *(asubha bhāvanā)*, mindfulness of death *(maraṇānussati)*, the four foundations of mindfulness *(satipaṭṭhāna)*, meditation on loving kindness *(mettā bhāvanā)*, mindfulness of breathing *(ānāpānasati)*, and calming *(samatha)* and insight *(vipassanā)* meditation. Despite learning many different types of meditation, novices generally practice loving kindness *(mettā bhāvanā)* and mindfulness of the breath *(ānāpānasati)* at their own temples. At Polgoda Vihara and at many other temples I visited throughout Sri Lanka, moreover, the practice of meditation was limited in the daily schedule; there were two brief fifteen- or twenty-minute sessions, one in the morning and one in the evening.

The fifth dimension of the elementary *pirivena* education is temple activities. This area of study comprises a very wide range of monastic duties that include how to clean one's robes, look after one's teacher, clean the shrine room and temple grounds, sweep, wash the dishes, clean the toilets and bathing area, visit other temples and monastics, and receive alms.[18] Along with these day-to-day activities, novices are also taught, in the more formal setting of a *pirivena* classroom, how to perform several monastic rituals: paying homage to the Buddha *(namaskāra)*, going for refuge to the Buddha, *Dhamma* and *Sangha (tun saraṇa)*, as well as administering the five and eight precepts. They are also taught about the meaning and content of the ten precepts that regulate their lives as novices.

Related to the performance of Buddhist rituals are the whole host of verses *(gathā)*, discourses *(sutta)*, and protective texts *(paritta)* that novices are asked to memorize, including the three discourses that make up smaller protection rituals (e.g., the *Mahāmaṅgalasutta*, *Ratanasutta*, and the *Karaṇīyamettasutta*) and other discourses and verses that make up part of longer protection rituals (e.g., *Aṭavisiparittaṃ*, *Jinapañjaraya*, *Jayamaṅgalagāthā*, *Aṅgulimālaparittaṃ*, and *Āṭānāṭiyasuttaṃ*). Novices also memorize the verses that are recited when receiving *dāna*, when transferring merit to the dead, when performing funeral rituals, when tying protection threads, when inviting the gods prior to a sermon, and when blessing the audience after preaching or performing protection rituals.

By the time a novice completes his five years of elementary *pirivena* studies, he should be able to complete a wide range of Buddhist rituals such as worshipping the Buddha *(Buddhapūjā)*, worshipping the past Buddhas (*suvisi* and *aṭavisi Buddhapūjā*), performing protection (Sinhala: *pirit;* Pali: *paritta*) and funeral *(paṅ-*

sukula) rituals, administering the five and eight precepts to laypeople, reciting verses to extol the merit earned from giving, and reciting brief sermons (particularly after receiving alms).

IDEAL MONASTIC DISCIPLINE: THE TEN PRECEPTS, *SEKHIYA* RULES, AND *DASADHAMMASUTTA*

The last component of a novice's education is discipline. Although one dimension of learning about monastic discipline concerns studying the ten precepts that govern the lives of Buddhist novices, novices also learn and commit to memory two important disciplinary texts: the *Dasadhammasutta* and the *sekhiya* rules.[19]

The *Dasadhammasutta* is a key source of information for monastics regarding who is a monk and how a monk should act. This text, which is found in the fifth section of the *Aṅguttara Nikāya* (V.87f.) and is taught to novices in their first year of *pirivena* studies (Hettiaracci 1994), contains a list of ten *(dasa)* qualities *(dhamma)* that must be reflected upon *(abhiṇhaṃ paccavekkhitabbaṃ)* by those who have "gone forth" *(pabbajitena)*:

> (1) that they have now come to the state of having a different color [or appearance], (2) that they are dependent on others for their sustenance, (3) that their appearance and deportment must be different, (4) whether or not they censure their own selves as a result of a lapse of virtue, (5) that change and separation will befall everything that is dear and pleasant to them, (6) that they are responsible for their actions, that they are heirs of their action, and the source of the results of action, (7) that whatever they do, they will reap the results, (8) that they are not wasting their nights and days, (9) whether or not they take delight in their dwelling places, and (10) whether or not they have experienced any superhuman powers or knowledge.

Although this short 139-word text is memorized in its entirety by all elementary *pirivena* students, the first three reflections—which were taught as a closely interrelated unit—are discussed the most inside and outside of the classroom; in reminding students that their own existence as monastics is dependent upon the generosity of others (reflection 2), many teachers (including Narada) encouraged them to reflect on the distinctiveness of their own appearance and deportment (reflections 1 and 3).

The Sinhala term that is commonly used to refer to both appearance and deportment is *ākalpa*.[20] Even though *ākalpa* is sometimes translated simply as "appearance," it actually encompasses a whole range of meanings including "suitable appearance, attitudes, and performance."[21] In the *pirivena* classes and Narada's advice sessions that I attended, the term *ākalpa* was used largely to distinguish monastic life from lay life. By employing the term to clarify (in the novices' minds) the distinctiveness of their own appearance, attitudes, deportment, and performance, as well as by correlating that distinctiveness to the monastics' reliance on the generosity of laypeople, Narada and many of the *pirivena* teachers I met also sought to emphasize the need for their own students to *please* and *satisfy* the laity, particularly their own patrons, on whose generosity they directly depended.

The *Dasadhammasutta* does not explain what "other actions and appearance/deportment" actually mean; the second "text" that novices studied, the *Sekhiya* rules, does.[22] Memorized during their second year at *pirivena*, the seventy-five *sekhiya* rules instill a vision, in the novices' minds, of a monastic who is physically disciplined and serene. By providing an image of a monastic's tempered external deportment and appearance, the rules work to transform a novice or a monk into an aesthetically pleasing object: one who wears his robe evenly, one who is well covered, one who walks quietly through towns and villages, one who walks with his arms by his side, one who walks with a downcast gaze, one who eats methodically and with manners, one who sits in a calm manner, one who preaches in a correct manner and with proper intention, and so on.

DIFFUSE WAYS OF LEARNING: PERFORMANCE THEORY AND AN ACTION-ORIENTED PEDAGOGY

The *sekhiya* rules continue to inform contemporary ideas of ideal monastic behavior and appearance; however, as I maintained in chapters 1 and 2, the aesthetic standard can never be fixed to a single set of rules. Besides changing over time—such as ideas about what is acceptable hair length[23]—aesthetic sensibilities are also influenced by local concerns, needs, and histories, as Carrithers (1990), Silber (1995), Collins (1998), Abeysekara (2002), and Hayashi (2003) have intimated. The very fluidity and adaptability of the aesthetic standard must involve, then, a type of monastic education that is not solely limited to learning certain "fixed" images of ideal monastic deportment and appearance (such as through reading the *Dasadhammasutta* and the *sekhiya* rules). Novices need other ways to learn about how to attract the hearts of others. In saying this, however, I do not mean to imply that learning and memorizing texts within a *pirivena* setting is not irrelevant; instead, I am suggesting that ideas about how to act as a monastic and what it means to be a monastic are also communicated through other, more diffuse, methods. Learning by doing and learning by performing are two such pedagogical methods that enable a monastic to learn about appropriate behavior and appearance while accounting for regional variations.[24]

When I began asking novices about their own training, particularly how they came to learn to be a Buddhist monastic, I was surprised to find little, if any, reference to monastic texts and discourses such as the *Dasadhammasutta* and the *sekhiya* rules. Even though most novices knew the title of these and other texts, conversations with them about their own training focused on a host of atextual, body-oriented ritualized activities. For many, learning about monastic life was intimately related to *doing* and *performing*.

When I asked Anuruddha, a fifteen-year-old novice, about what helped him to learn about being a monastic, he replied,

> Doing religious rituals is very important to the process of becoming a monk. You have to learn these activities for your whole life. The two activities in particular that affected my thoughts were worshipping the Buddha and cleaning the temple. I found cleaning the temple to be closely related to keeping the precepts. By worshipping the Buddha every day, I got used to being a monastic and began to think like a monastic.... Those who do not do the temple activities correctly are not following the [monastic] precepts well. By worshipping the Buddha you begin to develop your faith and that helps you acquire more feelings [or understanding] about being a monastic.

Anuruddha's comment exposed, quite plainly, the problems inherent in my own tendency to separate what I viewed as "real" classroom learning from what I saw to be the various responsibilities and distractions that usually encumber monastics. Although Anuruddha learned a number of discourses, languages, and stories while attending a nearby *pirivena*, his assessment of his own training reveals that texts may actually play a less central role in informing his understanding about how to dress, act, and perform as a Buddhist monastic. For Anuruddha, worshiping the Buddha led him to develop faith, which, in turn, helped him to understand or even feel what it is like to be a monastic. Performing other types of temple activities (such as sweeping) in a ritualized manner further shaped Anuruddha's attitudes and thoughts about the meaning and content of monastic life.[25]

Many other novices made a connection between doing, performing, and learning. Dhammika, the novice from Ampāra discussed in the previous chapter, shared with me his own reflections on his monastic training shortly after coming to Polgoda Vihara: "By seeing the activities going on around me in the shrine room, I got used to [being a monastic]. . . . The activities done in the shrine room made me closer to being a monastic. Cleaning the temple and making offerings to the Buddha made me closer to a monastic's role."

When I asked nine novices in 2003 to photograph an important temple activity, six of them took a picture of a monk sweeping the compound of the temple. Although I had my own conception of where monastic learning occurs (e.g., in a monastic college and during the nightly advice of the head monk), the novices, by discussing their photographs, pointed to the close relationship that exists between doing and learning. Piyananda—Gunasena's second son and one of the six who took a photograph of a novice sweeping—explained to me in the weeks following his ordination: "I started feeling like a monastic the day after the head monk advised us to think that we are monastics. What helped cause that change was doing the work of monastics that the head monk assigned to me. For example, when I was a layperson, I was not asked to sweep [*atugāṇavā*]. Now, I have to do it methodically. . . .[26] Now we can help with the activities in the alms hall such as organizing the alms food. Also, now we worship the Buddha with the other novices. I feel ready to accept everything. I am learning to be a novice."

The connection that these and other novices drew between learning and performing has not been explored too widely within the field of Buddhist studies. Nevertheless, it has been discussed in other disciplines, such as within the field of ritual studies. In *Ritual Theory, Ritual Practice,* Catherine Bell draws on the works of the ritual theorist Pierre Bourdieu to discuss the interrelatedness between mind and body by noting how ritual participation inscribes dominant symbols, structures, and beliefs of a particular community on a ritualized agent. She posits, for instance, that

> the molding of the body within a highly structured environment does not simply express inner states. Rather, it primarily acts to restructure bodies in the very doing of the acts themselves. . . . [W]hat we see in ritualization is not the mere display of subjective states or corporate values. Rather, we see an act of production—the production of a ritualized agent. . . . Hence, ritualization, as the production of a ritualized agent via the interaction of a body within a structured and structuring environment, always takes place within a larger and very immediate sociocultural situation. (1992:99f.)

What is notable about this process of ritualization is how performing rituals and participating in other types of ritualized activities (such as sweeping) instill Buddhist norms in the participants' minds and bodies.[27] As one older novice, after reflecting on the education he received at the local monastic school, explained, "It was not what we studied. It was the way we were supposed to act in the temples, such as standing up when the teacher came in, cleaning the temple, and talking properly to our teacher." This method for learning how to be and act in the world is also discussed in Michael Carrithers's comparative study of Buddhism and Jainism, where he notes that the aesthetic standard is not successfully communicated through lists of rules and injunctions but rather in "poems and images, in figural and patterned language, in ritual and in plastic art" (1990:158).

Conversations with head monks about the monastic training process suggest that Carrithers is correct in highlighting the pedagogical function of patterned language and speech. In Sinhala, as in Thai, a different vocabulary is used when addressing or speaking about members of the *sangha*. The different vocabularies, as W. S. Karunatillake (1997:4) has pointed out, shape understandings about monastic life by naturally differentiating it from lay life.[28] Charles Hallisey raises a similar point. Drawing on the concept of performative utterances developed by Tambiah (1968), Sesonske (1965), and Austin (1975), Hallisey discusses the performative dimension of language, specifically how particular utterances may alter formal relationships, such as the relationship between a Buddhist devotee and the Buddha (1988:82–88). Discussing the role that a specialized vocabulary plays in the training of novices, Narada explained,

> You have to develop your behavior pattern like a monk. . . . There should be a difference between a layman and a monk. For a simple example, take food. Everybody says "eat." For laymen it is *käma kanavā* but for monks it is *dāna valaṇdanavā*. The words *kanavā* and *valaṇdanavā* are different. They do not mean the same thing. It is the same act but two different actions. You can *kanavā* [or eat] when you walk, talk, or even stand. There are no limitations. *Valaṇdanavā*, on the other hand, is completely different. You have to think about the food, you have to sit properly, and you have to do it with manners. You have to do it while thinking that you are a monk. That is how the novices are trained.

This relationship between language, ways of conducting oneself, and ways of related to others appears to be founded on a multistep process in which the novices are first taught about ideal monastic behavior and deportment through learning texts, watching their peers, and attending Narada's nightly advice sessions, during which he frequently comments on the behavior—appropriate and inappropriate—of other monastics. These behavioral patterns are then correlated to a specialized vocabulary. As this process becomes reinforced over time, the words and their respective worldviews become automatically fused. It is this dimension of language that the sociologist Pierre Bourdieu (1977:94) alluded to when he said that a whole cosmology is instilled in the command "stand up straight." For Narada, words such as go *(vadinavā)* and eat *(valaṇḍanavā)* are not just verbal indicators of a monastic's higher status in society. Words that contain whole cosmologies and their utterance instill in the minds of their referents a whole way of being, acting, thinking, and relating.

My own study of monastic education and pedagogy suggests that Carrithers (1990:158) is also correct to highlight the role that rituals play in transmitting the contours of the aesthetic standard. To understand better the pedagogical role of ritual performance, I will turn my attention in this section to an extremely popular ceremony that almost every newcomer to the *sangha* learns in the first several years of his training: protection rituals.[29] After briefly examining the practices and settings in which novices are trained in *paritta* performance, I will discuss how learning *paritta* provides novices with a more culturally sensitive understanding of how to attract the hearts of lay patrons, including how to establish and maintain proper relationships with them.

Learning *paritta* and *paritta* performance largely occurs through a twofold process: (1) in *pirivena* and ancillary groups and (2) in more informal communities of learning and practice. Through the former, novices work toward memorizing key texts as well as learn how to pronounce the texts' words. Through the latter—informal learning communities—novices gradually come to an understanding and appreciation of the *aesthetics* of *paritta* performance and, thus, what is expected of them—in terms of deportment and appearance—within and outside of the ritual arena as Buddhist monastics.

One important component of learning *paritta* is, of course, memorizing the necessary texts. Although it is not uncommon to see novices working individually to learn the texts by heart (especially during the morning and evening hours when other monastic commitments are reduced), memorization (*kaṭapādaṃ*) work is often first tackled in monastic schools. At the *pirivena* attached to Polgoda Vihara as well as at several other *pirivenas* where I had the opportunity to spend time in Sri Lanka, the texts and verses were frequently recited line by line by a teacher, and repeated, line by line, by the students in unison. Through this more formal method of learning, students gradually came to memorize the texts. Their pronunciation was also corrected in the process.

Alongside repeating the *paritta* texts with their teachers, novices practiced reciting large sections of the texts in smaller groups of students of a similar level.

During these so-called *vat pirit* periods, which usually occurred in the evenings and during the weekend, each novice was given the opportunity to recite whole portions of *paritta* texts from memory while having any mispronunciations corrected by the group. Novices also learned where to break up Pali words so as not to change the words' meaning, as well as how and when to stretch the Pali syllables.

The other component to learning *paritta* is acquiring an understanding of how best to perform the texts in a ritual context. This type of learning mostly occurred in more informal *communities of practice,*[30] as well as through a process that Jean Lave and Etienne Wenger (1991) have referred to as "legitimate peripheral participation." By first listening to and watching the ritual being performed, novices become immersed in the complete world of *paritta* performance and, thus, readily acquire a firsthand understanding of what constitutes pleasing *paritta;* once novices have watched and listened to a number of rituals being performed, they are encouraged to participate further in these communities of learning and practice by imitating the actions, behavior, and speech of more experienced monastics.

What is compelling about the training that occurred through such communities of practice is that it collapses the distance between the learner and the learned, thus making the learning process more immediate and tangible. It also entails a more active process of learning and a more socially grounded manner of training. Susan Schwartz discusses such a form of training in reference to the performing arts in India. She writes,

> Accounts regarding the ancient *guru-shisha-parampara* system indicate that the student [*shishya*] lived with the *guru* [teacher] both to serve and to learn the tradition [*parampara*]. . . . Sources often maintain that very little talking was done. Rather, the guru would provide, in measured doses, lessons by example, which the student would absorb, copy, and rehearse until the teacher was satisfied. The atmosphere in which teaching and learning took place was oral/aural/kinesthetic. . . . If we are to understand the performing arts in India, however, this is one aspect that must be grasped. A distancing occurs between the student and the knowledge to be gained when the mode of transmission is the written word. The physical distance between the eye and the page is symbolic of a greater distance between the learning and the learned. However, when the transmission is experienced physically, as sound enters into the body through the ears and movement is physically internalized, it is more active, more engaged,

> and it is immediate, that is, unmediated. Those who learn physically learn differently, and experience their knowledge differently as well. It becomes ingested, becomes, like food, part of the one's cell structure. When the guru *shows*, rather than *tells*, absorption by the student is of a different quality altogether. (2004:5)

As learning to perform *paritta*, like learning to perform dance in India, demands the "full participation in the socio-cultural practices of a community" (Lave and Wenger 1991:29), it necessitates a type of learning that is much more encompassing than simply reading and memorizing. Included in this oral/aural/kinesthetic learning process for the novices is a whole social world; by participating in communities of practice, newcomers to the *sangha* become socialized into the wider world of Buddhist monastic culture and practice, thus coming to understand, in a qualitatively different manner, how to attract and please the laity by maintaining proper monastic appearance and ideal behavior.

When I asked Venerable Sujata, the novice discussed in the previous chapter, to describe a good *paritta* performance to me *("honda pirit kiyanne mokadda?")*, I expected his response to center on the need to recite the ritual texts correctly, with a proper cadence *(talaya)* and in a melodious *(mihiri)* manner. Although our conversation did eventually touch upon the issue of cadence, I found it surprising that Sujata's initial response focused largely on his own appearance and demeanor as a member of the Buddhist *sangha*. Making an implicit connection between the ritual's efficacy and the performers' ability to please and attract the hearts of the audience through their physical appearance, Sujata, like other monastics, said, "According to our lineage [*nikāya*], the robe has to cover both shoulders. Then, we should speak well to the people. The head and face should be shaven. Then we should walk according to a method/in a straight line. There is a procedure [*piliväla*]—we have to have a bath, then we have to shave our head and face, then we have to go beautifully in order to attract the people's hearts."

It is because of the relationship that is commonly drawn between the ritual's outcome and pleasing the hearts of the laity that make such occasions as learning *paritta* a unique opportunity for reflecting on what constitutes ideal monastic appearance. Even though several older novices and monks made reference to how the words recited of the ritual have an inherent power to them (literally, *vag śaktiya*),[31] my conversations with most novices undergoing training focused quite specifically on the reciters' physical appearance. Dhammadassi drew such a relationship when comparing protection rituals chanted by monastics with protection rituals chanted by laypeople *(gihi pirit)*:

> It is more important to see monks chanting *pirit* than laypeople. Monks have nicely worn robes. They have shaven heads. With a proper demeanor, a monk becomes a pleasing image. He is beautiful to the eye. He should also have a sweet/melodious [*mihiri*] voice and he should properly pronounce the words. Wearing a robe well, with a shaven head, and a shaven face, one looks like a proper monk. Then, as they listen and see things that are pleasing, their hearts become concentrated [*yomuvenevā*].

As I noted above, novices read about the importance of wearing their lower and upper robes evenly around them (*parimaṇḍalaṃ nivāsessāmi/pārupissāmi'ti*), of traveling in inhabited areas well covered (*supaṭicchanno antaraghare gamissāmi'ti*), and of sitting in inhabited areas well covered (*supaṭicchanno antaraghare nisīdissāmi'ti*) in the seventy-five training (*sekhiya*) rules. For a number of novices, however, their own understanding about pleasing monastic appearance occurs, in a much more visceral manner, through learning to perform rituals. As a result of the connection expressed between pleasing the hearts of the laity, the monastics' physical appearance and demeanor, and the ritual's power or outcome, *paritta* becomes a important means through which novices are provided with the opportunity to mentally absorb and physically embody prevailing conceptions of ideal monastic appearance. This process of learning, as a number of performance theorists point out, is not something that passively affects a doer or watcher; rather it is a dynamic process in which society and the people involved are constantly reflecting on their state and status. Explaining how performing shapes ritual agents by providing them with the opportunity to reflect on their state and status, Bell notes that

> In describing the construction of new cultural images, dispositions, and situations, performance theory has also focused creative attention on the importance of concomitant processes of self-reflection and interpretation termed "reflexivity." Many have seen the dramatic or performative dimension of social action as affording a public reflexivity or mirroring that enables the community to stand back and reflect upon their actions and identity. (1997:75)

Another pedagogical dimension to ritual performance is learning about monastic behavior. Conversations with novices and head monks revealed a similar understanding regarding how their own behavior as members of the *sangha* affects the attendees of the ritual and, in turn, the ritual's outcome. Venerable

Piyananda, who is often called upon to perform shorter *(set pirit)* and longer *(mahāpirit)* protection rituals, expressed to me the need for monastics to act appropriately. Describing what he considers proper monastic behavior to be, he explained,

> He has to recite it by only looking at the *pirit* text. He should not look around. He should not look at the people. People will be displeased if they see that the monk is looking around. The monk has to work in a way that pleases them.... When we go to recite *pirit*, if the householder is not displeased with us, his heart will be attracted to the *pirit*. If the *pirit* is chanted to bless the householder and his house, we should think, "may the householder receive peace." Then, the householder will be grabbed by us.

Venerable Atthadassi used our discussion of protection rituals as an opportunity to reflect, in a more tangible manner, upon what he understood ideal monastic behavior to be

> When *pirit* is recited, there has to be a sense of calm. When our head monk is seated, he doesn't shake even his legs. Seated like that, one has to recite it with an appropriate *talaya* [or cadence], that means, recite it in a normal way and beautifully.... If we behave in an agitated way among the people, they might feel disgusted.... We have to be restrained [*saṅvaraya*] when the exhortation [*anuśāsanaya*] is made. During that time, we should not be chatting with the other monks... [and] we should not be resting our heads on our palms or fall asleep. That is a mistake. The people will become fed up.... They will be fed up with listening to *pirit*, too.

Talking about the ideal *paritta* behavior exhibited by his own teacher and comparing those images with less pleasing reflections of monastic behavior provided Atthadassi with the chance to reflect, in a much more heightened manner, on his own identity and behavior.

It is worth noting that many of the novices' reflections on appropriate and pleasing *paritta* behavior are quite similar to canonical portrayals of ideal monastic conduct. In the training *(sekhiya)* rules discussed earlier, we read that monastics should go about with downcast eyes *(okkhitacakkhu antaraghare gamissāmī'ti)*, should sit with downcast eyes *(okkhittacakkhu antaraghare nisīdissāmī'ti)*, should sit with little sounds *(appasaddo antaraghare nisīdissāmi'ti)*, should not sit while shaking the body *(na kāyappacālakaṃ antaraghare nisīdissāmī'ti)* or swaying the arms *(bāhuppacālakaṃ)*, should not sit while shaking or bobbing one's head *(na sīsappacālakaṃ antaraghare nisīdissāmi'ti)*, and so on. Just as monks and novices are able to arrive at an intellectual understanding of proper monastic behavior through reading texts (such as the *sekhiya* rules) that provide specific instructions on how to act, so too do newcomers to the *sangha* come to learn about, through the oral/aural/kinesthetic manner that Schwartz discusses, ideal behavior both within and outside of the ritual arena by learning to perform *paritta* within a community of practice.[32]

CONCLUSION

One point I made when examining the connection between personal relationships and the socialization of newcomers to the *sangha* is that affective ties established among groups of monastics as well as between members of the *sangha* and lay Buddhists sustain Buddhist communities. As I continued to delve more into the topic of monastic training and education, especially during my later visits to the island, I came to see and appreciate how such ties sometimes influence choices that monastics make in regard to vocation. To illustrate this connection between affective bonds and vocation, let me turn to a case study of one monastic whom I have been closely following since 1999.

Venerable Kassapa first became a novice under Narada in 1991. He was twelve years old at the time. After spending eight years by Venerable Narada's side, Kassapa was sent to Ganegoda Vihara, the temple where Narada was first ordained. Although Devamitta was still running the temple when Kassapa arrived, Devamitta had become, as a result of his old age and more limited mobility, more and more disconnected from the temple's daily activities and, thus, the temple's patrons. Narada hoped that Kassapa's presence there would transform the temple into a vibrant community. Narada also assumed that Kassapa, already quite well known for his poetic form of preaching *(kavi baṇa)*, would take over the temple's administration when the time came. He did. After Devamitta passed away in 2003, Kassapa officially became the temple's new head monk *(vihārādhipati)*. What is perhaps most relevant about Kassapa's story, however, is not the temple's transformation, but how the Kassapa's relationships with his teacher and donors affected his own views about himself as a monastic.

In 1999 and 2000, Kassapa had expressed to me on several occasions his wish to move to a forest hermitage *(arañña)* and take up the full-time practice of meditation. Although Kassapa agreed to move to Ganegoda Vihara, he admitted that he did so out of a sense of commitment he felt toward his teacher, Narada. Kassapa stated that there was no way he could disregard his teacher's request, especially after his teacher raised him with such love and affection. When I asked him more directly why he was unable simply to leave the temple and start practicing meditation on a more full-time basis, Kassapa first spoke about the need to "guard his teacher's respect" and then added, "I have to think about the head monk. I have to satisfy him.... I have to fulfill his request to take care of little ones and donors' needs.... I have to keep in mind all that he has done for us. He uses me as an example to the group [of novices currently residing] there [at Polgoda Vihara]. I should be an example to the younger ones. I have to be good to him." The close relationship between him and his teacher—as well as between him and the younger novices living at Polgoda Vihara—has had a profound effect on the manner in which Kassapa has envisaged vocation and role performance, thus implicitly calling into question the view that viable role performance only occurs when deep religious motivations prompt monastic ordination (see, for instance, Gombrich 1998:379 and Obeyesekere 1981:41f.).

Another factor that shaped Kassapa's self-identity, including his own short- and long-term goals, was the bonds he began to form with the patrons from Ganegoda Vihara. Indeed, when I interviewed Kassapa in 2003 and 2004, he appeared well ensconced in his role as the temple's head monk. During our conversations together, moreover, Kassapa never once, on his own accord, mentioned the wish to go to a forest temple. When I casually reminded him of his earlier plan, he—after nodding his head and shrugging his shoulders—responded that he would still like to practice meditation but now had other responsibilities. He further explained that he has his own patrons to consider and that they often need him to help solve their own problems.[33] The implicit connection that Kassapa made between his own role as a member of the Buddhist *sangha* and the types of bonds he had formed with the patrons of Ganegoda Vihara was, in short, noteworthy.

Since moving to Ganegoda Vihara in 2000, Kassapa has done an excellent job of reviving the temple. Whereas the temple was often void of visitors during my numerous visits there in 1999, the temple has become, since 2000, a bustling center of Buddhist activity. During most evenings one would encounter several groups of donors spending time at the temple; the Buddhist *dharma* (Sunday) school connected to the temple is also heavily attended. Explaining the changes that occurred after becoming the head monk of the temple, Kassapa said, "Now I am busy handling the administration work here: taking care of small ones [novices] and serving the donors.... Before I came here, the donors did not come. The temple was deteriorating. Now they come because I am here. They come steadily from 5:30 to 9:30, especially the young ones [from the village] who come and talk to me about their problems. Making them happy is the pleasure I get from temple work."

The connections between social bonds and decision making do not imply that all monastics who develop affective ties with the laity remain in the order. Nonetheless, in thinking through the types of commitments that laypeople and monastics make to each other, the community, and the *sangha*, it becomes evident that such bonds are central to the formation and maintenance of Buddhist monastic culture in contemporary Sri Lanka. In fact, Venerable Sumedha overtly made such a connection when he explained,

> As monks become older, they have to be given responsibilities. When they are doing well they need to be given responsibility. That is why Venerable Piyaratana [the deputy head monk from Polgoda Vihara] did not disrobe. . . . That is why Venerable Ananda and Venerable Kassapa did not disrobe. They were given responsibilities and they did well. And as they developed a group of devotees around themselves, they came to know that they had to fulfill their requirements. Venerable Sivali, the former principal of the *pirivena* [attached to Polgoda Vihara] left and disrobed because he didn't do that. He didn't even administer the five precepts to the laity. He never performed religious activities. Never! Ultimately he felt isolated. No devotees liked him. No one was affectionate toward him. Ultimately he had to go.

As I will illustrate more fully in the following chapter with case studies of two monastics who were unable to develop ties with their teachers and patrons, such affective bonds are not only important in ensuring proper role performance; they are also central to the enterprise of Buddhist institution building.

5 Temple Building as Social Service
Family, Community, and Emotion

During a sermon following the ordination of seventeen boys in October 2004, Venerable Narada spoke at length about his work as the head monk of Polgoda Vihara to the crowd who had assembled at the temple to celebrate the ceremony. Addressing the crowd, Narada said,

> I have ordained about a hundred and eight boys in this temple here. With these seventeen, it will become one hundred and twenty-five. A hundred and twenty-five boys have ordained in this preaching hall. These seventeen young monastics are not alone. They are connected to the larger group here. They will have a huge number of brother-monks. Some of [the brother-monks] have already finished their studies. Others are still doing their education. They are now spread all over this country. They are providing a great social service to [our] society and to the religion. They are fulfilling the needs of donors in a number of places.
>
> I would also like to mention that we have a very good group of donors here. They always pay attention to our well-being. Some of them visit the temple daily. When we are sick, they give us medicine. We are pleased to have such a group of donors, not only here in this village, but thousands all over the country. With these seventeen children another group of people will also become donors of this temple. We can all come together and serve the religion and the world. You can also do more and more religious activities in your villages there.

When I first began researching Polgoda Vihara in 1999, there were only two branch temples associated with it: one under the administration of Venerable Sumedha in Uduvela and one run by Reverend Ananda in Banvelgolla. Before leaving Sri Lanka in May 2000, two new branch temples were opened: one in Baṭuaṃbē and one in Tēkkavatta.[1] The number of branch temples began increasing at an even greater rate since 2003; by May 2009, when I last saw Venerable Narada, he and his students had taken over ten additional temples: three in Kandy District, two in Anurādhapura District, one in Kurunägala District, and four in Mātalē District.[2] He is also in the process of taking over another temple in Anurādhapura District, bringing the total number of branch temples to fifteen.

Drawing on the voices of lay patrons associated with two temples that Narada recently acquired, as well with several monastics directly involved in the running of those new temples, I consider, in this chapter, monastic institution building. In exploring the various factors that drive particular groups of laypeople to seek new avenues of monastic patronage, I suggest that temple building occurs through a very dynamic process in which ideas regarding what constitutes an ideal temple, monastic, and lay devotee are constantly negotiated and renegotiated. Even though ritual needs may drive some people to associate with particular groups of monastics, I suggest that people's desire for close, affective bonds with monastics remain quite central to the temple-building process.

While investigating temple patronage and temple management in contemporary Sri Lanka, I pay special attention to the vocabulary of emotions that laypeople and monastics employ when describing the process. I suggest, by considering certain caste attitudes that have affected one Buddhist community, that people's histories and cultural practices make certain emotions possible and certain social bonds more likely. Finally, treating emotion as cultural appraisals that, in turn, shape people's aesthetic sensibilities, I explore how certain affective states (such as anger, hatred, love, affection, desire, and hope) shape people's aesthetic sensibilities, which, in turn, determine subsequent emotional responses and judgments. Before turning to the first of two case studies that make up the core of this chapter, I will situate the recent increase of temple building at Polgoda Vihara within Narada's expanding notions of social service.

TEMPLE BUILDING AS SOCIAL SERVICE

As I discussed in chapter 1, soon after Narada completed his university degree, he decided to devote his time and energy to serving society. Feeling a sense of obligation to the society that helped him pursue his studies as a monk, Narada resolved not only to turn his attention to the religious needs of his local patrons, but also to the social and economic needs of children living throughout Sri Lanka's disadvantaged areas *(duṣkara paḷāt)*. By bringing such children to his temple and ordaining them as Buddhist novices, Narada sought to provide them with a quality and level of education that would not have been available to them in their native villages.

As Narada's monastic enterprise began to expand, since the late 1990s, from several dozen students to 125 in 2004, over 140 in 2006, and almost 175 in

2008,[3] so did his understanding of social service. With an ever increasing number of senior students and qualified novices, Narada has begun expanding the reach of his social service enterprise to include lay Buddhists living in distant villages. When I returned to Sri Lanka in 2005–2006, I asked Narada about some of the changes that had taken place over the past year. In response to my query, Narada began discussing six temples that had recently come under his administration or were in the process of being transferred to him. When I mentioned that his idea of social service now appears to have two distinct dimensions—providing education to poor boys from harsher areas and establishing temples in villages around Sri Lanka—he agreed. After briefly speaking about the difficulties that many villagers face in fulfilling their own religious needs, Narada went on to suggest how the two dimensions of social service that I mentioned are interrelated:

> One [aspect of social service] is that when we go [to these villages], the people there give us their children. When they give us their children, we train them. After that, we are able to begin religious activities in these other places through these ones [who ordained from there]. . . . Now, [the villagers living in these other places] cannot fulfill their own religious needs because there are no monks. Those people still have religious needs: protection rituals, alms-giving, and funeral rituals. Even though they have these needs, there are no monks. It is good if we go there and do some work. We could also bring back boys [to ordain].
>
> . . . Of the crowd who is here, 99.9 percent are from North-Central Province.[4] Because of that, we have to do some service over there. Right? There are numerous temples which are closed. Because of that, more work should be done over there than here.

One point I made in chapters 1 and 4 was how close bonds that develop between monastics and their patrons hold Buddhist communities together and shape ideas about monastic vocation. In particular, I maintained that ties cultivated with their patrons inspired Narada and Kassapa to question earlier choices (e.g., disrobing or taking up the practice of meditation full time) and to reconsider their commitment to the *sangha* and society.

In regard to Narada's temple-building enterprise, the same may be said: that as his webs of relationships with the families of his own students broadened and deepened, Narada began to reevaluate his own understanding of social service. Now, rather than strictly focusing on the religious needs of his temple's patrons and the social and economic needs of poor children living in disadvantaged areas,

Narada has begun considering the religious needs of his students' families living far away from his own Kandyan temple. Acknowledging the commitment and sacrifice that many families from areas such as Huruluväva and Kumbukväva made when they handed their own children over to the *sangha*, Narada felt it only appropriate to reciprocate by establishing temples there.

Something in addition to the obligation he feels toward those who have given their sons to the *sangha*, however, is driving Narada's temple-building enterprise: that the perceived dearth of monastics on the island is threatening the very survival of the *sangha*. Although there are no reliable statistics that would help us determine the relative strength or weakness of the *sangha* in such areas as Madavala, Huruluväva, and Kumbukväva over the past fifty years, newspaper editorials, government reports, and personal accounts certainly corroborate Narada's perception. Descriptions of the insurmountable problems that laypeople sometimes encounter to secure a sufficient number of monks for their larger Buddhist rituals (e.g., death-anniversary alms-giving ceremonies)[5] are quite common, although, as Narada explained, such problems are not evenly felt:

> Let's take the total national income of the country. Let's say that that amount works out to about 150 dollars per month. Not everyone makes that. That figure is on paper only. It is wrong to divide the aggregate income by the entire population. There are very few people with money. Many people are poor.
>
> The problem with monks is similar to that. There are monks. When you divide them into the total population, you might say that there is one monk for every 400 people.[6] However, that number is not correct. Most of the monks today live in Galle, Colombo, Kandy, and Matara. In other places, the ratio is not 400:1 but 4,000:1.[7] You can see that in other places. There are plenty of temples around Kumbukväva. There are temples; however, there are no monks.

For Narada, there is a real pressing need for monastics to fulfill people's religious needs; if not, he argued, people will be forced to turn to other religious traditions.[8] Although Narada would not go so far as other monastics (including several of his senior students) to support the recent National Sinhala Heritage (Jathika Hela Urumaya) Party legislation to stop "unethical conversions,"[9] Narada believes that the very survival of the *sangha* is dependent upon a form of social service that includes serving the religious needs of all lay Buddhists, regardless of location, economic status, and caste.[10]

AMBANA AND KUMBUKVÄVA: SOCIAL BONDS AND THE DYNAMICS OF TEMPLE BUILDING

In discussing temple building in contemporary Sri Lanka, there are several case studies from which I could have drawn, including two temples that I discussed more recently in an article on monastic patronage (Samuels 2007a). My decision to focus on the temples in Ambana and Kumbukväva is based on several factors.[11] First, both case studies provide ample opportunity to reflect on the role that social relations and affective states play in the construction of monastic communities in contemporary Sri Lanka. More specifically, both cases illustrate how harmonious ties between a temple and its patrons occur through a dynamic process of negotiation and renegotiation that is, itself, driven by a whole range of emotions.

Ambana

The Ambana temple is located right in the middle of the village and sits on about an acre and a half of land. The village itself, an agricultural colony created in the 1950s, consists of about 200 families, 186 of whom belong to the village welfare society. When I visited the village in December 2005, the temple complex consisted of a four-room monastic residence, a large preaching hall (which also functioned as a *dharma* school and as a meeting place for the welfare society), and a mid-sized Buddha-image house *(buduge)* with a Buddha statue that is, I was told, more than a hundred years old. Construction was also under way on a two-story monastic college–*cum*–residence hall. No one with whom I spoke was able to tell me the date that the temple was actually founded, though one donor ventured that the temple's roots go all the way back to the period of King Valagambahu I (circa first century B.C.E.), a claim that did not seem to be substantiated by any evidence (such as inscriptions).

Prior to the 1970s, Ambana Vihara functioned as a branch temple of another nearby Rāmañña Nikāya temple. Unfortunately, that connection was severed thirty years ago when a wide river channel that was part of the larger Mahaveli irrigation project divided the two temples. Despite helping the villagers with their agricultural work, the river impinged upon the relationship between the two temples as the new route via the bridge increased the distance between them from a little over one kilometer to more than ten kilometers. The relationship between the temples was further hampered when the head monk from the main temple (with whom the villagers from Ambana were quite close) passed away. With his teacher gone, the monk in charge of the Ambana temple left, feeling an obligation neither to the villagers nor to his deceased teacher.

One would expect that the temple's regular annual income of about 60,000–70,000 rupees from its coconut trees and black-pepper plants would provide enough incentive for a monastic to make the temple his permanent home. The promise of a continuous cash flow, however, did not attract the most honest and committed monks to the temple. Unable to staff their remote temple on a permanent basis, the Ambana villagers began to turn to a monastic college seven kilometers away to fulfill their religious needs. Irrespective of the added costs for transporting monks to and from the *pirivena,* the villagers tolerated their situation for some time.

Soon things began to change. As it was explained to me, in 2000 the head monk from the *pirivena* decided to hold a large celebration *(piṅkama)* to raise money for needed repairs and construction projects. The villagers from Ambana were invited; they were also asked by the local patrons of the *pirivena* to contribute 10,000 rupees toward the needed repairs. The residents from Ambana were unable to raise the money. Rather than arriving to the celebration with partially filled hands, they decided to skip the event altogether. Unfortunately for them, the head monk of the *pirivena* did not take their absence lightly. As Venerable Ananda, the head monk who now oversees the Ambana temple, explained to me, "After that [celebration] day, that [*pirivena*] monk did not come to the village [when requested]. He didn't send anyone either.... When there was a religious event, they were unable to find monks.... The [Ambana] people became fed up." With their ties to the *pirivena* irreparably rent, the villagers began turning to other temples to fulfill their own ritual needs. By and large, their search was unsuccessful mostly because of the area's poor transportation and shortage of monks.

In discussing with me the problems that the Ambana patrons faced in running their village temple, Mr. Tilakaratana—a principal donor and head of the village welfare society—noted that most of the monastics who came to reside at the temple were "outsiders." Explaining what he meant by outsider, Tilakaratana added: "[Outsider] means that they didn't come here through a teacher or a temple. Monks from various places were simply taken by the donors. They came, stayed one or two years, and left. The reason for that is because of the mistakes that the monks made and mistakes that the donors made. There was no person or place to complain about the monk." Whereas "insiders"—i.e., monastics who come through people's personal connections and are closely tied to a teacher—would ensure that the temple's patrons retain some desirable "control over the affairs of a group of men who have left society" (Kemper 1980:35), the outsiders who came to Ambana remained too cut off from the villagers there. For the donors from Ambana, there was a real concern that the absence of such avenues of communication (i.e., between the temple's leader, his teacher, and the temple's patrons) may result in a monk who not only lacks the necessary level of commitment to his vocation but also is unwilling to adapt to the specific religious, emotional, and aesthetics needs of his patrons.

The patrons faced an insuperable problem to locate a nearby "insider" to run their temple on a permanent basis. As a result, they decided to look beyond Mātalē District, and, in 2003, formally decided to hand over their temple to Venerable Narada. The decision to hand over their temple to a monk living fifty kilometers away, however, was not completely unanticipated; a number of the residents in Ambana had relatives living nearby Polgoda Vihara.

One such family living nearby Narada's temple with connections to Ambana is the Pereras. The Pereras' proximity to the temple is not just physical; Mr. Perera has, over the years, become quite close to Narada and his students. Indeed, most evenings before setting off to his night job as a sorting officer in the main post office in Kandy, Perera visits the temple. The love that Perera displays toward the temple's residents is reflective, I observed, of his own deep-seated devotion to Buddhism. Besides maintaining a large shrine room in his own house, Perera performs lay protection rituals for others on a somewhat regular basis, including a number of residents from Ambana.

In June 2000, Mrs. Perera's father, who was living in Ambana at the time, died. Mrs. Perera's relatives were unable to procure a sufficient number of monastics for the funeral *(paṅsukula)* and seventh-day alms-giving *(dāna)* rituals. Well aware of Perera's close ties with Narada, Mrs. Perera's relatives asked him to intervene.[12] He accepted. For the *paṅsukula* ritual Perera brought Narada and several other novices to Ambana; for the alms-giving ritual he brought nine monastics.

After bringing another twelve monastics from Polgoda Vihara to Ambana for a second alms-giving ritual, Perera decided to do more for the village than simply act as their booking agent for Buddhist rituals. Refusing to watch the temple wither away, Perera suggested to the members of the village welfare society that they hand over their temple to Venerable Narada. Even though many welfare society members were receptive to the idea, a disagreement broke out between them and other members who had already entered into negotiations with a nearby monk to find someone for their temple. They were embarrassed to retract their offer and the welfare society declined Perera's proposition.

For the next several years nothing became of the Ambana temple. Although the monk repeatedly promised to find someone for the temple, it remained empty. After seeing the temple languish, Perera suggested again in 2003 that he be given the authority to intervene. This time speaking more forcefully to the welfare society members, Perera argued, "Until now, no monk has come. The monks who came here in the past were neither connected to a temple nor to a teacher. They had no connections. When someone among you dies, you have to go by motorcycle to bring someone. You bring anyone for the funeral ritual, even those with hair and beards. Then you bury the body. You don't even know if he *(ū)*[13] [who is brought] is drunk on hooch *(kassipu)*.[14] You are only interested in getting the job done. . . . I will take the responsibility [for bringing a monk]." After negotiating among themselves and with Perera the type of monastic that would be best suited for the temple, the welfare society entrusted Perera with the responsibility of locating a head monk.

Perera took his new duty to heart. On returning home from Ambana, Perera went straight to Polgoda Vihara and spoke to Narada about the possibility of sending a monk from Polgoda Vihara to the Ambana temple. Narada agreed and appointing Suvata, a sixty-year-old novice who had only donned the monastic robes several months earlier, to the post. Perera, however, was caught in a bind. Knowing quite well that Suvata would be ill suited for the task, on the one hand, and wanting to preserve his own social standing in Ambana, on the other, Perera felt obliged to object. He returned home to mull over how he might broach the issue with Venerable Narada. While at home, however, Suvata (who had learned about Narada's choice only minutes before) showed up at his door to express enthusiasm for taking over the temple. Describing Suvata's unbecoming behavior, Perera said,

> This shit [*mē pōra,* literally, "this manure"] started begging me, "Oh sir, I am unable to worship you right now because I am wearing a robe. Please give the temple to me." In fact, there were some problems between him and the other monks at Polgoda Vihara. They didn't like the way that Suvata acted. . . . I felt that I had no choice but to send that one [*ōka*].[15] If not he would have been killed [by the others]. [Suvata said to me] "May you, sir, become a buddha. Give me freedom [away from here]. May you become a buddha. If you send me there I would be free [of the situation here]." I couldn't refuse. He was about to worship me. I spoke to the head monk and we sent him.

Suvata was sent to the temple in Ambana in September 2003. Despite getting off to a good start, Suvata's relationship with the temple's devotees became strained when Suvata, whom I saw to be superciliously set in his own ways, refused to heed to the laity's needs and requests. When the patrons confronted the old novice, Suvata boiled over with rage, unable to accept the fact that a group of laypeople could actually have the audacity to challenge him. Rather than work at establishing a relationship in which the needs and expectations of all parties are considered, and a mutual process of give and take occurs, Suvata reacted in a way that irreparably damaged the mutually sustaining monastic-patron bond that is so essential for the successful running of a temple. Summarizing the conflict, Venerable Ananda explained: "When the people yelled, the old monk yelled. When the people blamed him, the old monk blamed them. That was the conflict. They blamed Suvata by saying: 'We will chase you away because you acted incorrectly. The truth [about how you acted] is known by the Bodhi tree and the temple.' The people said that to Suvata's face. Rather than try to calm the situation, he began arguing back. In an unexpected retort, Suvata said: 'Even though Prabhakaran [the leader of the Liberation Tigers of Tamil Eelam] blasted the Palace of the Tooth [i.e., Daḷada Māligāva], no one could chase Prabhakaran away.'"[16]

It was a good thing for Perera and the Ambana villagers that Suvata was not an "outsider." His connection to a teacher (Narada) and a temple (Polgoda Vihara) through a common link (Perera) provided the patrons of the Ambana temple not simply with a way out, but with a way to make their own needs and desires heard. Tilakaratana explained the situation at the time by noting that "[Suvata] didn't have good qualities [i.e., *gatiguṇa*]. He gets very angry. He is unable to work with the donors. We informed Narada about that. After that, he was brought back to the [Polgoda Vihara] temple. We got another monk to stay here." Indirectly calling into question the belief that for most Sri Lankan lay Buddhists any traditionally ordained monk would suffice, the exchanges between the temple patrons, Suvata, Perera, and Narada point to other concerns and needs. In particular, their interactions illustrate that while ritual needs and a desire to make merit may draw monastics and laypeople together from time to time, social bonds and affective ties are also important for sustaining Buddhist communities.[17]

Empathetic with his donors' concerns, Reverend Narada appointed Venerable Ratnasiri as the temple's new head. As a monk who had been in the *sangha* for six years, Ratnasiri was much more accommodating toward the Ambana patrons. According to Tilakaratana, a problem still remained:

> What happened with Venerable Ratnasiri was that he was not that talkative. He didn't talk to the people. However, he was able to do the religious work [i.e., *āgamika kaṭayutu*] quite well. He recited verses well. . . . He was good. He conducted himself well. Nonetheless, he couldn't speak well.

> He didn't keep contact with the others. He just kept to himself.... When we came [to the temple], the only thing he used to say was "Oh, patron sir has come." Other than that, he didn't speak. He used to sit quietly. We used to stay [at the temple] for a short while and then return home. Generally, it is not good for an administrator to be like that.

Although the patrons of the Ambana temple were interested in locating a monastic who could fulfill their religious needs, they clearly had other concerns and needs, including the desire to find a monk who could lead, develop their temple, and establish close ties with them.

After learning about his donors' feelings, Ratnasiri decided that it would be in everyone's best interest if he relinquished his position as the temple's leader *(vihārādhipati)*. The patrons' dissatisfaction had even further repercussions. Shortly after returning to Polgoda Vihara, Ratnasiri concluded that he was not cut out to be a monk and left the *sangha* altogether. He returned to Kumbukväva, his native village.[18]

Reconsidering the needs of the Ambana patrons, this time more carefully, Narada decided to hand over that temple's administration to his own elder student, Ananda. Although Narada would soon send one of his own students (an eighteen-year-old half-Tamil, half-Sinhala novice) to run the Ambana temple, Narada felt that the temple needed a much more skilled administrator, at least for the first year or so.

Ananda had heard about the problems at Ambana from Suvata and Ratnasiri. Nonetheless, Ananda decided to see for himself what actually went wrong. He traveled to Ambana and called for a meeting with the members of the welfare society. Worrying that the meeting might become a staging ground for the patrons to vent their anger and frustration, Ananda sought to set a more constructive tone. In order to test the level of the patrons' dedication to the temple before making any personal commitments toward the temple himself, Ananda suggested that the welfare society host an auction at the temple, with the proceeds going directly into the temple's coffers.[19]

The auction was a success. The welfare society raised about 10,000 rupees (approximately $100 U.S.), which Ananda believed was reflective of the patrons' commitment and devotion. Elucidating his own views about what went wrong, Ananda said,

> I quickly noticed the people's enthusiasm. The people are more encouraged and dedicated than here [in Kandy]. They kept coming to the temple

> and doing various things. They gave *dāna*. They helped out. Even when they saw me in the bus, they volunteered to buy a ticket for me. I thought [to myself] "These people are good."... The problem was that our people did not understand the villagers. They didn't know how to speak to the people there, how to understand them, and how to help them. I went there, worked, and helped them.... If the monk is good, the people would accept anything he says.... Recently some of our older students said "Having an administrative post is similar to getting married. It is like marrying a woman." That was the simile that the older ones used: "There are a lot of problems, just like marrying a woman." But I decided to prove that their attitude was wrong. I decided to carry out the work in Ambana unceasingly.

Ananda was unable to leave his own temple in Banvelgolla for any length of time; nonetheless, he realized that work at Ambana would only succeed if he became personally involved in the temple's administration. Along with sending one of Narada's students, Sumana, to reside there, as the temple head *(vihārādhipati)* on a permanent basis, Ananda continued to play an active role in developing the temple. Since they took over the temple, the patrons have remained pleased with the manner in which the temple has been running and developing. Their pleasure, I believe, is well illustrated in the fact that the construction that was under way for the two-story *pirivena*-residence hall in December 2005 was completed in 2007.

Although each case of temple building in Sri Lanka involves a particular past and, perhaps, specific needs and concerns, I believe that the Ambana case study points to several larger themes that relate to social relations and the social construction of monastic vocation. According to Ananda's interpretation of the events, the very enterprise of temple building is not solely driven by the desire to locate a properly ordained monastic (Suvata and Ratnasiri) or a monastic proficient in ritual performance (Ratnasiri); it is also based on a need for monastic-lay relationships that are founded on feelings of understanding, empathy, and trust. It is only when such relationships have been established that a temple leader is able to lead. Narada, perhaps, stated this most eloquently when, responding to my question about the successes and failures of temple building at Ambana, he said, "You need to understand the disposition [i.e., *svabhāva*] of the people and when doing activities [for them], not bother them. That is the way we do our work. We do that work in a proper manner. We give something to the people. As a result, the people feel close to us. Those [other] monks there bother the people. That is the problem. You must fulfill their requirements without bothering them."

Implied in my discussions with Tilakaratana and several other patrons, temple building for members of the welfare society is influenced by local social experiences and affective needs which, in turn, shape the selection process. Decisions about the type of monastic they would like to have access to and the type of institution they would like their temple to become is not only circumscribed by inherited understandings of the past and current hopes and interests; it is also something that dynamically evolves based on the bonds the patrons forge with particular monastics. Indeed, learning about what does not work (e.g., monastics who are unbending and those who are too shy) as well as what does (monastics who take the initiative and are more humble and willing to be corrected or even questioned) influences, in turn, both the patrons' and monastics' understanding of who constitutes an ideal member of the *sangha* as well as what is an ideal monastic institution. Explaining the need for close bonds, Tilakaratana noted,

> A connection [between a monk and patron] means this: to get together with the people, one must do religious rituals. There is also the side of the temple's development. There needs to be a monk who has the strength to bring the people together. One must say "Oh donor, sir, please come [*dāyaka mahattayā enḍa*]. Let's do this little work [*api mē ṭika väḍa karamu*]. These are the shortcomings [*mēvā aḍhupāḍu*]." Speaking in this manner, the monk should have the ability to arrange a meeting. After that, the people will help the monk. It is the monk, not the devotees, who should take the leadership. If not, the people will not feel like doing the work. The people must feel that "This temple needs to be built. It is our temple." When a monk comes forward, the people begin to feel it.

Rather than confronting the temple's patrons—as Suvata had done—or shying away from the patrons—as Ratnasiri had done—Sumana struck a more conciliatory tone. It was, in particular, the type of relationship that he and Ananda formed with the patrons—a relationship that continually evolved through a process of negotiation and renegotiation—that not only brought the Buddhist community at Ambana together, but also shaped their understandings of monastic vocation, patronage, and temple building.

Kumbukväva

The second case study focuses on a temple in Anurādhapura District. The temple sits approximately 1.5 kilometers from the village, which is named after a small nearby reservoir, Kumbukväva. Quite smaller than Ambana, the village consists of about a hundred families. Both the temple (which is located in the midst of large tracts of paddy fields) and the village are quite difficult to get to via public transportation.[20] At the time of my visit there in December 2005, the temple complex consisted of a mid-sized residence hall, a small image house *(buduge)*, a large assembly hall *(dharmaśālāva)*, and three reliquary mounds containing the relics of the temple's first three leaders.

The original temple, established around 1915, was located on a fifty-meter-high rock, several hundred meters away from the current temple. In the beginning that temple was the home of a meditating monk—Gunacanda—who, from his single-room hut *(kuṭī)* that more closely resembled a cave dwelling, used to provide the villagers with advice *(avavāda)* and religious instruction *(anusāsanāva)*. Finding life in his *kuṭī* increasingly unbearable during the dry, hot season (which lasts around seven months), Gunacanda asked his patrons to build another residence for him. A small room *(āvāsayak)* was quickly constructed for him where the present temple sits today. Gunacanda's new residence was quite meager: built on small pillars to help with ventilation, the room consisted of four clay walls and a straw roof.

During the time that Gunacanda alternated between the two dwellings—the *kuṭī* on the rock during the rainy season and the small clay hut during the hot season—the residents decided to build yet another residence for him. This new three-roomed building, built around 1925, was large enough to house five monastics. Although it is quite dilapidated today, it functioned as the residence for the temple's monastics until 2007, when a new residence hall, large enough to house ten monastics, was completed.[21]

After Gunacanda died, the temple complex was taken over by one of his students, Piyatissa. At his passing, the temple fell under the administration of another of Gunacanda's students, Amaravamsa. When Amaravamsa, a native of Kumbukväva, died in 1980, so too did the temple's administration; none of Amaravamsa's four students were willing to take over the temple's administration. In fact, prior to his death, all four students had already left the area and moved to Vidyāsāgara Pirivena in Gaṇēgoḍa.[22] Finding no one to reside in the temple on a full-time basis, the Kumbukväva residents handed the temple over to the head monk of Vidyāsāgara Pirivena, who, in turn, successively sent a number of his own students there. Most of them remained at the temple for only short periods of time before returning back to Gaṇēgoḍa.

Even though the head monk of Vidyāsāgara Pirivena helped the Kumbukväva villagers keep their temple running, the arrangement was less than ideal from the donors' perspective. Despite showing their devotion and allegiance to the temple and *sangha* by supporting the various monastics who made their way to the Kumbukväva temple, the patrons felt that the monastics lacked any long-term vision and commitment. With the exception of one Tamil monk who stayed at the temple for a little over a year,[23] the majority of the monastics sent from Gaṇēgoḍa treated their stay there simply as a temporary assignment, hardly ideal for a group of patrons interested in developing the temple and village.

Recognizing the detrimental effects that the temple's provisional administration had on the villagers themselves, the Kumbukväva donors decided to take matters into their own hands. After calling the head monk from Vidyāsāgara Pirivena to the Kumbukväva temple, the patrons requested he either send a permanent monk to reside at the temple or return the temple to the donor association *(dāyaka sabhāva)*. Facing a shortage of students himself, the head monk had no other option than to choose the latter. With the temple back under their control, the donor association began actively looking for other suitable monastics. The monks they found, however, were similar to their Gaṇēgoḍa predecessors: most came and went within a period of several months. Since 2000, the temple has been vacant.

Despite the dearth of Rāmañña temples in the area and fewer number of Rāmañña Nikāya monks in the country,[24] the Kumbukväva residents remained committed to maintaining the temple's original Rāmañña Nikāya affiliation. When I asked the group of patrons why they preferred to have the temple sit vacant than to hand it over to monks living in the nearby Siyam Nikāya temples at Mayilagasväva, Upuldeniya, and Himbutugolväva, one donor within the group openly responded:

> There is a lineage. The person who has tasted being hit by burning wood is said to be afraid even of fireflies [*giṇipellen bäṭa kā minihā, kaṇamädiriyāṭat bayayilu*]. . . . There are fewer monks in Siyam Nikāya temples. They don't ordain many boys. They are only interested in ordaining their own relatives. They only ordain their brothers' and sisters' sons. They only ordain from their own lineage [*paramparāva*].
>
> That is not the situation in the Rāmañña Nikāya. It doesn't matter who they are. They ordain them.[25] By understanding that situation, we felt that it would not be good to hand over this temple to the Siyam Nikāya. If we gave it to the Siyam Nikāya, then that situation would arise. If we hand over our temple to another temple where there are few monks, we would be in the same situation [as we are now].

In justifying the decision to maintain the temple's Rāmañña affiliation, the donor mentioned three specific problems inherent within the Siyam Nikāya: few monks live in each Siyam Nikāya temple, monks from that lineage only ordained their own relatives, and monks from the Siyam lineage restrict ordination to their own caste.[26] Further conversations with the donors in more private settings as well as with those familiar with the area revealed that it was the third issue—caste attitudes within the Siyam Nikāya—that was the burning wood that had permanently scarred the Kumbukväva residents. When I mentioned to Sumedha how interesting I found the patrons' vehement commitment to the Rāmañña Nikāya to be, he responded by briefly outlining the history of the three Sri Lankan Nikāyas. Focusing more specifically on the issue of lineage within the Siyam Nikāya, Sumedha began discussing the negative effects that their caste attitudes had for lower-caste people:[27]

> On the other side of Kumbukväva is Mayilagasväva. That is a Goyigama village. Kumbukväva belongs to another group. As far as I know, they are Batgama. . . . Those people were trampled upon [*pāgeṇavā*] in the past by the Siyam Nikāya. As a result of that and various environmental factors,[28] that place became very troubled [*duṣkara*]. No one came to help them. At that time, a monk called [Udunuvara] Sarananda went to those villages, ordained boys, and built temples. He ordained boys from those villages and taught them. . . . It is said that that monk had visited Kumbukväva during those days.[29] It is true. He is said to have gone to Kumbukväva. He went to the next two villages as well. That monk started temples in those villages. Because of that, the people from those villages liked the Rāmañña Nikāya. The Siyam Nikāya temples didn't help the people at all.
>
> . . . The upcountry rebellion was mostly confined to Kandy. The people living in Kumbukväva were pleased that the country was handed over to the British. . . . The reason for their happiness is because the caste system had crushed them. . . . There is a saying that goes "When the country went to the white people, the status of the low caste people went up."[30]

A slightly different explanation was espoused by a novice from Kumbukväva, Nanodaya, who ordained in Polgoda Vihara in 2000. When I asked him why he thought the Kumbukväva patrons (including his own father) were unwilling to hand the temple over to monks from *another* lineage (I did not mention the Siyam Nikāya by name), he explained,

> There are a number of Siyam Nikāya temples in that area. However, not much good can be said about them. I should tell you the truth. During the reign of Kīrti Śrī Vikrama Rājasiṃha it was said "Do not ordain those of low caste [*adukula*]."[31] That is their custom. They don't like to ordain just anyone. They don't like to accept temples in low-caste areas. The other thing is that they are mostly interested in money. [Those monks from the Siyam Nikāya] treat the others lowly [*pahat vidhihaṭa salakannē*]. . . . Venerable Sarananda . . . dedicated himself more to ordaining boys from low castes. With that in mind, the people would have thought "We wouldn't like to give the temple which belongs to the monk who fought for our caste and our race to outsiders [*apē jatiya venuven kulaya venuven saṭan karapu hāmuduru kenekge pansalak piṭayana vaṭa akamätiya*]."

One issue that Sumedha and Nanodaya raised in their discussions of the patrons' commitment to the Rāmañña Nikāya is the manner in which monks from the Siyam Nikāya interact with low-caste members: not helping them, refusing to reside in their villages, treating them harshly. Regardless of whether or not the residents of Kumbukväva were *directly* affected by monks from the Siyam Nikāya, such stories about how monastics from the Siyam Nikāya disregarded and continue to disregard the concerns and needs of non-Goyigama Buddhists are, from my own experience, quite pervasive in the consciousnesses and experiences of those who belong to Sri Lanka's service castes.[32] Although handing over a temple to one's nephew and restricting ordination to the Goyigama caste may seem ordinary and even acceptable to many people living in Sri Lanka, the very thought of losing control of their village temple to a community of monks who prefer handing their temples down to their own relatives[33] and restricting ordination to their own kind serves as a poignant reminder, to the Kumbukväva residents, of the caste biases that plagued late nineteenth- and twentieth-century Sri Lanka.

In December 2004, the administration of the Kumbukväva temple was transferred to Venerable Narada and his students. One of Narada's students—Anuruddha—has, since that time, been the temple's head monk or *vihārādhipati*. Besides looking after the temple, he also cares for seven other novices, ranging from ten to fifteen years of age. To understand how and why a temple in a remote village in Anurādhapura district came to be associated with Polgoda Vihara in Kandy (approximately 150 kilometers away), it is necessary to return to the late 1980s, when Sumedha was the head monk of the Madavala temple.

Shortly after his ordination at Polgoda Vihara, Sumedha left his teachers (Narada and Devamitta) for Anurādhapura. Prior to taking over the temple in Madavala, Sumedha spent a short time at Nikkaväva Pirivena in Anurādhapura. During that time, Sumedha would often accompany the *pirivena*'s head monk to the area's numerous villages. Kumbukväva was one of those villages. After that initial visit, Sumedha returned to Kumbukväva several times to perform religious rituals there for many of the village's residents.

Sumedha eventually returned to Kandy to administer his temple in Uduvela. While living in Kandy he continued maintaining ties with Kumbukväva. Such ties grew even stronger after Ajit, a teenage lay boy from the village, began living at Sumedha's temple while studying at a private school outside of Kandy. During one of Ajit's father's many visits to see his son, Sumedha requested that Ajit's father find a boy to ordain from Kumbukväva. Sumedha was soon informed about a twenty-four-year-old man who was interested in becoming a monastic. Sumedha went to Kumbukväva, returned with the man, and ordained him at his Uduvela temple in 1998. He was given the name Ratnasiri and would, within five years, return back home after trying his hand, somewhat unsuccessfully, at running the Ambana temple.

With Ratnasiri's ordination and several more children from Kumbukväva following suit, ties between the village, Sumedha, and Narada quickly burgeoned; Sumedha and Narada began making visits to Kumbukväva on occasion in order to perform religious rituals for the villagers. It was during one of those rituals there in 2004 that Narada began expressing an interest in the Kumbukväva temple. Discussing with me the course of events that led the donor association to transfer the Kumbukväva temple to Narada, Jayasekara, the association's chair, explained: "When the head monk had come for a celebration recently we came to know that he had expressed an interest in the temple saying 'I feel that if I had a temple like this, I would develop it.' Hearing that, we felt a sense of hope and handed the temple over to him. . . . The monk accepted it at once. We then wrote a letter [of agreement] and handed over the temple."

At one point in a group interview I conducted at the Kumbukväva temple, I inquired further into the factors that led the association to hand over its temple to Narada; several people began discussing Narada's qualities *(gatiguṇa)*,[34] particularly his humility. One donor explained: "The head monk, [Venerable Narada], is humble. . . . We saw that. We felt that the head monk is the only one suitable enough for this temple." When I asked him what he meant by humility, several others who were present began recounting to me their own experiences of visiting Polgoda Vihara. For instance, Jayasekara explained,

> We saw that our head monk is very humble. He is not harsh toward the young monastics. He takes good care of them. We saw that when the head monk goes to bed, he checks on all the young monastics: Have they been bitten by mosquitoes? Are their robes all right? He checks everything. That means that he looks after them better than a parent. That is what we saw when we went to [Polgoda Vihara]. . . . He does the same thing here.
>
> Anyone can easily see that this monk is good. If we are interested in ordaining a boy, we feel that we should bring them to that temple. Why? Because the children are loved. He doesn't hit the children. They can learn [secular subjects]. They can study *dharma*. They do both. That is our experience. We clearly know that the students of the head monk are more knowledgeable in terms of the *dharma* than the other monks in other temples. Recently there was a funeral. For that, a monastic who had only been in the *sangha* for four or five years participated. He preached better than a scholar monk. . . . I felt a sense of longing toward the sermon.

It was clear from my interview that in terms of a monastic leader, the patrons were not simply looking for any properly ordained monastic. They were interested in finding someone who embodies the qualities of love and affection that more closely resemble how a parent might feel toward his or her own child.

Perhaps the quality that impressed the patrons most about Narada is his own sense of commitment both to his students and to the *sangha*. During a more casual conversation with Jayasekara, he mentioned how Narada has devoted his life to the *sangha*, a fact that could be seen, he noted, not only in the development that is currently going on at Polgoda Vihara but also in the number of students that Narada ordained over the years. Drawing a comparison between Narada and many of the previous residents of the village temple, one donor explained,

> After [Gunacanda's] original disciples [i.e., *mul gōlayo*] died, there was no one else. . . . After that, many of the monks who came here were strangers [*piṭin apu*],[35] coming from the outside [*agantuka*]. They stayed for a month or two and left without even telling the mat on the floor. No one knew. The patrons treated them with food and such. [They] didn't say anything. [They] just left. That was the situation. This temple was devastated [*naṭabun*].
>
> Now that Narada has taken over the temple, other monks will not come and stay here. Most monks do not want to look after a temple for someone else. . . . If they think that the [temple's] ownership is for them,

only then will they look after the temple. That is what happened in Mayilagasväva. Mayilagasväva temple was handed over to a monk in Colombo. That monk sent several outside monks to look after the temple. Those ones had no interest whatsoever in staying there.

BEYOND KUMBUKVÄVA: SOCIAL CAPITAL AND THE BUILDING OF NEW NETWORKS

Since Venerable Narada took over the temple in December 2004, a new residence hall large enough to house ten monastics was completed. Such developments are not only reflective of close ties between the temple's residents and patrons, but also the means through which new interpersonal bonds between the temple's patrons and other villages are established. Within Kumbukväva itself, the temple has now become a vibrant gathering point for its villagers (despite being 1.5 kilometers from the actual village), as well as an avenue by which the villagers could receive respect and longing *(āsāva)* from outsiders. Speaking to me almost one year after Narada took over the temple's administration, several donors explained:

Donor 2: Laypeople from the surrounding villages are now connected to this temple

Donor 1: There are groups in several villages that bring alms to this temple.

Donor 2: We have a lot of monks.

Donor 3: Patrons from the surrounding villages have no chance of giving alms. There is a shortage of monks. When there is an alms-giving or a funeral, there is no place from where to bring monks. There are some temples. There is usually, however, only one monk living there.

Donor 1: Now from here eight monks can be brought [to a religious function]. If there is a protection ritual or an alms-giving, monks can be brought. Because there are many monks staying here, other villagers have begun to feel a sense of longing toward this temple. There are a lot of monks staying here. With them living here, [the residents of the surrounding villages] can fulfill all their [religious] needs—merit work [*piṅ väḍa*] and alms-giving [*dāna väḍa*]. They can do that. Many people from the surrounding villages bring alms here.

In the first six months after Narada took over the temple, alms food was largely provided by the Kumbukväva residents themselves. As the number of novices there began to increase and as work on the new living quarters got under way, new social connections began to be forged not only between the temple and new groups of patrons, but also between those new groups and the residents of Kumbukväva. While a close look at the temple's alms register reveals that the Kumbukväva patrons do not regularly cross paths with patrons from other villages,[36] recent temple activities have brought the different groups of patrons together. Much like the community gatherings that Hanifan (1916) referred to in his discussion of social capital,[37] these groups have recently joined hands during several temple-based fund-raising activities; the Kumbukväva patrons have also begun tapping into the temple's larger patron base to collect money for the temple. Although it is too soon to see whether or not the Kumbukväva temple will truly become a catalyst for building larger social networks and personal bonds, recent activities indicate that such a potential is there and with proper leadership, the temple may make cooperative action between the patrons and other Buddhists possible.

Along with facilitating ties between the Kumbukväva residents and other groups of Buddhists, the recent work under way at the temple has helped Narada forge new connections with other, more outlying villages. In one conversation I had with him in December 2005, he mentioned that he is currently in the process of establishing two new temples, one in Maradan Maḍuva and the other in Vāhalkaḍa.[38] When I asked Narada how that came to be, he echoed some of the discussions I had with the Kumbukväva patrons—particularly how the Kumbukväva temple has become a source of envy or longing *(āsāva)* for the people living around the area—by saying,

> The people [from Maradan Maḍuva and Vāhalkaḍa] came and recently asked me for monks [to start a temple]. Why is that? Because of the news that spread there [in Maradan Maḍuva and Vāhalkaḍa] via the relatives living in Kumbukväva. The Kumbukväva people would have gone there and said "Our temple is now like this. Now there are several monks living there. The work is going well." When they say that, the other people feel longing/desire. Why is that? Because those temples [in Maradan Maḍuva and Vāhalkaḍa] are abandoned. Those are poor areas. We could do a lot in terms of religious work. . . . I told them that I will come to see the temples. We are now thinking about going to those temples in the near future.

When I asked the residents from Kumbukväva to comment on Narada's plan of starting temples in Maradan Maḍuva and Vāhalkaḍa, two donors explained the role that the ground-breaking ceremony held at Kumbukväva played in the process:[39]

Donor 1: That happened because there are relatives [there] who have connections with this village. Those people come here from time to time. They were here when Venerable Narada preached a sermon [during the ground-breaking ceremony].

Donor 5: Several boys who ordained from this village have relatives in Vāhalkaḍa. When the ground-breaking ceremony took place, the people from Vāhalkaḍa came.

Just as ordaining children from certain villages enabled Narada and his students to build close bonds with groups of parents living far away from Polgoda Vihara, so too has the whole enterprise of temple building become a means by which Narada can establish new networks with people living even farther away. Moreover, just as the ties developed between Narada and a growing number of parents and families resulted in a continued flow of new recruits to Polgoda Vihara, so too has temple building resulted in not only a continuous flow of new recruits to Polgoda Vihara,[40] but also continued expansion of Polgoda Vihara's reaches to a number of regions in Sri Lanka.

CONCLUSION

As one looks more closely at the events leading up to the reestablishment of the Ambana temple, one finds that despite the willingness of several monastics living outside of the village to fulfill the laity's religious needs, the donors wanted more: they yearned for a monk who would not only take a more active role in the patrons' lives but also understand the patrons' past, their needs, the challenges they faced, and their hopes. Although Ratnasiri was able to fulfill the laity's religious needs and expectations, Sumana was a better fit. As a monastic who was considered humble, more willing to learn and grow, and sensitive to his patrons' needs and wishes, Sumana was better able to attract the hearts of his patrons than his previous two predecessors. Indeed, it is partially Sumana's willingness to help and serve the people combined with his ability to connect to the temple's patrons that has led to the temple's current development. In the words of Tilakaratana, "Now he has gone to everyone's house. Everyone knows him. In that way, people feel like helping out."

Suvata and Ratnasiri, on the other hand, lacked the ability—perhaps "facility" is a better term—to establish close ties with their patrons. The first monk,

Suvata, was not only combative but, similar to perceived qualities of monks who ordain late in life, was also too set in his own ways.[41] His successor, Ratnasiri, was much less antagonistic. Nonetheless, his inability to face the crowd quickly led to tensions which resulted in Ratnasiri feeling quite incapable and the donors feeling that they still needed a head monk.

Along with lacking traits that would help them deal well with others—empathy, trust, and respect—both Suvata and Ratnasiri were, in a very different sense, outsiders. Despite being part of a lineage to which the laity could turn when problems arose, both monastics lacked a sense of commitment and the desire to adjust their appearance and behavior in accordance with people's needs or expectations. Moreover, unlike the sense of obligation and the feelings of respect and gratitude that Kassapa felt and exhibited toward Narada (see chapter 4), Suvata and Ratnasiri were, according to their teachers, much more independent minded.[42] While such a quality is not bad in itself (as it would enable a monastic "to take the leadership"), it becomes a problem, from the patrons' perspective, when it is not tempered with an attitude of humility.

Just like the Ambana residents, the patrons of the Kumbukväva temple had very poor assessments of monks coming from the "outside." Whereas the Ambana residents used the term "outsider" to describe monastics who lack the necessary connections with teachers or temples (and thus, the means by which donors could reign in wanton monastics), the Kumbukväva patrons used the term somewhat differently: to refer to those monastics who lack a sense of ownership and pride toward the temple. Even though the phenomenon of monastics owning temples—which is commonly referred to as monastic landlordism (see Evers 1972:16; see also Bechert 1970; Gunawardana 1979; and Rahula 1993)—is sometimes regarded with disdain, for this donor (and a number of patrons who echoed a similar perspective during the interview) ownership is beneficial. Rather than rupturing the monk-patron relationship (as monastic landlordism sometimes does),[43] ownership came to be associated with a sense of commitment toward the temple and the temple's patrons. Indeed, for several of the Kumbukväva donors, locating a group of monastics personally devoted and committed to the temple and its donors is essential. As one lay patron rhetorically asked me, "Would I really want to go and look after *your* home?"

What strikes me most, perhaps, about the two case studies of temple building is the relationship between history, aesthetics, emotion, and cognition. As I have suggested above and in earlier chapters, ideas about acceptable monastic deportment and appearance are partially shaped by the past. Further influenced by local social experiences, the aesthetic standard produces certain affective responses (e.g., anger or displeasure toward monks from the Siyam Nikāya and pleasure toward monks from the Rāmañña Nikāya). The emotional reactions, in turn, make particular relationships and bonds possible (such as bonds with Rāmañña Nikāya monks) while the bonds themselves, as they deepen and develop over time, further shape and determine one's aesthetic sensibilities (e.g., a loving monk is pleasing). It is to such an interconnectedness, I believe, that Martha Nussbaum is concerned about when she contends that as emotions are concerned with the person's flourishing (2001:31), they cannot possibly be "simply blind surges of affect, stirrings or sensations that arise from our animal nature and are identified (and distinguished from one another) by their felt quality alone. Instead, they themselves have a cognitive content; they are intimately related to beliefs or judgments about the world in such a way that the removal of the relevant belief will remove not only the reason for the emotion, but also the emotion itself" (1990:291). Although some scholars (e.g., Gombrich 1998 and Spiro 1982) have sought to separate affect and cognition when studying the relationship and tensions between religious belief and practice, such a division seems somewhat untenable; the many emotions that underlie the patrons' experiences—anger and distrust vis-à-vis the monks from the Siyam Nikāya, disappointment and disillusionment with regard to the "outside" monks, and love, attachment, and compassion in relation to Narada and Ananda—play a constitutive role in religious praxis and in social life by shaping people's vision of who is a model Buddhist monastic, what is an appropriate monastic vocation, what is appropriate practice, and what is an ideal Buddhist institution.

Conclusion

Social Relations and the Aesthetics of Emotion

In the preceding chapters I have discussed Buddhism as a human activity by attending to the range of emotions, social bonds, and shared aesthetic sensibilities that draw and hold together communities of Buddhists. Although such an examination does not necessarily preclude the importance of Buddhist texts, I have focused largely on the emotional textures and multi-moment histories of groups of laypeople and monastics with the goal of recovering and highlighting specific conjunctures in which ideas about vocation, patronage, recruitment, and institution building are dynamically negotiated and further refined. I maintained that overlooking emotion and its place in Buddhist practice and social relations may increase the tendency to reduce ideas about recruitment, socialization, lay-patron relations, and institution building to economic needs, the memorization of Buddhist texts and the enactment of the monastic disciplinary rules *(Vinaya)*, economic exchange, and ritual needs, respectively.

Turning to specific moments in which ideas of aesthetics and vocation are constructed and subsequently defined, I have posited that local social experiences, as well as the affective needs of individuals and communities, sometimes shape the interpretive and selection process through which Buddhists develop an understanding of what kind of institution to support or what type of monastic to become. Understandings of vocation and monastic behavior are certainly influenced by the manner in which monks are ideally portrayed in texts and art; nonetheless, I contended that affective states and social bonds function to curb the extremes of an overly rigid orthopraxy.

In examining what is accomplished in the field of affect and aesthetics, I have highlighted the relationship that sometimes exists between emotion and action. Using several case studies, I explored how emotion functions expressively and strategically in determining and influencing the bonds and commitments that laypeople make to specific monastics, to particular monastic institutions, and to the Buddhist religion. Turning first to the Buddhist community that surrounded Venerable Narada, I illustrated how ties that formed between Narada and his immediate group of supporters inspired further commitment to Narada as a Buddhist monastic, to his vision of the role that the *sangha* should play in contemporary society, and to Polgoda Vihara as it grew from housing a single monk in 1978 to more than seventy-five monastics thirty years later. Concentrating on one of Reverend Narada's senior students, Venerable Sumedha, I illustrated how bonds forged between him and the patrons and children living in two different villages led to a specific form of commitment: giving a son to the *sangha*. Finally, I showed how affective states instilled though sermons may influence people's thoughts about Buddhism and their devotion toward the religion with respect to safeguarding it in the face of perceived periods of decline.

In a similar vein, I investigated the role that affective ties play in the social construction of monastic vocation. Turning to the language of emotion that relates to and is articulated in the context of institution building, I contended that bonds between monastics and lay patrons as well as between students and teachers are important to the process of socialization, especially in regard to ideas about vocation and practice. Considering the social relations that existed at Polgoda Vihara, I illustrated how Narada's decision to remain in the *sangha* as well as his decision to adopt a social service monastic vocation were largely the outcome of the relationships he forged with his patrons and teachers. Turning to one of his students, Venerable Kassapa, I maintained that the bonds that existed between him and his teacher, as well as between him and the patrons of Ganegoda Vihara, were important components to his decision to remain at the temple and to serve his donors' needs.

In several places in the preceding chapters, I have made reference to the nexus of affect and aesthetics. Conversations I had with monastics and laypeople suggest that pleasing the heart by embodying locally influenced aesthetic standards—whether in dress, in bodily movements, or in physical appearance—helps generate feelings of confidence among the laity. Without generating such feelings as trust, authority, affection, and hope, Sumedha would not have succeeded in drawing so many new recruits to his and his teacher's temples.

The term "aesthetics of emotion," however, implies not only that aesthetic responses trigger certain emotions, but also that personal and shared emotions, at the local level, may shape notions of beauty. Indeed, the feelings of humiliation that led the patrons of Sri Kirti Vihara to build Polgoda Vihara, the feelings of anger that led the donors of Ambana to seek different head monks, and the feelings of shame that led the residents of Kumbukväva to maintain the temple's Rāmañña Nikāya affiliation all functioned, in different ways, to mold their own conceptions of what type of temple and monk attracts the heart. The affective bonds that then develop between a monastic and his patrons play yet a further role in refining the contours of what constitutes acceptable or pleasing behavior.

If we are to take seriously the connection that exists between emotion, volition, cognition, and aesthetics—as we should—examining emotion and its place in religion becomes central to making the behavior of religious practitioners, whether monastic or lay, intelligible by relating what people do to their shared histories, personal experiences, and future aspirations. As ideas about beauty, monastic vocation, patronage, and institution building are shaped and determined by the very relationships and affective bonds that exist among the laity and *sangha* as well as between monastics and their lay supporters, examining emotions and the constitutive roles they play in social life and religious praxis becomes paramount.

Notes

Introduction

1. The term *vihara* (*vihāra* in Pali and *vihāraya* in Sinhala) means "residence," specifically the residence in a Buddhist temple. More generally, the term, like the Sinhala word *pansala*, means "temple"; I have adopted that usage throughout the book. Thus, Polgoda Vihara is the same as Polgoda temple.

2. Such an interpretation—which is often advocated by certain monastics who have broken away from the established monkhood (Carrithers 1979; Gombrich and Obeyesekere 1988:325–352), laypeople who have instituted various types of reform movements (Kemper 1978), and those sponsoring government legislation to curb monastic excesses (Samuels 2002)—is advocated in Kitsiri Malalgoda's (1976) history of Sri Lankan Buddhism as well as more recently in H. L. Seneviratne's (1999) *The Work of Kings*. For a critique of this particular understanding of decline and revival, see Steven Kemper (1980) and Anne Blackburn (2001).

3. In his work on the forest monks of Sri Lanka, Michael Carrithers, for instance, makes such a correlation when he writes (1979:297), "A simplified picture of the history of the Theravāda Sangha is as follows. The order of ascetics, separated from the world, gradually evolves towards the equilibrium state, the domesticated Sangha. Once this is reached, reformers may then arise from within the ranks, and though the majority of the Sangha remain domesticated, there appear groups, necessarily small because necessarily self-referring, of reform monks. As these settle and grow, they evolve towards domestication, and though associated in name with reform, come to entertain in fact the opinions of village literary specialists. Within this overgrown domesticated erstwhile reform groups there appear further reformers . . . and the process continues."

4. Steven Collins discusses this notion of "strategies of legitimation" in his work on the Pali canon where he argues that the *Pali canon = Early Buddhism* equation should be rejected in favor of seeing the canon "as part of a strategy of legitimation by the monks of the Mahāvihāra lineage in Ceylon in the early centuries of the first millennium A.D." (1990:89).

5. This notion of generalized exchange is discussed in Ivan Strenski's (1983) article "On Generalized Exchange and the Domestication of the Sangha."

6. These rules are clearly outlined in Rupert Gethin's *The Foundations of Buddhism* (1998), as well as in Mohan Wijayaratna's *Buddhist Monastic Life* (1990).

7. The episodes of his life in which he is seated under the Bodhi tree unmoved by lust or fear, or depicted as being emotionally detached as he abandons his wife and newborn

son in the name of enlightenment, come vividly to mind. It is no wonder, as the Buddhist studies scholar Kevin Trainor suggests, that "many undergraduates come away from their first introduction to Buddhism thinking that emotion itself is fundamentally problematic according to basic Buddhist teachings" (2003:524). This particular view of Buddhism's flight from the emotions or the exaltation of emotional detachment is sometimes also extended to include Hinduism and Jainism (see Masson 1981). Although there are passages in popular Buddhist texts such as the *Dhammapada* and *Sutta-Nipāta*, as well as early Indian traditions, that suggest that Masson is correct, it is important—as Maria Heim (2008), June McDaniel (1995; 2008), and others point out—to consider aspects of the Buddhist and Hindu traditions that see the emotions as valuable and playing a soteriological role.

8. One reason why there has been a tendency to overlook the emotions in Buddhism is because scholars and students have the propensity, in the words of Kevin Trainor (2003:524f.), to "associate religious emotion with feelings of devotion and to regard such devotional attitudes as inconsistent with early Buddhism." A key example of this is Walpola Rahula's *What the Buddha Taught*, where he notes that "in Buddhist countries there are simple and beautiful customs and ceremonies on religious occasions. They have little to do with the real Path. But they have their value in satisfying certain religious emotions and the needs of those who are less advanced, and helping them gradually along the Path." Inherent in Rahula's statement is the belief that Buddhism is a rational belief system. Such a depiction of Buddhism traces it roots back to the late nineteenth and early twentieth centuries and to such figures as T. W. Rhys Davids, whose interpretation of Pali Buddhism, argues Judith Snodgrass, "remains the basis not only of Western understanding of Buddhism but of many modern Buddhist movements in Asia" (2007:186; see also Hallisey 1995 and Obeyesekere 1991).

9. See Clough (1892) and Carter (1996). In Venerable Sorata's Sinhala-Sinhala Dictionary (*Śrī Sumaṅgala Śabdakoṣaya* 1998: vol. 1, p. 137), the term *äda* is glossed as *ākarṣaṇaya kara*, which means "attraction, dragging, gravitation."

10. Discussing its emotional, volitional, and cognitive dimensions T. W. Rhys Davids and William Stede (1972:266; see also Karunaratna 1979:172 and Sorata 1998:1044) define the term *citta* as "the heart (psychologically), i.e., the centre & focus of man's emotional nature as well as that intellectual element which inheres in & accompanies its manifestations; i.e., thought.... The meaning of citta is best understood when explaining it by expressions familiar to us, as: with all my heart; heart and soul; I have no heart to do it; blessed are the pure in heart; singleness of heart (cp. ekagga); all of which emphasize the emotional & conative side or 'thought' more than its mental & rational side (for which see manas & viññāṇa)." For a comparative discussion of the interrelatedness of one's affective and cognitive faculties in Buddhism and its separation in Western philosophical discourse, see Solomon (1995; 2003), Heim (2008), and Corrigan (2008).

11. I have used "heart-mind" in other publications (see, for example, Samuels 2007a and 2008). Other scholars using the term "heart-mind" to refer to this center of feeling and thinking are Jonathan Spencer (1990b:613) and Sid Brown (2001:9).

12. I thank Patrick Olivelle for bringing this particular point to my attention.

13. The phrase can also mean "to flatter" and, thus, may be used more manipulatively. I thank Stephen Berkwitz for noting this more calculating use of the phrase.

14. I am particularly indebted to the works of Arjun Appadurai (1990), Stephen Berkwitz (2001; 2003), Maria Heim (2003), Abu-Lughod and Catherine Lutz (1990), Catherine Lutz (1988), Owen Lynch (1990a; 1990b), Steven Parish (2004), Michelle Rosaldo (1984), Andy Rotman (2003), Margaret Trawick (1990a; 1990b), and Kevin Trainor (2003). For a critique of what he believes is extreme constructionism in the writings of Rosaldo, Lutz, and Abu-Lughod, see Reddy (1997).

15. For a discussion of regarding universalism and particularlism, see Corrigan (2008; 2004) as well as Lutz and White (1986).

16. The notion of the emotions as sites of reason and judgment, "as intelligent responses to the perception of value," has been explored at great length in Martha Nussbaum's *Upheavals of Thought: The Intelligence of Emotions* (2001).

17. This relates to J. L. Austin's work *How to Do Things with Words* (1975; see also Tambiah 1968), where he notes that saying "I do" at a wedding performs a function in that it weds one to another.

18. As I noted in an earlier publication (Samuels 2004b:957ff.; see also Hansen 2007:8ff.), scholars such as Charles Keyes (1983), Steven Collins (1990), and, more recently, Anne Blackburn (1999b) have begun to challenge the very notion of a Buddhist Pali canon by pointing to other local texts—for example, ritual manuals, vernacular texts, popular commentaries, and Buddhist narratives (e.g., pseudo *Jātaka* stories)—that play a role in constituting the Theravāda teachings, or *dhamma*.

Not all scholars, however, are willing to endorse such a trend. In an article in the *Journal of the International Association of Buddhist Studies*, Oliver Freiberger points out the risks involved in such a movement. For instance, he argues that "canonical texts are, in contrast to the common view, a rich source for current scholarly interests (such as the issues of religious practice and diversity) [and] that by excluding the canon, Buddhist Studies runs the risk of canonizing other sources for research and, at the same time, enhances particularism in teaching" (2004:262; see also Cabezón, 1995).

19. This reorientation has also had an effect on teaching Buddhism in an academic setting. The essays in *Teaching Buddhism in the West* (2002; Victor Hori et al., eds.) are certainly reflective of this trend, particularly those written by Frank Reynolds (2000) and O'Hyun Park (2002). See also Frank Reynolds's article "Buddhist Studies in the United States" (2000:134).

20. Abeysekara (2002:3) writes, "I want to demonstrate modestly some of the ways in which the relations between what can and cannot count as Buddhism, culture, and difference, alter within specific 'native' debates. That is, to demonstrate the ways in which what I call 'minute contingent conjunctures' make possible and *centrally* visible the emergence and submergence, the centering and marginalizing, the privileging and subordinating of what and who can and cannot constitute 'Buddhism' and 'difference.'"

Yukio Hayashi (2003:3) expresses a similar idea, though with a greater concern about the *longue durée*, in his recent publication *Practical Buddhism among the Thai-Lao*, where he explains that "concepts such as 'religion,' 'magic,' or even 'Buddhist temple' are actually born within the multi-faceted statements of people who live in a particular culture or locality.... [I]t is therefore essential to look at the context within which indigenous criteria are articulated."

21. For a history of the Rāmañña Nikāya, which was established in Sri Lanka in 1864, see Medhālaṅkārā (2003), *Buddha Śāsana Komiṣan Vārtāva* (1959:46ff.), and Vākaḍa Hadrā Bhikṣhuṇi's *Bāratiya Saha Laṅkā Sāsana Itihāsaya* [*The history of the sangha in India and Sri Lanka*].

22. Photo elicitation is a field method that involves inserting photographs into the interview process to elicit information from the interviewee. The majority of studies using photo elicitation insert photographs taken by people other than the interviewee. My decision to insert photographs taken by the subjects themselves—autodriven photo elicitation, as it is known in the field—is based on the belief that photographs taken by the research subjects themselves are more likely to represent their world in a more meaningful manner and, thus, better suited to bridging the culturally distinct worlds of the researcher and the researched. Cindy Clark (1999:40) discusses this same sentiment concerning autodriven photo elicitation in regard to children when she writes that "the autodrive technique—because of its ability to portray behaviors in context, as well as to explore the meaning of those behaviors to the actors—allowed children to visually show and tell aspects of their lives that were important to them."

1 Narada Thero

1. "Bodhi tree" (or tree of enlightenment) is the more common term to denote the *aśvattha* tree *(Ficus Religiosa)* under which the Buddha had meditated and became enlightened. The Buddhist nun Sanghamitta (daughter of King Asoka) is said to have brought a cutting of the actual tree under which the Buddha attained enlightenment to Sri Lanka at the invitation of the Sri Lankan king, Devānampiyatissa.

2. The *Jātaka* collection contains 547 stories of the Buddha's past lives (see Cowell 1990).

3. Although Gotama Buddha is sometimes referred to as the founder of Buddhism, the tradition recognizes him as one in a long lineage of fully enlightened buddhas *(sammāsambuddhā)*. This idea of previous buddhas—its significance and development—has been discussed in and Malalasekera (1971), Gombrich (1980), Reynolds and Hallisey (1987), Samuels (1997), and Nattier (2004).

4. In another temple outside of Kandy where I briefly conducted research, a university education was treated much more apprehensively, as the head monk viewed secular education as a corrupting force to traditional Buddhist monasticism. After asking many of the temple's residents whether they were interested in studying at a university, an option that became available to monastics in the mid-1900s, I no longer felt welcome there.

5. Uncovering the tension between cognition and religious action—what one says one believes and does and what one really believes and does—or between the affective and cognitive is the primary concern of Richard Gombrich's *Precept and Practice* (1998:5ff.).

6. At ordination, boys are given a new monastic name. Although Venerable Narada was known by another name before he became a novice, for simplicity's sake I will refer to him only by his monastic name. I will follow this convention for other monastics as well.

7. Although monastics perform the majority of protection rituals, those performed by laypeople have grown in popularity in more recent times. Overnight lay protection rituals cost much less and are easier to arrange, particularly for those living in more remote areas where locating a sufficient number of monks and providing them with transport and lodging is difficult.

8. This rule was put in place after the Buddha ordained his own son, Rahula, and the Buddha's father, King Suddhodana, protested the boy's ordination (see Vin I.83).

9. The term "brother-monk" denotes someone who shares the same ordination lineage and who is ordained under the same preceptor *(upajjhāya)*. Both Devamitta and Sudhammananda became novices and later received higher ordination *(upasampadā)* under Sri Udunuvara Sarananda, a very charismatic monastic from the Rāmañña Nikāya. I will discuss Sarananda and the effects that his own life had on Narada's notion of social service below. As Devamitta was Sudhammananda's senior, the latter may be referred to as Devamitta's younger brother-monk.

10. Personal communication, May 2003. The importance of finding a Buddhist institution where one's son will be loved and treated well is not uncommon and will be discussed further in chapters 3 and 5.

11. Sometimes the term *dhammadūta/dharmadūta* is translated as Buddhist missionary. As the term missionary is often associated with a more active form of religious conversion, I have decided to use the more literal translation "messenger of the teachings" or "messenger of the *dhamma*." The concept of missionizing in Buddhism, including possible meanings of the term *dhammadūta* or *dharmadūta*, is discussed in Lothe (1986), Walters (1992), and, most recently, in Linda Learman's (2004) edited volume *Buddhist Missionaries in the Era of Globalization* (see especially Steven Kemper's contribution in that volume).

12. The German Dharmaduta Society was founded in 1957 by Asoka Weeraratna, a lay Buddhist who had a penchant for spreading Buddhism to Western Europe. The society, which was originally called the Lanka Dhammaduta Society (established 1952), went hand in hand with another of Weeraratna's achievements: the founding of the Berlin Buddhist Vihara in Germany. Rather than merely being content with training German monks in Sri Lanka, Weeraratna believed that it would be ideal to establish a Buddhist center in the heart of Germany and to house that center with Sri Lankan–trained monks. In 1957, Weeraratna organized the first Sri Lankan Buddhist mission to Berlin. For a full discussion of that missionary society, see Bhikkhu Bodhi (2000) as well as Agganyani (2002).

13. These very problems are believed to have sparked the 1971 insurgency that was instigated by the Marxist-oriented People's Liberation Front (Janata Vimukti Peramuna).

Although the insurgency was short lived, the problems that gave rise to the insurgency were not. Examples of some of the problems that continued in the years following the insurgency were "a fourfold rise in the price of crude oil... accompanied by a spectacular upward movement in the prices of wheat, rice and sugar in the international market" in 1973 and 1974 (C. R. de Silva, 1999:290). The further overall drop in food production due to unfavorable climatic conditions led to the rationing of some staples in Sri Lanka during the same period, such as a one-pound weekly ration of rice and a three-quarter-pound monthly ration of sugar (ibid., 292). This is also detailed in Kearney and Jiggins (1975). For more detail on the 1971 insurrection, see also Politicus (1972), Arasaratnam (1972), Obeyesekere (1974), Kearney (1975; 1977), Jiggins (1979), Seneratne (1997), and Wickramasinghe (2006:234ff.).

14. This handbook, which is reprinted in a number of editions (e.g., Dhammatilaka 1997 and Vanaratna 1990), is commonly used for the training of Buddhist novices. Included in the handbook are sections on the *sangha*'s history, ordination procedures, rules of etiquette *(sekhiya)*, subjects commonly used for meditation, a selection of discourses recited during protection rituals, a selection of verses recited during worship *(pūjā)* rituals, and so on. The other training handbook found in Buddhist temples is the *Śāsanāvataraṇaya* (Candavimala 1998). As this handbook contains information about Theravāda monasticism that goes beyond the novice stage and is written in a language that is mostly inaccessible to the young novices, it is not as commonly used as the *Sāmaṇera Baṇadaham Pota*.

15. There are two categories of teachers in charge of the training and education of Buddhist novices: *upajjhāya* and *ācariya*. The former is the one who leads the ordination *(pabbajjā)* ritual and who provides novices with their formal and informal monastic training, both disciplinary and educational. The latter generally functions as a substitute or deputy to the *upajjhāya* and may be a *piriveṇa* teacher or another older monk living in a temple.

16. Narada has pointed out that it was after Sudhammananda's return from Germany that he began to show interest in meditation and living in forest temples and meditation retreat centers.

17. Sarananda Pirivena was founded in 1952 by one of Sudhammananda's and Devamitta's brother-monks, Venerable Kumbukgamuvē Śrī Guṇaratana Thero, and is affiliated with the Rāmañña Nikāya (although qualified students from any monastic fraternity are able to attend). Venerable Gunaratana's life and the types of caste biases he faced is described in Ñaṇānanda and Kīrtiratna.

18. The passing of Pirivena Act 11828 in 1959 is largely accredited for the secularization of the *pirivena* curriculum (Adikari 1991:301f.). The two educational paths are outlined on the final page in Adikari (1991).

19. Narada's views about monastic education will be examined more fully in chapter 4.

20. See, for instance, Rahula (1974:91).

21. Gunasekera (1994:112) mentions a similar impetus behind the establishment of new temples in the village of Rangama: "During the baseline period all castes in the community worshipped at the Rangama Vihāraya. In the 1940s, however, two new *vihāra* were built

in the area—one in Devideniya and one in West Galewala. Both *vihāra* were financed by the people of these villages and significantly neither belongs to the Siyam Nikāya, which restricts ordination to the Goigama. The establishment of these *vihāra* has enabled the majority of Batgama and Vahumpura of this community to maintain a high degree of caste segregation." Both Batgama (palanquin bearers) and Vahumpura (jaggory makers) are considered, like the *beravā*, to be service castes.

22. Further discussions with the lay devotees suggests that "our group" refers to patrons from the *beravā* caste. The neighboring villages of Palledanda and Godavela are mostly inhabited by the high-caste Goyigama.

23. Conch blowers, like drummers, belong to the service castes.

24. Traditionally, *rājakāriya* (literally, "service to the king") was a compulsory labor/land tax system administered through an official called the *disāva* or *disāpati*. In addition to the burden of compulsory service (military or otherwise) owed to the king or *disāvas* (Dewaraja 1988:226), all landowners and cultivators in the kingdom were subject to a grain tax, called *kada rājakāriya* (Dewaraja et al. 1995:330). Along with *rājakāriya* and *kada rājakāriya*, lower-caste members who occupied and tilled paddy lands were subject to perform "services of a professional nature" related to their caste (Dewaraja 1995c:393).

Although the system of *rājakārikya* was abolished by the British in 1833 and the feudal political establishment was gradually replaced after the signing of the Kandyan convention in 1815, the head monk's reference to *rājakārikya*—especially his tone and choice of words—may have served as a poignant reminder of the feudal system for the low-caste *dāyakas*. This may be the case because, as Malalgoda (1976:74) has noted, conspicuous parallels between the political and religious authorities had already existed: "Important monasteries were endowed with land grants in much the same manner as the important chiefs were. . . . The chiefs who received lands *(nindagam)* were entitled to the dues and services *(rājakārikya)* which were formerly rendered to the Crown by the tenants of those lands. The dues and services were similarly transferred to the monks and monasteries in the case of *vihāragam*, or temple lands."

25. The Harispattuve monk they mentioned is Devamitta.

26. Sinhala words for the pronoun "you" and its accompanying verbal imperative are (see Karunatillake 1997):

Degree of Respect/Disrespect	**Pronoun "You"**	**Associated Verb (in the imperative)**
Very respectful (Monks)	*Oba vahansē*	*Vaḍinna, vaḍinna* (go, come)
Respectful (MPs, and so on)	*Obatumā*	*Yanna/yanḍa, enna/enḍa* (go, come)
Equality (friends)	*Oyā, Ohē*	*Yanna/yanḍa, enna/enḍa* (go, come)
Disrespectful	*Umba*	*Palayan, varen* (go, come)
Very disrespectful	*Tamusē*	*Pala, vara* (go, come) *palayan, varen yanna, enna*
Extremely disrespectful	*Tō*	*Pala, vara* (go, come); *palayan, varen* (can also be used)

While some of the pronouns and verbs are considered to be very respectful (such as when addressing a monk *(oba vahansē)*, a member of parliament *(obatumā)*, or certain people of respectable professions such as doctors, lawyers, or university professors *(obatumā)*, other forms of the pronoun are not only more informal (like the French *tu* or the Sinhalese *oya*), but quite demeaning (*umba, tamusē,* and *tō*). Although it is not uncommon to hear young friends using *tō* and *palayan* among themselves, or to hear grandparents endearingly address their own children and grandchildren by the pronoun *umba* or *tamusē,* the same words are inappropriate and disrespectful in other contexts, such as public, mixed-caste encounters between a head monk and his patrons.

27. When I asked another villager, an internationally renowned drummer, about the history of Polgoda Vihara, he began by noting, more generally, that "a problem [*praśnaya*] occurred in the village. When they went to observe *sil* at [Sri Kirti Vihara], there was a small division among the people. That is why our fathers got together and decided to start a small separate temple." Having heard the story already from Dharmadasa, I asked the drummer, quite pointedly, if the problem had to do with caste *(praśnaya kiyannē kula gäna da)*. He emphatically responded, "That *indeed* was the very problem [*anna ēka tama praśnaya*]. Those were the very reasons that led to the construction of this temple [*anna ē hētu uḍa tamayi, mē pansala ārambha karannat hētuva*]....That is why our fathers got together and decided to start a small separate temple. Then, they brought a different [*nikāya*] monk and asked him to stay here."

28. Bryce Ryan (1953:171) has noted that whereas the term *umba* is a "'soft' term used by a Goyigama to, or in reference to, one of lower caste when the relationship is friendly...or if the lower caste person is wealthy," the term *tō* is used "by a Goyigama to, or in reference to, a low caste person generally...[and] in reference to, or in address to, a Beravāyā [drummer] or Roḍiyā [washer]."

In discussing caste stratification and overt demarcations during the seventeenth and eighteenth centuries, Lorna Dewaraja (1995:375, 379) points out that "the caste system entered into the administration, both secular and ecclesiastical, regulated taxation, determined judicial procedure and governed all social relationships....An unwritten code of behaviour governed all social relationships between different castes and overt caste symbols were fixed by custom. The length of the lower garment, the right to wear an upper garment, the forms of address, the prefixes and suffixes added to the names were all fixed by social usage" (see also Gombrich 1998: chap. 8). This relationship between vocabulary and social status was also noted by Robert Knox (1911:168; see also Davy 1821) when he wrote that the Sinhalese "have seven or eight words for Thou, or You, which they apply to persons according to their quality, or according as they would honour them" as well as, more recently by Wickramasinghe (2000:982), who writes that "in the Sinhalese society many such pronouns which indicate the social ranking or respect are used, for example, Obavahanse, tamunnaanse, oyaa, tamuse, umba, too, ban, bolan, etc."

29. One example of this within the context of Polgoda Vihara will be explored below.

30. This will be discussed below.

31. As I have discussed elsewhere, Narada's preference for studying over religious activities in no way implies that a monastic's religious obligations may be shirked. For Narada, a monk is like a soldier who should be ready, at all times, to fulfill the laity's religious needs (Samuels 2003:118).

32. Disapproval about offering secular subjects in *pirivenas* and monastics studying in university is discussed in chapter 3 of George Bond's (1992) *The Buddhist Revival in Sri Lanka: Religious Tradition, Reinterpretation, and Response*. Along with some laypeople and monastics, a number of government-sponsored reports, such as the report of the University Commission, also argued against monks pursuing a university education, believing that it is a "step in the wrong direction, leading the bhikkhus further and further away from the serene calmness of bhikkhu life" (Gunawardena 1963:40).

33. Similar to the baccalaureate exams in countries such as France or the SAT or ACT exams in the United States, the advanced-level exams are a key determinant for university admissions.

34. Statistics from 1997 reveal that of those who were qualified to enter a university (73,574), only 15.49 percent (10,450) were actually granted admission into one of the country's twelve public universities. The granting of university status to two large monastic colleges in Colombo in 1958—Vidyālaṅkāra and Vidyodaya—made it easier and more acceptable for monks to pursue a traditional university degree rather than a *paṇḍita* degree at one of Sri Lanka's monastic colleges.

35. Discussing the role that patriotism played in the second uprising, Nira Nickramasinghe (2006:244) explains that "the rise of the JVP is closely linked to a patriotic issue, what has been referred to as the 'Ruhunu spirit' by scholars who draw parallels between the JVP's opposition to Indian intervention and King Dutugemunu's heroic and patriotic fight for motherland against the Tamil king Elara and his army."

36. Even though Narada was not sympathetic to the JVP's ideology, he, like many others, were forced to participate in several of their strikes or *hartals* against the government. The JVP were, in fact, quite successful in coercing people into following its demands by using a variety of tactics, such as attacking, humiliating, and even killing those who refused to submit to the JVP appointed "national strike" days (see C. R. de Silva 1999:304; see also Senaratne 1997:121 and Wickramasinghe 2006:239).

37. Writing on the involvement of monks in the JVP, Nira Wickramasinghe (2006:241) notes that "young monks who constituted a sizeable proportion of the university population had been recruited into the movement and formed one of the three front organizations of the JVP, together with the fronts for workers and youth. In 1987 they marched on the streets to the cry of 'Motherland First, Pirivena Second,' and they were generally deployed for JVP propaganda on issues such as the privatization of the Medical College." Matthews (1988–1989) discusses other political monastic groups such as the Young Monks' Patriotic Front (Dēsaprēmi Taruṇa Bhikṣu Peramuna), the Monks' Authority for Humanity (Manavahitavadi Bhikṣu Saṁvidhānaya), the Upcountry Monks' Tri-Nikāya Organization (Kandurața Trinikāya Bhikṣu Sangamaya), and so on.

38. Identification cards are supposed to be carried by all laypeople. Although there have been attempts, from time to time, to require monastics to carry identity cards, they have always balked at such suggestions. To this day, monastics are not required to carry identity cards.

39. The tendency to disrobe is, as Jonathan Spencer (1990a:46) noted, particularly high for university graduates who have secured, for themselves, government jobs.

40. This phrase about the "*dharma,* when protected, protects" *(dharma rakṣati rakṣitaha)* is a proverb that is found throughout Buddhist and Hindu literature (e.g., the *Mānavadharmaśāstra* and the *Mahābhārata*).

41. Although this image of laypeople giving to monastics what they themselves ate appears quite similar, in spirit, to the early Buddhist practice of going on alms rounds (Wijayaratna 1990:71), laypeople in contemporary Sri Lanka (as in other countries within the Theravāda world) more often than not cook special meals for monastics. Several religious laywomen I know even refuse to taste the food they prepare for monastics, believing that by doing so, they would taint it.

42. This idea of eating solid food at night and, thus, breaking one of the key monastic precepts will be examined below.

43. Novices in Sri Lanka, as in other areas of the Buddhist world following the Pali *Vinaya*—Myanmar, Thailand, Laos, Cambodia, Southwest China, and South Vietnam—follow ten monastic precepts: not taking life, not taking what is not given, not engaging in any sexual activities, not lying, not taking intoxicants, not eating after midday, not sleeping on high or soft beds, not wearing jewelry or perfume, not watching shows or other entertainment spectacles, and not handling gold and silver.

44. This will be discussed further in chapter 3.

45. The ideologies of both the Sinhala Heritage Party and the more recently formed, monk-led National Sinhala Heritage (Jathika Hela Urumaya) Party is discussed in Mahinda Deegalle (2004). For a further elaboration on the factors that contributed to the emergence of the National Sinhala Heritage Party, see also Hennayake (2004).

46. Although Narada has shunned any involvement with politics, he did not prevent his more senior students from becoming involved in the monk-led National Sinhala Heritage Party in 2004.

47. The types of politically based divisions that sometimes plague village life in contemporary Sri Lanka has been well documented in Jonathan Spencer's *A Sinhalese Village in a Time of Trouble* (1990a).

48. One donor who knew several people from the dissenting group surmised the factors that brought the group back to Polgoda Vihara when he said,

> Those who protested against the head monk's refusal to take part in the procession [*perahära*] were unable to sustain it [i.e., their protest]. In fact, there were many from that group among the crowd who recently came to the temple to bless the head monk after his illness [with dengue fever]. . . . [I]f they have some religious activity at their own home, they have to come to the temple, talk to the head monk, and finally pay their respects to him by saying "Reverend sir, excuse me." By doing that, their disgust is removed from their hearts. This time, it was because

of politics. There may be some other reasons or because something else happened. These kind of things are common.

49. This idea of minute conjunctures is drawn from Ananda Abeysekara's *Colors of the Robe* (2002:3). I should note that my own interest in using this concept is examining how monastics and laypeople work together, over the *longue durée*, to negotiate shared visions of acceptable monastic appearance and deportment.

50. The monastic articles that Narada is referring to here are the eight requisites given to ordinands during their ordination: three robes (an upper robe, a lower robe, and vest), a bowl, a belt, a razor, a needle, and a water strainer.

51. Sarananda's life and social service agenda are described in Gamini Senadhira's (2000) *Bahu Jana Hitāya* [*For the sake of all*] as well as in Debatgama Nārada's (1990) *Uḍunuvara Śrī Sārānanda Mahā Svamipādayāṇan Vahansē: Saṅkṣita Jīvana Caritaya* [*A brief biography of Uḍanuvara Śrī Sārānanda, the great honorable reverend*].

52. Sarananda was from the Batgama (also called Padu) caste, which is fairly numerous in the Kandyan highlands and the north-central jungle. From the perspective of high-caste members, Batgama are only fit for menial outdoor labor, although their traditional service, which has long been lost or forgotten (see Knox 1911:45), is palanquin bearer for officials. Ryan (1958:127) further notes that most of those who refer to themselves as Batgama nowadays are "economically depressed, lacking in land, and are often wage laborers."

53. Sarananda was able to improve the quality and standing of low-caste villagers by opening the monkhood to them as well as by establishing a network of public schools. For instance, during one sermon he reportedly gave in Aṭabāgē, the village where Sudhammananda and Devamitta received their monastic training, Sarananda critiqued the prevailing class and caste system by saying,

> We all have the strength and knowledge to attain *nibbāna*. But, you don't possess the heritage of the religion or to become ordained. Lord Buddha's *sāsana* is common to all who have devotion and energy. Anyone who wants to fulfill those principles can ordain there. Lord Buddha has clearly described the people who should not ordain. But there are no obstacles of caste, lineage, and nationality in the buddha *sāsana*. Monks who were after King Kīrti Śrī Rājasiṃha were the ones who introduced caste into the monkhood. It is serious discrimination. It is enough that we tolerate these unrighteous [*adharmic*] activities of the evil people who created them. . . . Our country is being developed rapidly; Colombo is like a small England. People are developing rapidly. Houses are coming up. In this area, roads are being developed. However, there is no one to save you. It wouldn't work if you don't have a proper education according to the present developing environment. If you don't have education and if you don't have religion, what is the meaning of humanity. There are many people who converted to Christianity and have the chance to receive Christian ordination. However, we are traditional Buddhist; yet we don't have the right to be ordained (Senadhira 2000:115f.; see also Suravīra 2003).

54. For instance, Pannasekhara sought to improve the economic and social lives of villagers through improving the village educational system, organizing volunteer groups, and coordinating various constructions projects (e.g., reading rooms and homes for the destitute). Silaratana (1913–1982) also believed that monastic service must be oriented toward the economic well-being of Sri Lankans. In his *Gramasamvardhana* (1:6; cited in Seneviratne 1999:119) he posits that the temple

> must provide guidance for this fivefold development [i.e., economic, health, behavioral, intellectual, and moral]. It is only when such social needs are met [*siddhavana kalhi*] by the place of worship, that it will become one [*siddhastanaya*] in the literal sense. In my view, it is with that expectation that the ancient kings donated hundreds of acres of land and paddy fields to the old Buddhist places of worship.

I might add that such calls for a more socially engaged *sangha* is not only restricted to Sri Lanka; laypeople and monastics living in other Asian countries with substantial Buddhist populations have demanded that the *sangha* take a more active role in improving the lives of laypeople both economically and socially (e.g., Larung Gar monastery [*bla lung sgar*] in Tibet, which contains an old-age home; Venerable Wei Wu's Tan Hsiang temple in Penang, Malaysia, which has a free medical clinic, preschool, and old-age home; and programs offered through Mahamakut Buddhist University that prepare their students for community development work such as building bridges, schools, and wells [see Gosling 1980 and Tambiah 1973]).

55. Seneviratne argues that the main thrust of Rahula's *Heritage of the Bhikkhu* is to validate the role of political activism for the twentieth century by showing how monks have played a role in politics throughout Sri Lanka's history. In the same way, a number of monastics from Vidyodaya—by referencing such texts as *Mahāsāḷa Sutta* and the *Mātuposaka Sutta* and the *Sigālaka Sutta*—legitimate their version of social service by contending that it goes all the way back to the Buddha.

56. Belonging to a family of flower scavengers in Rājagaha, Sunīta Thero earned his living as a street sweeper. As Malalasekera points out (1960:2:1212), Sunīta's rebirth as a laborer is said to have been the result of speaking disparagingly of a Pacceka buddha.

57. There are two Sopāka Theras identified in the Pali canonical texts. The first was born the child of a cemetery keeper (Malalasekera 1960:2:1303), while the second the son of a very poor woman who had died shortly after giving birth (ibid., 1302).

58. Rāhula, Ānanda, and Anuruddha are all members of the Sākya clan (Katthiya or Kṣatriya caste), whereas Moggallāna is a member of the Brahmin caste.

59. Richard Gombrich arrives at this particular conclusion—that what people say now is remarkably similar to what was said 1,500 years ago—in his book *Precept and Practice* (1998:372, 382). Although he is careful to distinguish what people say and what they do, Gombrich argues that Buddhism has changed little since, at least, the times that the commentaries were composed.

60. Jonathan Spencer (1990c) has noted, for example, that, because Buddhism's break from kingship after 1815, the tradition has become increasingly open to a variety of perspectives concerning the role of the *sangha*, particularly in regard to a number of lay initiatives that have positioned their own particular vision of the *sangha*'s place in society over others.

61. During one conversation I had with Narada about embarking on his social service agenda, he explained, "I understand that in most of the temples, the majority of monks are not educated. They just focus on their religious duties. Then I thought "It is better to introduce the path of education to the *sangha*. I believe that without an education [i.e., an educated group of monastics], this temple would decay. I decided to take action to prevent that decay. We have to protect the religion [*sāsana*]. We have to protect ourselves."

62. There have been numerous editorials in newspapers over time (e.g., Jinadasa 1957; Wimalaratana 2003) that have called on Buddhist monastics to adopt a more socially oriented role in society.

63. In advancing his vision of the role that the *sangha* should play in contemporary society, particularly in regard to poor children and street boys, Narada also supports a system of temporary ordination in Sri Lanka. Although, in doing so, Narada has challenged the pervasive view in Sri Lanka that monastic ordination should be lifelong commitment *(javājivaṃ)*, he is not alone in advocating such a change (see Gombrich 1984; Wickremegamage 1999; Gunaratne 2002).

64. The four divine abidings are compassion *(karuṇā)*, loving kindness *(mettā)*, sympathetic joy *(muditā)*, and equanimity *(upekkhā)*. The idea of these emotions being unbounded is found in Harvey Aronson's book *Love and Sympathy in Theravāda Buddhism*. Speaking specifically of the quality of sympathy, Aronson writes, "The bonds of fondness and attachment that bring worldly individuals together influence their sympathy. However, Gotama's interest in others' happiness was free from all normal worldly bias and attachment, and, thus, it was unbound" (1986:6). What is clear from my conversations with Narada is that his feelings of sympathy and love are very bounded, much like the bonds of fondness and attachment that bring people together.

65. One common assumption about such children is that their new stepmother would treat them poorly by favoring her own biological children over her stepchildren. Several young novices whose fathers had remarried discussed with me the poor treatment they received at the hands of their new mothers.

66. Discussing the Vinaya Vardhana Society, Steven Kemper points out that the importance that the Society placed on the *Vinaya* is not new and that other *Vinaya* reform movements (such as the forest ascetics or *tāpasa* movement) existed prior to as well as alongside the Society. One may also see such importance placed on the *Vinaya* in the writings of Dharmapāla (1965:223), the Buddhist reformer and founder of the Mahābōdhi Society: "The Bhikkhu who does not observe the precepts and leads an unworthy immoral life is called a 'Samana preta' which means a dead ghost and his is also called a 'mahacora' great thief."

67. This particular view is discussed in Rupert Gethin's *The Foundations of Buddhism* (1998:102), where he writes, "The onus is on a monk to make himself a suitable recipient of the laity's gifts. So long as a monk lives in accordance with the basic precepts of the Vinaya, he fulfils his obligation to society and renders himself a field of merit for the laity. The more fully a monk lives out the spiritual life, the more fruitful the field of merit."

2 Aesthetics of Emotions and Affective Bonds

1. Although most Buddhist monastics use traditional umbrellas to shield them from the sun and rain, some monastics from the Rāmañña Nikāya still use umbrellas modeled upon the traditional palmyra-leaf umbrella believed to have been used by the early monastic community.

2. Country-wide, the number of monks belonging to the Siyam Nikāya—the largest of the three fraternities in Sri Lanka—outnumber those from the Rāmañña Nikāya—the smallest of the three fraternities—by more than three to one (C. R. de Silva 2006).

3. The possibility that actual control and factual ownership of a temple and all temple land could lie with the chief monk (Phadnis 1976:98; Evers 1967:706) opened the door to a form of pupillary succession (*śiṣyānuśiṣyaparamparāva*) through which monasteries and their properties have remained in the hands of certain families. With the rise of another rule of succession—*jñātiśiṣyaparamparāva* or *sivuruparamparāva*—only a relative of a head monk may succeed him (Bechert 1970:768). It is worth noting, though, as Steven Kemper (1984:408f.) has, that sometimes the issue of pupillary succession is decided upon by the family members of individual monks and not necessarily by the monks themselves.

4. Although Narada's and Sumedha's use of ordination as a way to effect change is somewhat unique, they are certainly not alone. Venerables Sōmānanda from Puttalam District (Vanigasinha 2004) and Dammaratana from Hantana have worked to improve the lives of poor children by ordaining them and providing them with an education. Another monk I met, Venerable Jinavamsa from Dambulla regularly travels through war-torn areas looking for orphans and children from very impoverished backgrounds to ordain. Several of his students were subsequently sent to Venerable Narada's temple.

5. This idea about cultural reproduction, how the past and present work together to legitimate beliefs and practices, is discussed at length in Steven Kemper's *The Presence of the Past: Chronicles, Politics, and Culture in Sinhala Life* (1991).

6. There have been, especially since the 1950s, a number of politically sponsored ordination rituals. Like the *Budu Jayanti* celebrations held in 1956 to commemorate the 2,500-year anniversary of the Buddha's death and the *Mahindu Jayanti* or the celebration held in 1992 to celebrate the 2,300-year anniversary of the coming of Buddhism to Sri Lanka with the Arahant Mahinda (Ananda 1992; Vimalavaṅśa 1992; Yayasena 1992; and *Mahindu Jayanti Väda Saṭahana*), many of these politically sponsored ordination rituals are fueled by nationalistic sentiments which are, themselves, driven by the perception that the *sangha* is in a state of rapid decline.

7. Prior to putting on monastic robes, the ordinand requests monastic robes from his teacher. After the teacher places the robes on the ordinand's forearms, the teacher takes one end of the belt that is usually used to hold up the lower robes and ties it around the ordinand's neck. This is usually done at a time that is deemed auspicious. For a description of this event, see Dickson (1884), Htun Hmat Win (1986), and Samuels (2002).

8. According to Rhys Davids and Stede (1972: s.v.) *ākappa* means "attire, appearance, and deportment." The Sinhala term for *ākappa, ākalpa,* has a similar, though slightly expanded, meaning "appearance, attitudes, arrayment, guise, action, and performance."

9. This sentiment was shared by many head monks and parents of monastics. Although there are no statistics to validate or invalidate that perception, it is commonly thought that young novices living too close to their own families and friends would have a difficult time adopting to their new status as Buddhist monastics. Such a belief, Jane Bunnag (1970:89) notes, is also found in Thailand.

10. Within the first year, Sumedha began ordaining several students. Although the majority of them were transferred to Polgoda Vihara, several remained by Sumedha's side to assist him in the temple's everyday affairs.

11. The offering of daily alms to the temple usually includes one of the temple's monks leading the laity in the refuge formula, administering the five precepts, and reciting verses that extol the merit associated with giving *(piṁvākya)*.

12. Immediately following World War II and Sri Lanka's independence in 1948, Parliament allocated 700 million rupees for the restoration of abandoned reservoirs including the Padavilkulam, Kantalai, Huruluväva, Kandalama, and Kaudulla tanks. Part of this agrarian revolution was based on the perceived need to curb Sri Lanka's dependence on other nations for providing its own citizens with food (C. R. de Silva 1999:318). For a fuller account of D. S. Senanayake's life, see Hulugalle (1975).

13. Although the vision of curbing Sri Lanka's reliance on food imports is quite laudable, it is important to mention that the vision was also tinged with Sinhala pride and nationalistic sentiments. Discussing Senanayake's agricultural revolution, Deborah Winslow writes (2004:32f.) that his expansionist policies

> proved to be a policy with major ethnic implications. By 1954, well over half of the "pioneer colonists" who had been relocated into the newly irrigated areas were Sinhalese... while the populations of the northern and eastern areas into which they were being moved were either mixed Sinhalese and Tamil or predominantly Tamil. Thus the settlement schemes effectively readjusted dry zone population balances in favor of the Sinhalese.... What seemed a straightforward economic development plan... actually put the full weight of national economic policy behind one community's vision of the island's past and future identity, at the expense of competing visions held by members of other groups.

The ethnic implications of Senanayake's vision and policy is particularly acute in the Gal Oya region of Ampāra District (see, for instance, V. Thangavelu [n.d.], for more details).

Huruluväva, not part of the Gal Oya region, is associated with the Yan Oya scheme that Thangavelu also discusses.

14. See, for instance, de Mel (2006a), Ekanayake (2005), and Jayasuriya (1976).

15. Anurādhapura is listed as "educationally disadvantaged districts," in the *Statistical Handbook, 1997: Statistics on University Education in Sri Lanka* (University Grants Commission 1998:43). According to census data from 1981, the percentage of males who passed the General Certificate of Education (Ordinary Level) and General Certificate of Education (Advanced Level) is 4.7 percent and 1.0 percent, respectively (Abeysinghe, 1983:30). Speaking of these figures, Abeysinghe (ibid.) writes: "To continue education and pass G.C.E. (A. Level) had been a remote chance in the district as the percentages of that group were always below 1 since 1963."

16. This idea is based on conversations with a number of ordinands, novices, and parents from the area.

17. In one conversation with Sumedha, for instance, he explained that "poverty is not a thing that a boy can understand. Regardless of the types of delicious food a boy is given, he always prefers that which his mother gives him, even if it is only onion, chili, and rice."

18. See, for instance, Olcott (1928:297) and Copleston (1892:432), as two historical sources that speak about the Rāmañña Nikāya in very laudatory terms.

19. In his important historical study of the developments of the three Sri Lankan *Nikāyas*, Kitsiri Malalgoda (1976:167; see also Obeyesekere 1968) writes, the "'reformism' of the Rāmañña fraternity persisted, on the whole, longer than that of the (earlier) Amarapura fraternity; one reason for this, it could be supposed, was that it was more strongly motivated by religious ideals pure and simple."

20. In a number of conversations with laypeople in Anurādhapura and Kandy, monks from the Siyam Nikāya were characterized as being too worldly and only concerned with protecting their own interests. As the Siyam Nikāya tends to restrict ordination to the highest Sri Lankan caste and that many Siyam Nikāya temples own large tracts of cultivatable land which is leased to farmers (see, for instance, Gunawardana 1979), the Nikāya tends to be the target of many people's criticism.

21. There are approximately thirty-two temples registered as belonging to the Siyam Nikāya in the area. Besides the Madavala temple, the only other institution associated with the Rāmañña Nikāya is Bodhirāja Pirivena.

22. Wijayaratna goes on to discuss other examples of men and women whose decision to enter the *sangha* was based on the Buddha's appearance and demeanor: Kaccāna, Sigāla-Mātā, Paripuṇṇaka, Uttiya, Godhika, Subāhu, Valliya, Nanda, and Vakkali, to name only a few. I might add that the aesthetic appeal of monastic dress is not only limited to the Buddhist tradition. Several scholars (Falk 1980; Finke 1997; Wittberg 1996; Stark and Finke 2000) writing on the Catholic tradition have also noted that after Vatican Council II, Pope John Paul demanded that the Catholic religious orders experiment with different roles, structures, and even dress (per the Decree for Renewal of Religious Life of 1962).

Several of these same scholars have argued that the decision that a number of women's orders had taken to change their dress (including, for some, abandoning the habit altogether) after the decree has, in subsequent years, led to declining number of new recruits.

23. Although the Vinaya Vardhana Society and the *tāpasa* movement have largely died out in contemporary Sri Lanka, the propensity driving both groups to define ideal monastic behavior strictly along *Vinaya* norms have not.

24. *Dharma* schools or *daham pāsäl* (sing.: *daham pāsäla*) are often referred to as Buddhist Sunday schools in English as they traditionally meet on Sundays. These schools—modeled upon their Christian counterparts—are very popular among children and teenagers in contemporary Sri Lanka. Besides providing the opportunities for children to learn about various facets of Buddhist doctrine, the life stories of the Buddha and other important Buddhist figures, they, like Christian Sunday schools, also function as an important venue for socializing.

25. *Huruḷuvävē sisilen niti nähävena madavala rajamahāveherē, saṅghabōdhi daham pāsäl sisuvan vē apa raṭa däya sarasana.*

26. Discussing the purpose behind establishing the Buddhist Theosophical Society and the Buddhist Sunday schools, Olcott writes, "As the Christians have their Society for the diffusion of Christian knowledge, so this should be a society for the diffusion of Buddhist knowledge" (*A Collection of Lectures on Theosophy and Archaic Religions Delivered in India and Ceylon by Colonel H. S. Olcott, President of the Theosophical Society*, 1883:34; cited in Prothero 1996:97). Particularly interesting is that the specific brand of Buddhism that Olcott sought to instill through these Sunday schools was one that was, to a large degree, devoid of rituals and free of other "Buddhist superstitions" (see Dharmapāla 1965; Hallisey 1995; Prothero 1995, 1996).

27. Sumedha explained: "There are songs about Lord Buddha, his perfections [*paramitā*], and Bodhgaya [the place where the Buddha was enlightened]. I was very happy to listen to those songs during my childhood.... That might have been the result from a past life. I felt a longing toward them. I loved them." The one song that Sumedha mentioned by name and even sung to me as an example of what drew him to the *sangha* was the popular Amaradēva song "Paramitā Bala."

28. Both rituals have a wide aesthetic appeal in contemporary Sri Lanka largely because they contain Sinhala verses that are often beautifully sung. These two preaching styles are discussed in Mahinda Deegalle's recent publication, *Popularizing Buddhism: Preaching as Performance in Sri Lanka* (2006; see also Mahinda Deegalle 1995).

29. Discussing the appeal of all-night preaching performances or *dharmadēśanā*, H. L. Seneviratne (1999:45) writes that "a look at this sequence [of the all-night ceremony] makes it clear that the doctrinal content is limited to the core of the sutra and the commentary. Even there the sutra is not understood, because it is in Pali. Even the commentary may well be another text, in Pali or Sinhala, which is also memorized by the preacher and chanted. *The appeal of this was more poetic or musical within an overall structure of religious emotion*" (emphasis added). This particular preaching style, Seneviratne further notes, was

given up in favor of shorter sermons that were seen as effective tools for competing with their Christian counterparts by conveying, in the words of Anagārika Dharmapāla, the "pure psychology" of textual Buddhism (Dharmapāla 1965:530 and 638). This more "functional" form of preaching was later complemented by two other forms of ritualized preaching: poetic preaching *(kavi baṇa)* that Venerable Kumbukgamuvē Guṇaratana created in the 1950s and the very popular *bodhipūjā* that Venerable Pānadurē Ariyadhamma created in the 1970s (see Gombrich 1981 as well as Seneviratne and Wickremeratne 1980).

30. Another of Reverend Narada's senior students—Venerable Ananda—mentioned to me the importance that speaking affectionately to children has in the recruitment process:

> We say "Oh little one, shall we ordain? You can also study well. The [lay]people will help you. There is a lot of freedom. You can also develop the skills to preach *baṇa* well [*cūti babō, pävidi vemuda? Hondaṭa igenagannat puluvan. Minissun udav upakāra karanavā. Hari nidahas. Hondaṭa baṇa kiyanavā vagē häkiyāvat diyuṇu kara-ganna puluvan*]." That is what I say. The boys like [to hear] it a lot. Generally, to get them to ordain . . . we need to coax [*ravaṭanda ōnä*] them, just like parents who speak to their children in baby language. Otherwise it wouldn't work. If not, it would be difficult. It is through that that they ordain.

31. Since Sumedha left Madavala in 1994, the temple has been left vacant, with the exception of several short periods during which it was inhabited by other monastics from the area. In 2006 the temple was handed over to a monk who is one of Sumedha's close friends.

32. This other type of social service enterprise will be discussed in chapter 5.

33. See, for instance, *Census of Population and Housing, 2001. Population and housing data: Results from sample tabulations, Matale District*, 2003:2 and Ekanayake (2005).

34. The residents from Mahavela appear to have settled there from the southwest towns of Kodagoda and Balapitiya. The original occupation of the Salāgama caste was weaving; however, as a result of cinnamon gaining in importance during Portuguese and Dutch rule, the Salāgama caste members living in the south were encouraged to devote their energies to the cinnamon industry so that, by the eighteenth century, their "natural" occupation was considered to be cinnamon peeling (C. R. de Silva 1995:179f.; see also Ryan 1953). Their increased social and economic standing as well as their more diversified occupations opened them, along with members of the Karāva and Durāva castes, to numerous opportunities throughout Sri Lanka as well as abroad (see, for instance, Roberts 1982 and Arseculeratne 1991)

35. Although Sumedha referred to a dark age in Mahavela's past, other conversations with him suggest that the village's dark age is something that is still ongoing.

36. *Śrī siri narada lama samājaya, hadavata vēyi mahavela. Apa ipaduna mahavela rändi, anduru yugaya avasan karamin. Hiru sandu hamuvaṭa peraṭama pā tabamū.*

37. Sumedha claimed that the drop-out rate was around 80 percent. Even though that seems to be an exaggeration, census data from 1981 points to a higher than normal drop-out rate for older school children in Mātalē District. Although the school attendance rate

was hovering around 90 percent for boys living in rural Mātalē in grades 1–5, that rate dropped precipitously from the ages 13 to 18: 76.1 percent, 65.7 percent, 56.8 percent, 45.8 percent, 34.3 percent, and 24.4 percent (*Sri Lanka Census of Population and Housing, 1981*. Vol. 1, pt. 5: *District report, Matale* 1984:38). These statistics, however, may vary quite markedly from area to area as well as from village to village; unfortunately, there are no district secretary's statistics for areas within Mātalē District.

38. The *kaṭhina* ceremony is held at the ends of the rains retreat (usually in October/November) during which the laity offers new robes to the *sangha*. *Pirit*, to which Sumedha also referred, is a protection ritual that is commonly performed throughout Sri Lanka. This ritual, which I will discuss at greater lengths in chapter 4, includes the chanting of Pali verses and the tying of protective threads on lay Buddhists. For a fuller account of protection rituals, see Lily de Silva's *Paritta: A Historical and Religious Study of the Buddhist Ceremony for Peace and Prosperity in Sri Lanka*.

39. Discussing with me some of the factors that drew him to the *sangha*, Sumedha said, "There were three boys who ordained at Liyangastänna Vihara. That was about thirty years ago. When I saw the way that they ordained, the procession [*perahära*], the respect, and the consolation [*senäsīma*] I also wished to ordain during that occasion. Even though I didn't know it at the time, it affected me."

40. After ordaining the Madavala boy in Mahavela, Sumedha kept him in the temple, rather than sending him, like many of those who ordained in Madavala, to Polgoda Vihara in Kandy. In fact, to help him in what became a very active ritual performance agenda, Sumedha also brought several novices from Polgoda Vihara to Mahavela.

41. Merit transference rituals are quite common in South and Southeast Asia. For two scholarly discussions of this Buddhist ritual, particularly how it relates to the Buddhist doctrine of karma, see Gombrich (1971) and Keyes (1983).

42. The speech was much longer, lasting over eleven minutes. I have included parts of the speech that are most relevant to our present discussion of monastic recruitment.

43. This idea about the door being open to them concerns the tendency found within certain lineages and temples to limit ordination to certain castes. Like his teacher (Narada) and his great grand-teacher (Sarananda), Sumedha seeks to tear down any conditions—social and economic—that have prevented certain groups from entering the monastic order.

44. Although there are a number of ways to acquire merit, such as by any of the ten wholesome actions (Pali: *dasakusalakamma*), giving a son to the *sangha* is regarded as being one of the most potent ways to make merit. It is commonly believed that the merit that results from such an activity is powerful enough to propel numerous generations of relatives, on both the mother's and father's side, to enlightenment or *nibbāna*.

45. The subject of Buddhism's decline is sometimes raised in government reports (e.g., *Bauddha Toraturu Parikṣaka Sabhāve Vārtāva* 1956; *Buddha Śāsana Komiṣan Vārtāva* 1959; *Bauddha Śāsana Amātyāṅśaya Kāryabharya Piḷibhanda Sammantraṇa Vārtāva* 1990; Sumanatissa 1995) and in newspaper editorials (Vanigasinha, 2004) and articles (Sumana 2000;

Dhammananda 2001; and "PM Warns of Conspiracy against Buddhists" 2001). Discussions about the (perceived) decline of Buddhism on the island often function as powerful forces used to usher in changes within the *sangha* (e.g., revamping the *pirivena* curricula [the passing of Pirivena Act 11828 in 1959 or Act 64 in 1979] or to argue for new types of monastic training institutions [Pirivena Training Institutes in the early 1980s and Sāmaṇera Training Centers in the early 1990s]).

46. Venerable Sumedha and Venerable Ananda—another of Narada's senior students who has been quite active in recruiting newcomers to the *sangha*—acknowledged that novices with more pleasing appearances (e.g., fair skin color, well-proportioned faces, and so on) are more likely to please donors. After using the example of the Buddha to justify their comment, both monks qualified their statements by remarking that any advantage that is the outcome of a novice's pleasing appearance would, within a very short time, be equalized by his skills and abilities. As Sumedha explained, "At the beginning, sometimes those with bad appearances may not be treated well by the people. However, if they behave well and develop their skills, they will receive more attention and better treatment from the donors. Sometimes fair[-skinned] ones lose the people's acceptance on account of their behavior and skills. Their dedication towards the religion is important."

47. Another of Narada's senior students, Ananda, made a similar claim during a sermon he delivered in Davulagala: "We talk about country, race, and religion. However, people don't like sending their own children to the army nor to ordain. We should not do that. Children who are given to the army protect the country. Children who are given for ordination protect the religion." Speaking to me about his speech, Ananda added, "There is a saying that one should have four children to carry the coffin: one child to look after the parents, helping them when they are ill; another child for the army; another child to look after the business; and, another to give to the religion. I told them that when I went there for the sermon. I say that all over the place. I said that on the Davulagala day. I also said: 'There should be someone from the family to ordain; therefore give us a child.' A week after I said that I received a message [from there] about a child who is interested [in ordaining]. The parents are willing to give [the boy to the *sangha*]. I went there myself. I spoke to the boy and brought him."

3 Aesthetic-Affective Social Networks and Monastic Recruitment

1. This particular method of recruitment was also advanced in John Lofland and Rodney Stark's study of the American following of the "Lord of the Second Advent" movement. Since the publication of that study in 1965, other scholars—e.g., Gaede (1976); Frederick Lynch (1977; 1979); Richardson and Steward (1977); Lofland and Skonovd (1981), and Stark and Bainbridge (1985)—have also begun examining the role that such social ties play in recruitment and membership in a religious movement or cult.

2. The view of the *sangha* as providing poor children with an avenue for upward mobility has been used quite frequently since the 1960s as a way to account for monastic recruitment. Scholars of Thai Buddhism using such a model include David Wyatt (1966; reprinted 1996), Craig Reynolds (1972), Jane Bunnag (1973), Stanley Tambiah (1976),

and Charles Keyes (1977). For Burma, see Melford Spiro's work *Buddhism and Society* (1982). Concurrent with Spiro, Gananath Obeyesekere (1981) has also used that model to understand temple recruitment in Sri Lanka. Although the upward mobility theory is somewhat dated, it is still sometimes used to account for temple recruitment in contemporary society (see, for example, Obeyesekere 2001).

3. The Madavala temple shares a common boundary line with the Gunasenas' property. The close proximity meant an almost continuous flow of foot traffic between the Gunasenas and the Madavala temple.

4. Gunasena described to me the types of boys he seeks to bring to Polgoda Vihara during one conversation:

> I am the one who directed many of those children to the temple. All of them are innocent [*ahiṅsaka*] boys. Many of them are without shelter [*ata äriya lamayi*]. Some have no mothers. Some have no fathers. Some children belong to parents who are separated. Many of them are like that. There are four or five boys who are not like that. The father of the two smallest ones [here] had died. There is another young monastic whose parents are separated. His mother is not here today. She doesn't have a husband. That is one group. There is another one whose mother had left.

5. It was Gunasena who encouraged his first two sons to ordain; his third son ordained of his own volition.

6. You do not have to be a monastic to study in a monastic college or *pirivena*. According to statistics provided in Abayaratna Adikari's excellent study of *pirivena* education—*Śrī Laṅkāvē Sambhāvya Adhyāpanaya hā mahā Sangana* (1991:301f.)—only two fifths of all *pirivena* students are actually monastics.

7. There are no government statistics regarding disrobing rates. The monastic and laypeople I spoke with estimate the current rate of disrobing to be at about 85–95 percent. The belief that the numbers within the *sangha* is rapidly shrinking is one that is widely held, particularly by Buddhists living in more outlying areas where they face difficulties procuring a sufficient number of monastic for their more elaborate rituals.

8. Explaining the events that followed Piyadassi's disrobing, Gunasena said, "I didn't want to see my first boy disrobe and I refused his return. I didn't go to speak to him even. . . . Then I wondered what I should do as a parent. [I felt that] I had to accept him. . . . As he was no longer going to school, I asked him what he wanted to do. He said 'I want to work.'"

9. For a discussion of this quality of shame in a broader South Asian setting, see Parish (1994) as well as the works of Richard Shweder, particularly "Toward a Deep Cultural Psychology of Shame" (2003).

10. This exam was first initiated in the early 1920s. Although the scholarships, based on merit and the student's economic background, were suspended for a period of time, they were later expanded in number (12,500 in 1996) to accommodate the ever growing number of students (338,352 in 1992) sitting for it (Udagama 1999:28).

11. In addition to being granted entrance into a central school, children from poor families are given an annual stipend to help offset any additional fees or costs. In 1951, the awards were even extended to advanced-level and university education (Udagama 1999:28).

12. The stress that the fifth-grade scholarship exam has on children is colorfully portrayed in Nihal de Silva's (2006) new novel, *Paduma Meets the Sunbird: Stories from Paduma's World*, where, in the words of Tara de Mel (2006b), "the importance placed on the Grade five scholarship examination, the most rigorous ordeal for a ten-year-old, is reiterated by several characters in these stories." Udagama (1999:47) also notes that the importance placed on the exam had an adverse affect on the quality of the children's education as the exam itself has tended to dominate teaching and learning.

13. During a three-month period, I conducted four interviews with Sujata, including a photo-elicited interview that lasted well over two hours.

14. In Sinhala, as in Thai, a different vocabulary is used when addressing or speaking about members of the *sangha*. The different vocabularies, as W. S. Karunatillake (1979:4) has pointed out, shapes understandings about the monastic order as well as creates a distinction between the *sangha* and the laity. Examples of the different speech provided by Karunatillake (4 n. 2) includes such commonly used verbs as *be/exist*, *eat*, *drink*, *sleep*, *go*, *come*, and so on. B. J. Terwiel (1975) raises a similar point in his discussion of Thai Buddhism.

15. After mentioning dirty things, Sujata paused for what seemed like several minutes before going on. His awkwardness and hesitation during this point in our interview together may be interpreted as references to physical abuse and molestation. I did not feel it worthwhile or even productive at the time to press him on the issue.

16. This point of monastics helping their parents back at home is quite common and will be discussed below.

17. According to Sujata, Gunasena simply told the boy, "The temple is good. There are no problems. There are no shortcomings. There are facilities there to study. There are no strict rules. You can live there like brothers. There are no problems."

18. During the period, Sujata's sister was studying for the advanced-level exams. Her private tuition courses were a strain on the family's finances.

19. In Sri Lanka, people often refer to others by kinship terms. Sujata's parents are not related to the Gunasenas.

20. Mothers of some 40,000 children under the age of five were working in the Middle East in 1987 (Gunatilleke 1987; see also Eelens and Speckmann 1990).

21. Sarat's use of "our" in this quotation probably refers either to the fact that Sujata belonged to the same Huruluväva school or that Sujata hails from the same agricultural colony as Sarat's family. They are not relatives.

22. This point was raised in my conversation with Sujata. When I asked him whether or not he did anything special to attract his friends' hearts to Polgoda Vihara, he replied,

"There is a lake there [in Huruluväva]. We used to all go there together to have a bath. We played there."

23. As I discussed in note 26 in chapter 1, the verbal imperative *palayan* is quite demeaning and considered bad language for a teacher to use when addressing his students.

24. Venerable Dhammadassi was recruited to Polgoda Vihara through Gunasena.

25. Echoing and building on Sugathadasa's study, R. D. Wanigaratne (1975:5) mentions that "the lack of space for outdoor recreational facilities and the lack of an inclination for recreational activities because of the ceaseless struggle for day-to-day existence perhaps have paved the way for the marked presence of anti-social activities like addiction to liquor, gambling, etc., observed in the colony during the survey."

26. Dhammasiri became a novice at Polgoda Vihara in 2000.

27. Sumanasiri and Santasiri ordained at Polgoda Vihara in 2001, one year after Dhammasiri.

28. Like Sumedha, Narada believed that giving cakes and other things to the laity play a role in monastic recruitment. Discussing with me Ajit's story, Narada said, "When we go to that type of [difficult] area we buy something for the small [novices] to take there. When small ones go home, they take something with them. Taking it, the other children's hearts become attracted. He goes and gives a toffee or something else like that. Children become attracted when [the young novices] do such things."

29. Although *ayyā* means "elder brother," it is being used here to refer to Ajit's older cousin, Santasiri.

30. Although she refers to Dhammika's grandfather as her uncle, her use of the kinship term is out of respect; she is not a relative.

31. As Ananda explained, Santasiri's parents later discussed Polgoda Vihara and sending their son there with Ananda's family still living in Ampāra.

32. During our interview, for instance, she confided, "Even though there is a head monk in the village temple—I don't know whether I should say this here—but he has gone with a woman. Until it actually happened, nobody knew. Now, the second monk has become the head monk. When these things go on, we don't feel like sending our sons to those temples. If we can give the boys a good place like this, we know that they will be well."

33. One reason for this could be, as Sumedha noted in the previous chapter, the villagers lack of interest in Buddhism.

4 Learning to Be Novices

* Earlier versions of several sections of this chapter were published previously in Samuels (2005; 2002). I thank the *Journal of the International Association of Buddhist Studies* for granting me permission to reprint revised versions of sections of my article here.

1. Indeed, quite unlike several scholars (Wells 1960:136; Spiro 1980:246; and Wijayaratna 1990:3f. and 14) who have understood *pabbajjā* quite literally (e.g., "leaving the world, adopting the ascetic life"), monastic ordination, for Narada, should in no way imply the abrogation of ties with society or the novices' biological families. Narada's belief that the forging of close ties between his students and patrons are essential is also echoed in the writings of Ilana Silber (1981 and 1995) and Jane Bunnag (1973), who have argued that laypeople tend to treat monastics who have cut themselves off from this world with suspicion.

2. Silananda explained this phenomenon to me in 2003 when he discussed how the use of kinship terms facilitated the forming of close bonds with several principal temple donors: "I became used to calling them 'mother' and 'father.' When I came here I saw the head monk and others call them 'mother' and 'father.'. . . It touches the people's hearts. [Now,] if the head monk is not here, I go straightaway to the people and talk to them. I definitely talk to them. When I go to the preaching hall, I tell them 'Since our parents are far away, you have become our parents.'"

3. This will be discussed further at the end of this chapter.

4. Välamiṭiyāvē Kusaladhamma, the head monk of Vidyālaṅkāra Pirivena in Colombo, reflected on the training he received as an ordinand: "I became a monk after being in the temple for four years. I was a boy for four years in the temple and then became a monk. During that [ordinand] period, I became aware of my teachers. I became aware of the activities of a temple. I became aware of the devotees who were connected to the temple. I became close to the temple. Then I became a monk. Now, that method no longer exists. Now they bring boys, keep them for one month, ordain them, and send them to a monastic college after one month. . . . They don't teach them about the life of a monk." It was such reflections on the changes regarding monastic training that led to the creation of a new monastic training institution in 1992, the Sāmaṇera Bhikṣu Puhuṇu Madhyasthāna or Sāmaṇera-Bhikkhu Training Institute (Venerable Kusaladhamma, personal communication; see also Kusaladhamma 1994). I should note, however, that this particular belief that novices and monastics are not receiving sufficient training has a longer history in Sri Lanka. Several examples of government-sponsored commissions and reports that criticized the training of monastics are *Bauddha Toraturu Parikṣaka Sabhāve Vārtāva* (1956), which was published in an abridged form under the English title *The Betrayal of Buddhism* (Dharmavijaya Press, 1956), as well as the 1970 report that led to the passing of *Pirivena* Act 64 in 1980 (Deheragoda n.d.:195 and Adikari 1991).

5. For instance, during an interview in 2000, Narada maintained the need for monastics to study a wide range of subjects, including secular ones:

> The present world is always changing and a monk's education should reflect those changes. If we disregard those changes and try to explain everything in Pali and Sanskrit, we will be in trouble. The environment in which laypeople operate is much wider than the society of monks. Without those new technologies, monks cannot advise the laity. If the education for monks does not match the current world, they will be driven away [*pälavenavā*] from the present society.

> ...I think that the people in the twenty-first century will be more knowledgeable than the previous one. They will have well-developed minds. The twenty-first century will be a scientifically developed world. As I see it, in the new millennium the world will be smaller. Our mission is to teach the monks for that society. For example, the monks cannot say that according to the *Sassa Jātaka,* the rabbit in the moon was drawn by a person. That cannot be taught to the people in the new millennium. We have to develop our knowledge according to the world and teach people from our new understandings.

Overtly challenging numerous calls for limiting monastic education to religious subjects and classical languages (e.g., Pirivena Act 64 which was passed into law in 1980 [see Deheragoda, n.d.]), Narada has vociferously argued that the educational level of monastics must keep pace with the ever increasing knowledge base of laypeople. Echoing arguments that Walpola Rahula advanced over sixty years ago (1946; 1974), Narada asserted on several occasions that without a broad education, monastics would be rendered useless to society.

6. The textbooks I have referred to are those edited by Hettiaracci Dharmasena (1997; 1994a–d).

7. The Buddha's nine qualities are being (1) worthy or accomplished *(arahaṃ)*, (2) perfectly enlightened *(sammāsambuddho)*, (3) possessed with knowledge and conduct *(vijjācaraṇasampanno)*, (4) the well-gone one *(sugato)*, (5) the knower of worlds *(lokavidū)*, (6) an unsurpassable teacher of men to be tamed *(anuttaro purisadammasārathī)*, (7) a teacher of gods and men *(satthā devamanussānaṃ)*, (8) the enlightened one *(buddho)*, and (9) the blessed one *(bhagava)*.

8. The names given below are written in their Pali, not Sinhala, forms.

9. Rāhula is often seen as the paradigmatic child monastic. His life, particularly when he meets his father and becomes a monastic, is discussed in both secular schools and *pirivenas*. Rāhula is also the subject of study at Buddhist *dharma* schools.

10. The six factors are physical acts of goodwill, verbal acts of goodwill, mental acts of goodwill, sharing what one receives, living virtuously with others, living with good views, and helping others along the path.

11. The four divine abidings are compassion *(karuṇā)*, loving kindness *(mettā)*, sympathetic joy *(muditā)*, and equanimity *(upekkhā)*. The four foundations of mindfulness *(satipaṭṭhāna)* include mindfulness of the body *(kāyā)*, feelings *(vedanā)*, mental states *(cittā)*, and *dharmas (dhammā)*.

12. The four conditions are consistent effort, looking after one's wealth, having good friends, and balancing one's income with one's expenses.

13. The ten are being averse to the teachings, keeping bad friends, being fond of sleep and being indolent, not supporting one's mother and father, deceiving Brahmins or ascetics, not sharing one's wealth, being proud of one's birth, being a drunk and a gambler, practicing adultery, being jealous of one's young wife, handing over one's authority to a drunken woman, and living above one's means.

14. The *Sigālovādasutta* from the *Dīgha Nikāya* is, perhaps, the most famous discourse for laypeople. As this *sutta* covers many important themes that are still relevant today—not killing; not stealing; not lying; not practicing adultery; not committing acts out of desire, anger, ignorance, or fear; looking after one's wealth; having good friends; caring for one's parents; looking after one's teachers; caring for one's marital partner; treating one's friends well; caring for one's employees; and treating ascetics and brahmins well—many novices use one or more ideas from this discourse while preaching during their early preaching career.

15. The seven are being generous, hard working, patient, open, trustworthy, and helpful to those experiencing adversity, and treating others as equals.

16. The verses of the *Dhammapada* also form the prologue to a set of popular stories used in preaching throughout Sri Lanka. These stories are found in the fifth-century Pali commentary to the *Dhammapada* and in the thirteenth-century Sinhala text the *Saddharmarantāvaliya*.

17. These doctrine are discussed in most introductory texts. For a clear presentation of each of them, see Gethin (1998) and Harvey (1990).

18. These activities and duties are explained quite elaborately in another monastic handbook used by more senior novices, *Śāsanāvataraṇaya* (Candaratana, 1998).

19. These two texts appear to have had a much longer role in monastic training in Sri Lanka. For instance, in a number of twelfth- and thirteenth-century monastic injunctions or *Katikāvatas*, reference is made to the vital place that the *Dasadhammasutta* holds as a guide for monastic discipline. In the thirteenth-century Daṃbadeṇi Katikāvata written by King Vijayabāhu III (1220–1234), for example, we read that "All the senior bhikkhus, junior and those of the middle grade should contemplate on the *Anumāna Sutta* and the *Dasadhamma Sutta* without distraction at least once a day" (Ratnapala 1971:52, 145). One century earlier, in the *katikāvata* of King Mahāparākramabāhu (1153–1186), we read that "novices should be made to commit to memory the *Heraṇasikha, Sekhiya,* and the *Dasadhammasutta,* rehearse and practice these without lapse. They should be employed in the fulfilment [*sic*] of the functions of solitude and thus disciplined" (Ratnapala 1971:39 and 130; see also Blackburn 2001:149).

20. In Pali, the term is *ākappo* and appears in the third of the ten reflections listed in the *Dasadhammasutta* as "*añño me ākappo karaṇīyo ti pabbajitena abhiṇhaṃ paccavekkhitabba* (One who has gone forth should continually reflect 'For me there are other actions [*karaṇiyo*] and appearance/deportment [*ākappo*]')."

21. Carter (1996:85); see also Sorata (1998, 1:122).

22. Although I have called the *sekhiya* rules a "text," they do not actually form a text in their entirety. Instead, the *sekhiya* rules make up the penultimate section of the *Pāṭimokkha,* a list of 227 rules that are ideally recited by fully ordained monks during the full and new moons *(uposatha)* days.

23. While the allowable length for head hair according to the *Vinaya* is two fingerwidths *(dvaṅgula)*—a length similar to a long American crew cut—laypeople and even

groups of monastics living in contemporary Sri Lanka feel that that length is unsuitable for monastics.

24. I have also discussed these pedagogical methods in two recent (Samuels 2004; 2005) publications.

25. For a further discussion of cleaning and sweeping as an important temple activity, see Samuels (2007).

26. What Piyananda is referring to in this statement is how newcomers to the *sangha* are taught to complete various temple duties in a specific, even ritualized, manner. Sweeping is one such activity.

27. Applying Bell's work to the field of Buddhist studies, Kevin Trainor—in his recent work on Buddhist relics—points out that "the performance of the respective rituals serves as a process of inscription through which distinctive patterns of meaningful practice become embodied in the participants, or, in other words, ritualized agents are created" (1997:140). Charles Keyes makes a similar point when he suggests that "texts are invested by a people with a timelessness whose message becomes translated in ritual into meanings that inform ongoing social experience" (1983:273; see also Rappaport 1979:200).

28. Examples of the different speech provided by Karunatillake (1997:4, n. 2) includes such commonly used verbs as *be/exist, eat, drink, sleep, go, come,* and so on. One example of a difference in vocabulary pertains to the very "to eat" which is *kanavā* for laypeople and *valaṇdanavā* for members of the *sangha*. B. J. Terwiel (1975) raises a similar point in his discussion of Thai Buddhism.

29. The importance of this ritual is well attested to by the fact "that hardly a day passes without this ceremony being performed in some form or other in almost every locality" (L. de Silva 1981:3; see also Pertold 1923 and Saddhatissa 1991). The popularity of protection or *paritta* rituals appear to go back to the medieval period. The inscription of Kassapa V (r. 914–923), for example, states that knowledge of the *pirit pota* or the *Book of Protection* is a condition for acceptance into the order (Wickremasinghe 1904:1:48, line 38). In the inscription of Mahinda IV (r. 956–972) as well as in the monastic injunction of Rājādhi Rājasiṃha, monastics are enjoined to recite *paritta* daily (Wickremasinghe 1904:1:91, line 10f.; for the Rājasiṃha's injunction, see Ratnapala 1971:180). There are also references to *paritta* in the *vaṃsa* literature, such as the *Cūlavaṃsa* (Geiger 1973: chaps. 37, 46, 51, 52, 73, and 87).

30. The idea of communities of learning is developed in Anna Gade's (2004) recent work on learning to recite the Qur'an in contemporary Indonesia.

31. This point will be discussed below.

32. Reflecting with me further about how the very ideals of proper *paritta* apply more widely to his life as a Buddhist monastic, Venerable Sujata added, "Monks should go everywhere with shaven heads, with shaven beards, and with a clean physical appearance. Then only will people be pleased about monks. Then only will people listen to monks with accompanying feelings of trust." Dhammadassi also used our discussion of correct *paritta*

performance to discuss with me, more generally, how monastics should behave and work toward attracting the hearts of the laity: "The monk should be qualified to be worshipped by the donors. Monks should have restraint in order to be worshipped by the donors. He should treat all people equally, without making any distinctions based on caste and relations. All donors should be treated equally. The monk should help all people in the village without being concerned that it is night or day when they are suffering from illness and other things. The donors expect that the monks should develop the temple and live in a good manner as a monk."

33. In one interview I had with him in 2004, he explained: "a temple means the place where monks can provide solutions to all of the peoples' problems. They should address their problems and provide solutions. If there is a problem in the village, the monk should be able to resolve it. . . . The temple should have the strength to develop the villagers. At the same time, the monks should please the people."

5 Temple Building as Social Service

1. The temple in Batuambe was actually opened in May 1998; however, until 2000, the temple was only run on a temporary basis.

2. Although Narada had a plan, in 2006, to take over two more temples located near the border between the districts of Anurādhapura and Trincomalee, the tensions there as a result of the conflict as well as the difficulties that temples and monastics living there often face impeded the take over of those temples. The difficulties that monastics living in border regions face is described in Hēmakumāra's (1999) article "Kusagini Vaḷ̥andana Hamuduruvaru" [Monks who eat hunger].

3. A number of Venerable Narada's students have disrobed over the years. Currently, he has 129 students residing at Polgoda Vihara and its fourteen branch temples.

4. The ordination registry at the temple shows that only approximately 70 percent of the monastics living at Polgoda Vihara in 2004 were from the North-Central Province.

5. While there are no statistics that would show us whether the number of monastics living in various villages in the North-Central Province (such as around Anurādhapura) are decreasing or increasing, it is worth pointing out that according to the Buddhist Information Inspection Committee, there was a dearth of monastics in the North-Central Province (along with Uva and Eastern Provinces) as far back as 1956. In their report, for instance, the committee states that for people living around reservoir areas in Anurādhapura, Pollonnaruva, and Ampāra, "it is very difficult to find a monk to offer, at least, matakavastra at a funeral. They are unable to get a monk to perform funeral sermons and death anniversary alms-givings" (*Bauddha Toraturu Parikṣaka Sabhāve Vārtāva* 1956:105).

6. I was the one who gave Narada the 400:1 ratio. I arrived at that figure by roughly dividing 30,000 monks (a figure given by the Ministry of Buddhist Affairs) by the total Sinhala Buddhist population (approximately 13,000,000).

7. According to the census taken in 2001 (*Census of Population and Housing, 2001, Sri Lanka. District Report. Anurādhapura*, 2004), the clergy population of Galenbidunuväva, the division where Kumbukväva is located is 102. With the Sinhala population of the same division at 39,306, the monk to lay Buddhist ratio is approximately 385:1.

8. During one conversation I had with Venerable Narada in 1999 (Samuels 2003:116ff.), he described the following scenario:

> In Harispattuwa, I received letters from monks who were organizing a protest of the building of a new church. Later I met that group of monks and the one who sent me the letter. I realized, though, that we cannot blame the Christians for coming into the villages and started their activities. The fault should be placed on the monks. I found out that from the temple where the complaints were sent, no social service was being provided by the monks. The monks have enough money and a good life. They are not concerned about the devotees' religious requirements. As a result, the devotees might have felt fed up with the temple. The only option for them was to go to the next temple and ask them to fulfill their [i.e., laity's] religious needs. If they go to the next temple to invite monks for, say, a *paṅsukula*, the monks in that temple will be blamed by the monks in the first temple who are not providing the social service to begin with. What would happen to the people then? They will be in trouble as they have no other solutions after the monks in the second temple refuse. So, if the people need monks for a funeral and the monks in the first temple do not come and the monks in the second temple do not come out of a fear of being rebuked by the monks in the first temple, what can the laity do? They would go to the church. If people have nowhere to go, they will look to other possibilities such as the church.

9. The anticonversion bill titled "Prohibition of Forcible Conversion of Religion" was published by Venerable Omalpe Sobhita in 2004 and was discussed at length in numerous editorials in Sri Lanka's English and Sinhala newspapers since that time (see, for example, Perera 1999; S. Abeywickrama 2001; Bastians 2004; Abayadīra 2004; Jinapriya 2004a, 2004b; and Senanayake 2004). For a more general discussion of the concept of decline within Buddhism, see Jan Nattier's (1991) excellent book *Once Upon a Future Time: Studies in a Buddhist Prophecy of Decline*.

10. A number of lay Buddhists belonging to Sri Lanka's service castes have discussed with me the problems they sometimes face getting monks from the high-caste Siyam Nikāya to perform rituals for them (see Samuels 2007a). Also, a number of lay Buddhists who are less financially secure have complained on several occasions that the demands of certain monks (e.g., payment, private transportation, and choice food) have made all-night protection rituals as well as larger alms-giving rituals too costly for them.

11. The temples in Ambana and Kumbukväva were taken over by Narada in 2003 and 2004 respectively. While both temples were established much earlier, recent problems with the temples' administration left each group of patrons with little choice but to seek alternatives.

12. Mrs. Perera was working as a house maid in the Middle East at the time of her father's death.

13. The term *ū* is a form of the third-person pronoun used, primarily, to refer to animals and people such as thugs. Perera's use of the pronoun to differentiate Narada's students from those monastics previously brought to Ambana is quite telling.

14. *Kassipu* is illegally produced alcohol. Besides being quite inexpensive, it is known for causing a variety of health problems and even death.

15. *Ōka*, which literally means "that one," is very ill suited for speaking about monastics. More respectively, laypeople would refer to "that monk" as *ē hāmuduruwo*, literally, "that reverend" or "that lord."

16. The bomb blast at the Daḷada Māligāva took place on January 25, 1998.

17. I have suggested elsewhere (2008) that making merit is not just predicated on finding a properly ordained monk but also on an emotional dimension in which the donor feels pleased and happy prior to, during, and following a donative act.

18. According to Sumedha, who was Ratnasiri's preceptor *(upajjhāya)*, Ratnasiri preferred a more solitary, forest-like existence to living in a village temple and focusing on studying, ritual performance, and social service. Although Sumedha attributed Ratnasiri's preference to the late age (twenty-four) at which he became a monk—echoing a commentarial view that people who ordain late in life are not fit for studying (DhpA p. 8)—it could very well be that Ratnasiri's preference for the forest was based upon his recognition of his own shyness.

19. Holding auctions on temple grounds is not an uncommon way to raise money for a temple. Usually, people donate various goods to the temple for the auction. Those goods are then auctioned off, with all of the proceeds directly benefiting the temple itself.

20. The Kumbukväva temple is not that far from Huruluväva and Madavala, but the poor roads in the area made our journey there quite long and arduous. Although the village is served by government run bus service, the service is very infrequent.

21. That residence hall was expanded to house fifteen monastics in 2009.

22. This *pirivena* was one of many established by Saranandа. With the state of today's roads, it would probably take four to five hours to drive from Ganegoda to Kumbukväva.

23. Although Buddhism has been often associated with the Sinhalese, there have been, throughout Sri Lanka's history, Tamil Buddhists. Some Tamil Buddhists have also gone on to become monks and run their own Buddhist temples.

24. Although there are a number of Siyam Nikāya temples around the area (thirty-two according to Sumedha), there are only two temples/*pirivenas* with monastics from the Rāmañña Nikāya. According to Sumedha, there are no Amarapura Nikāya temples in the area.

25. This conception of the Rāmañña Nikāya as being open to members from all castes is somewhat problematic. Gananath Obeyesekere (1968:35), Richard Gombrich (1998:

chap. 8), and Ananda Abeysekara (2002:177) have found that caste biases also exist within the Rāmañña Nikāya, as they do within the other Buddhist fraternities.

26. There are some recent exceptions to this rule. For instance, the idea of caste-based ordination has been challenged both by members of the Siyam Nikāya (see, for instance, Abeysekara 2002:174–200) and by laypeople who, like R. Amaravaṇśa Baṇdhāra (2005), have expressed the need for eradicating all caste-restricted ordinations and caste-based fraternities.

27. I examined the relationship between caste affiliation and temple patronage more recently in an article in *Modern Asian Studies* (Samuels 2007).

28. Sumedha's reference to environmental factors pertains to the area's dry, hot climate.

29. *Bahu Jana Hitāya*—the historical narrative on Sarananda's life—did not mention Kumbukväva by name; however, it does recount that Sarananda built a number of temples in twelve separate districts, including Anurādhapura (Senadhira 2000:170).

30. This idea, particularly as it relates to the low-caste Salāgamas in the south of Sri Lanka, has been discussed by scholars such as John Rogers (2004:55), A. P. Kannangara (1993:112f.), and Michael Roberts (1982). The view of the British as being anti-caste has also been challenged in John Rogers' (1990; 1993; 2004) and Nicholas Dirks' (2006) important studies.

31. In fact, it was during the reign of King Rājādhi Rājasiṃha when the Siyam Nikāya became restricted to Goyigama caste members.

32. See Samuels (2007a). One dimension of disregarding the needs and desires of low caste members—even the desire for making merit—concerns the important activity of alms-giving. Speaking about how some Siyam Nikāya monastics refuse to eat the alms food given to them by low-caste members, a monk, describing his experiences living in a Siyam Nikāya temple approximately fifteen kilometers from Kumbukväva, said,

> I was ordained as a monk in the Siyam Nikāya. [From that experience] I came to know that some monks refuse to take meals from low-caste people.... When it is from a low caste, some monks living in the temple refused to eat the *dāna* from them. Those are the kinds of things that took place there. They refused to associate or to chat with those kind of people.... [The monks] just answered the laypeople's questions and went back to what they were doing. They only spoke to certain groups of people. They even made tea for them. There are monks who act like that.

This preference for not eating with or taking food from members of the lower castes is also commented upon by Robert Knox (1911:105), who in discussing the restrictions placed upon the Radaḷa—the highest subcaste of the Goyigama—writes that the Radaḷa "abhor to eat or drink, or intermarry with any of Inferior Quality to themselves." The relationship between attitudes toward caste and food is, not surprisingly, something that is mentioned in other studies of Sri Lankan monasticism. For instance, Michael Carrithers's anthropological study of the forest movement (1983; 1979a), particularly the ascetic or *tāpasa* movement that began in the early twentieth century and grew in popularity in the 1950s, hints at the role that caste may play in giving alms. He notes, for example, that the majority of supporters of the *tāpasa* movement were poor people, particularly from low castes. He also remarks how low-caste members "were often poorly and disdainfully served by the village monk." It was out of this situation, Carrithers suggests, that the ascetics became a favorite of low-caste groups: "Tāpasa Himi probably followed the pattern of that for other tāpasayō and monks. . . . : though they receive alms from those of all castes, they are particular favourites with low-caste groups because they do not discriminate between donors" (1979a:306; see also Kemper 1978:232, n. 19).

33. According to the monastic disciplinary code, temples and their property were not to be treated as private property. In effect, they were *saṅghika*, that is, belonged to the whole monastic community. Although some monastics acted in the role of temple caretaker, all property, ideally at least, remained the property of the community with the Buddha at its head (see, for instance, *Cullavagga* II.169, as well as *Pācittiya* rules 82 [for monks] and 160 [for nuns] of the *bhikkhu* and *bhikkhunī Pāṭimokkha*, which forbid the diversion of temples and temple property to an individual).

When we turn to Sri Lanka, however, even though it is quite true that according to the Buddhist Temporalities Ordinance of 1931 (Section 20) all monastic property (temples and temple property) should be vested to a trustee, Section 4 of the same Temporalities Ordinance allows the chief monk or *vihārādhipati* of a temple to appoint himself as the trustee (see H. W. Tambiah, 1962). As Phadnis (1976:98) has noted and Hans-Dieter Evers has illustrated, with chief monks taking control of their temple and temple property arose the desire to keep temple property in the hands of certain families by restricting pupillary succession to a chief monk's relatives (most commonly their nephew). Evidence from monastic injunctions or *katikāvata* points to traces this phenomenon to as far back as the Daṃbadeṇi period (Ratnapala 1971:147).

34. The term *gatiguṇa* refers to the quality or virtue *(guṇa)* of one's manner or customs *(gati)*. Used in this manner, the term refers more generally to one's quality of being.

35. The term *piṭin apu* implies no feelings of familiarity or closeness; perhaps a better English term would be "foreigners."

36. There are, in general, three families responsible for bringing alms in the morning, and three for the midday meal. According to the temple's register, for fifteen days a month, *dāna* comes from families living in Kumbukväva; for fifteen days, from families living in other villages.

37. Since Hanifan's groundbreaking article, other social scientists have begun examining the idea of social capital, which, for many, is based on the "stock of active connections among people: the trust, mutual understanding, and shared values and behaviors that bind the members of human networks and communities and make cooperative action possible" (Cohen and Prusak 2001:4; see also Bourdieu 1986:248). Although there are certainly many tangible and intangible benefits associated with social capital—increased tolerance, improved character traits, facilitating a flow of information (see Putnam 2000)—well-being is regarded by many as being its key outcome (Helliwell 2004).

38. As I noted at the beginning of this chapter, the plan to establish these two temples was interrupted as a result of the conflict at the time.

39. The highlight of the ceremony is burying a foundation stone in the ground. That is then usually followed by speeches given by the head of the temple's donor's association, monastic leaders, and, if possible, local and national politicians.

40. Since the development of close ties between Narada and the Kumbukväva temple, seven more boys have made their way to Polgoda Vihara from Kumbukväva and become novices.

41. I had seen Suvata asserting his own opinions and ways of being with other, more senior, monastics at Polgoda Vihara several times. When I began discussing what I observed with other monks (including Narada) and laypeople, I came to understand that while older, more senior, monks are regarded very highly in Sri Lanka, monastics who choose to ordain at a late age are not. It is commonly believed that such monks are too set in their own ways to be properly trained—somewhat analogous to the expression "You cannot teach an old dog new tricks." These types of monks are sometimes referred to as a shard of earthenware (*vaḷanda kaḍa vāgē*). As one Sri Lankan head monk from the United States explained to me, "Just as a piece of earthenware belongs neither to the category of pots nor to the clay in the earth, so too do such types of monastics belong neither to the category of 'monastic' nor to the category of 'layman.'"

This particular view regarding those who ordain late in life is also be found in certain Pali canonical texts (where the Buddha is purported to have observed that the life of renunciation is difficult for those who have already enjoyed the comforts of worldly life [as in the *Laṭukikopamasutta,* M.1.447–456]) and commentarial texts (where such people are depicted as being ill suited for the path of study [DhpA p. 8; see also AA p. 22]). Such views challenge Gananath Obeyesekere's (2001) belief that the decision to become a monastic should be reserved until later in life (see also S. Karunaratna 2001).

42. Sumana, on the other hand, was much more willing to listen to and even heed his teacher's wishes, not to mention the wishes of the Ambana patrons. He also had and exhibited respect for his teacher; he spoke about his desire to "protect Narada's respect" by attracting the hearts of the temple's patrons.

43. This is discussed, for instance, in Gunawardana (1979); see also Bechert (1970:767f.; 1966:1:224ff.).

References

Abayadīra, Manoj. January 11, 2004. "Kavadā Pāsadda Apa Dinisurāṇō? [When will the sun dawn on us?]." *Divayina*, Kalina.

Abeysekara, A. 2002. *Colors of the Robe: Religion, Identity, and Difference*. Studies in Comparative Religion Series. Columbia: University of South Carolina Press.

Abeysinghe, S. 1983. *Population Profile of the Anuradhapura District*. Colombo, Sri Lanka: Department of Government Printing.

Abeywickrama, S. May 4, 2001. "Safeguarding Buddhism." *The Island*, Opinion, 18.

Abu-Lughod, L., and C. A. Lutz. 1990. "Introduction: Emotion, Discourse, and the Politics of Everyday Life." In *Language and the Politics of Emotion*, eds. Catherine A. Lutz and Lila Abu-Lughod, 1–23. Cambridge: Cambridge University Press.

Adikari, A. 1991. *Śrī Laṅkāvē Sambhāvya Adhyāpanaya Hā Maha Sangana* [Classical education and the great *sangha* of Sri Lanka]. Colombo, Sri Lanka: S. Godage.

Agganyani (Christa Bentenrieder). 2002. "The Prospects for the Growth of Buddhism in Germany and other Western Countries." Keynote address at Savsiripaye, Colombo to commemorate the 50th Anniversary of the founding of the German Dharmaduta Society (1952–2002).

Ananda, Girambe. March 20, 1992. "Kula Daruvan 2300 Pävidi Karavīma Budu Sasunē Cira Jīvanaya Sandahāyi [The ordination of 2300 boys is for the long life of the buddha sasana]." *Dinamina*.

Anuruddha, Räkmalē. August 4, 2005. "Vartamāna Bhikṣuva Hā Nāyakatvaya [The present monk and leadership]." *Budusaraṇa*.

Appadurai, A. 1990. "Topographies of the Self: Praise and Emotion in Hindu India." In *Language and the Politics of Emotion*, eds. C. Lutz and Lila Abu-Lughod, 92–112. Cambridge: Cambridge University Press.

Arasaratnam, S. Autumn 1972. "The Ceylon Insurrection of April 1971: Some Causes and Consequences." *Pacific Affairs* 45 (3): 356–371.

Aronson, H. B. 1986. *Love and Sympathy in Theravada Buddhism*. Delhi: Motilal Banarsidass.

Arseculeratne, S. N. 1991. *Sinhalese Immigrants in Malaysia and Singapore 1860–1990: History through Recollection*. Colombo, Sri Lanka: K. V. G. De Silva and Sons.

Austin, J. L. 1975. *How to Do Things with Words*. 2nd ed., eds. J. O. Urmson and Marina Sbisa. Cambridge, MA: Harvard University Press.

Baṇdhāra, Amaravaṇśa R. February 20, 2005. "Śāsana Cirasthtiya Sandahā Äti Kaḷa Katikāvat [The kativatas made for the sasana's long existence]" *Divayina*, Supplemental section.

Bastians, Dharisha. August 1, 2004. "Conversion Battle Reaches a Climax." *The Sunday Leader*, Issues section.

Bauddha Śāsana Amātyāṅśaya Kāryabharya Piḷibhanda Sammantraṇa Vārtāva [Conference report on the activities of the buddha sasana ministry]. 1990. Colombo, Sri Lanka: Government Printers.

Bauddha Toraturu Parikṣaka Sabhāve Vārtāva [Report of the Buddhist information inspection committee]. 1956. Balangoda, Sri Lanka: Dharma Vijaya Press.

Buddha Śāsana Komiṣan Vārtāva [The report of the Buddha Sasana commission]. 1959. Colombo, Sri Lanka: Government of Ceylon, Sessional Papers XVIII.

Bechert, H. 1970. "Theravada Buddhist Sangha: Some General Observations on Historical and Political Factors in Its Development." *Journal of Asian Studies* 29 (4): 761–778.

———. 1966. *Buddhismus, Staat Und Gesellschaft in Den Landern Des Theravada-Buddhismus*. Berlin: Alfred Metzner Verlag.

Bell, C. 1997. *Ritual: Perspectives and Dimensions*. New York: Oxford University Press.

———. 1992. *Ritual Theory, Ritual Practice*. New York: Oxford University Press.

Berkwitz, S.C. 2003. "History and Gratitude in Theravada Buddhism." *Journal of the American Academy of Religion* 71 (3): 579–604.

———. 2001. "Emotions and Ethics in Buddhist History: The Sinhala Thupavamsa and the Work of Virtue." *Religion* 31 (2): 155–173.

The Betrayal of Buddhism: An Abridged Version of the Report of the Buddhist Committee of Inquiry. 1956. Balangoda, Sri Lanka: Dharmavijaya Press.

Bhikkhu Bodhi. July 2000. *Promoting Buddhism in Europe*. Buddha Sasana (available at http://www.buddhanet.net/budsas/ebud/ebdha194.htm).

Blackburn, A.M. 2003. "Localizing Lineage: Importing Higher Ordination in Theravadin South and Southeast Asia." In *Constituting Communities: Theravada Buddhism and the Religious Cultures of South and Southeast Asia*, eds. John Clifford Holt, Jacob N. Kinnard, and Jonathan S. Walters, 131–150. Albany: State University of New York Press.

———. 2001. *Buddhist Learning and Textual Practice in Eighteenth-Century Lankan Monastic Culture*. Princeton, NJ: Princeton University Press.

———. 1999a. "Looking for the *Vinaya:* Monastic Discipline in the Practical Canons of the Theravāda." *Journal of the International Association of Buddhist Studies* 22 (2): 281–311.

———. 1999b. "Magic in the Monastery: Textual Practice and Monastic Identity in Sri Lanka." *History of Religions* 38 (4): 354–372.

Bond, G.D. 1988. *The Buddhist Revival in Sri Lanka: Religious Tradition, Reinterpretation and Response*. Columbia: University of South Carolina Press.

Bourdieu, P. 1986. "Forms of Capital." In *Handbook of Theory and Research for the Sociology of Education*, ed. J.G. Richardson, 241–258. New York: Greenwood Press.

———. 1977. *Outline of a Theory of Practice*, trans. Richard Nice. Cambridge: Cambridge University Press.

Brown, S. 2001. *The Journey of One Buddhist Nun: Even against the Wind*. Albany: State University of New York Press.

Bunnag, J. 1973. *Buddhist Monk, Buddhist Layman: A Study of Urban Monastic Organization in Central Thailand*. Cambridge: Cambridge University Press.

———. 1970. "Monk-Layman Interaction in Central Thai Society." In *Memoriam Phya Anuman Rajadhon: Contributions in Memory of the Late President of the Siam Society*, 87–106. Bangkok: Siam Society.

Cabezón, J.I. 1995. "Buddhist Studies as a Discipline and the Role of Theory." *Journal of the International Association of Buddhist Studies* 18:213–268.

Candavimala, R. 1998. *Sāsanāvataraṇaya* [The raft of the teachings]. Colombo, Sri Lanka: Anula Mudranalayayehi Mudrapitayi, 1966. Reprint. Polgas Ovita, Sri Lanka: Sikuru Prakashakayo.

Carrithers, M. 1990. "Jainism and Buddhism as Enduring Historical Streams." *Journal of the Anthropological Society of Oxford* 21 (2): 141–163.

———. 1983. *The Forest Monks of Sri Lanka: An Anthropological and Historical Study*. Calcutta: Oxford University Press.

———. 1979. "The Modern Ascetic of Lanka and the Pattern of Change in Buddhism." *Man: The Journal of the Royal Anthropological Institute* 14 (2): 294–310.

Carter, C. 1996. *Siṁhala Iṅgrīsi Akārādiya*. Colombo, Sri Lanka: The Ceylon Observer Printing Works, 1924. Reprint. New Delhi: Asian Educational Services.

Carter, J.R. 1993. *On Understanding Buddhists: Essays on the Theravada Tradition in Sri Lanka*. Albany: State University of New York Press.

Census of Population and Housing, 2001. Population and Housing Data: Results From Sample Tabulations, Matale District. 2003. Colombo, Sri Lanka: Department of Census and Statistics.

Census of Population and Housing, 2001, Sri Lanka. District Report. Anuradhapura. 2004. Colombo, Sri Lanka: Department of Census and Statistics.

Chakravarti, U. 1987. *The Social Dimension of Early Buddhism*. Oxford: Oxford University Press.

Cohen, D., and L. Prusak. 2001. *In Good Company: How Social Capital Makes Organizations Work*. Boston: Harvard Business School Press.

Collier, J. 1957. "Photography in Anthropology: A Report on Two Experiments." *American Anthropologist* 59:843–859.

Collier, J.J., and Malcolm Collier. 1986. *Visual Anthropology: Photography as a Research Method*. Albuquerque: University of New Mexico Press.

Collins, S. 1998. *Nirvana and Other Buddhist Felicities: Utopias of the Pali Imaginaire*. Cambridge: Cambridge University Press.

———. 1990. "On the Very Idea of the Pali Canon." *Journal of the Pali Text Society* 15:89–126.

Copleston, R.S. 1892. *Buddhism: Primitive and Present in Magadha and in Ceylon*. London: Longmans, Green, and Company.

Corrigan, J. 2008. "Introduction: The Study of Religion and Emotion." In *The Oxford Handbook of Religion and Emotion*, ed. John Corrigan, 3–13. Oxford: Oxford University Press.

———. 2004. "Introduction: Emotions Research and the Academic Study of Religion." In *Religion and Emotion: Approaches and Interpretations*, ed. John Corrigan, 3–32. New York: Oxford University Press.

———, Eric Crump, and John Kloos. 2000. *Emotion and Religion: A Critical Assessment and Annotated Bibliography*. Westport, CT: Greenwood Press.

Cowell, E.B., ed. 1990. *Jataka Stories*, 6 Vols., trans. R. Chalmers. New Delhi: Motilal Banarsidass.

Daniel, E.V. 1996. *Charred Lullabies: Chapters in an Anthropology of Violence*. Princeton, NJ: Princeton University Press.

Davy, J. 1821. *An Account of the Interior of Ceylon and of Its Inhabitants*. London: Longman, Hurst, Rees, Orme, and Brown.

Deheragoda, E. R. K. n.d. *Legislative Enactments of the Democratic Socialist Republic of Sri Lanka, Vol. XIV.* Colombo, Sri Lanka: Government of the Democratic Socialist Republic of Sri Lanka.

de Mel, Tara. October 12, 2006a. *Sri Lanka Report: Status of Education MDG Implementation.* Electronic document available at http://southasia.oneworld.net/article/view/127169/1/.

———. May 28, 2006b. "Enter a Kid's World with Paduma." *The Sunday Times*, Plus.

de Silva, C. R. 2006. "Buddhist Monks and Peace in Sri Lanka." In *Buddhism, Conflict and Violence in Modern Sri Lanka*, ed. Mahinda Deegalle, 202–209. London and New York: Routledge.

———. 1999. *Sri Lanka: A History.* 2nd ed. 1987. Reprint. New Delhi: Vikas Publishing House.

———. 1995. "Expulsion of the Portuguese from Sri Lanka." In *History of Sri Lanka, Volume II*, ed. K. M. de Silva, 163–181. Peradeniya, Sri Lanka: University of Peradeniya.

de Silva, L. 1981. *Paritta: A Historical and Religious Study of the Buddhist Ceremony for Peace and Prosperity in Sri Lanka.* Spolia Zeylanica, vol. 36, ed. P. H. D. H. de Silva. Colombo, Sri Lanka: Department of Government Printing.

de Silva, N. 2006. *Paduma Meets the Sunbird: Stories from Paduma's World.* Colombo, Sri Lanka: Perera Hussein Publishing House.

Dēvanārāyana, Vilpred [Wilfred]. February 13, 2000. "Piṇḍapātayā Vädīma Bhikṣuvakaṭa Avanambuvakda?" *Divayina.*

Dewaraja, L. S. 1995. "The Social and Economic Conditions in the Kandyan Kingdom in the Seventeenth and Eighteenth Centuries." In *History of Sri Lanka, Volume II*, ed. K. M. de Silva, 375–397. Peradeniya, Sri Lanka: University of Peradeniya.

———. 1988. *The Kandyan Kingdom of Sri Lanka: 1707–1782.* Colombo, Sri Lanka: Lake House Investments, LTD.

———, S. Arasaratnam, and D. A. Kotelawele. 1995. "Administrative Systems: Kandyan and Dutch." In *History of Sri Lanka, Vol. II*, ed. K. M. de Silva, 321–374. Peradeniya, Sri Lanka: University of Peradeniya.

Dhammananda, M. April 22, 2001. "Budusāsuna Rakinnaṭa Kumak Karamu da? [What should we do to protect the buddha sasana?]" *Divayina.*

Dhammatilaka, Pälavatta, ed. 1997. *Theravāda Sāmaṇera Baṇadaham Pota.* Colombo, Sri Lanka: M. D. Gunasena.

Dharmapāla, A. 1965. *Return to Righteousness: A Collection of Speeches, Essays and Letters of the Anagarika Dharmapala*, ed. Ananda Guruge. Ceylon: The Anakarika Dharmapala Birth Centenary Committee.

Dirks, N. B. 2006. *Castes of Mind: Colonialism and the Making of Modern India.* 3rd ed. Princeton, NJ: Princeton University Press, 2001. Reprint. Delhi: Permanent Black.

Eelens, F., and J. D. Speckmann. 1990. "Recruitment of Labor Migrants for the Middle East: The Sri Lankan Case." *International Migration Review* 24 (2): 297–322.

Ekanayake, S. B. May 11, 2005. "Disparities in Education and Challenges." *The Island.*

Evers, H. 1972. *Monks, Priests and Peasants: A Study of Buddhism and Social Structure in Central Ceylon.* Leiden: E. J. Brill.

———. December 1967. "Kinship and Property Rights in a Buddhist Monastery in Central Ceylon." *American Anthropologist* 69 (6): 703–710.

Falk, M.M. 1980. "Vocations: Identity and Commitment." *Review for Religious* 39 (3): 357–366.

Finke, R. 1997. "An Orderly Return to Tradition: Explaining the Recruitment of Members into Catholic Religious Orders." *Journal for the Scientific Study of Religion* 36 (2): 218–230.

Freiberger, O. 2004. "The Buddhist Canon and the Canon of Buddhist Studies." *Journal of the International Association of Buddhist Studies* 27 (2): 261–284.

Gade, A. 2004. *Perfection Makes Practice: Learning, Emotion, and the Recited Qur'an in Indonesia*. Honolulu: University of Hawai'i Press.

Gaede, S. 1976. "A Causal Model of Belief-Orthodoxy: Proposal and Empirical Test." *Sociological Analysis* 37:205–217.

Geiger, W., trans. 1973. *Cūḷavaṃsa: Being a More Recent Part of the Mahāvaṃsa*. London: The Pali Text Society.

———. 1964. *The Mahāvaṃsa or the Great Chronicle of Ceylon*. London: Luzac and Company.

Gethin, R. 1998. *The Foundations of Buddhism*. Oxford: Oxford University Press.

Gilbert, Elizabeth. 2007. *Eat, Pray, Love: One Woman's Search for Everything across Italy, India, and Indonesia*. New York: Penguin.

Gokhale, B.G. 1965. "The Early Buddhist Elite." *Journal of Indian History* 42 (2): 391–402.

Gombrich, R. 2006. *Theravada Buddhism: A Social History from Ancient Benares to Modern Colombo*. 2nd ed. Oxon, UK: Routledge Press.

———. 1998. *Precept and Practice: Traditional Buddhism in the Rural Highlands of Ceylon*. Oxford: Oxford University Press, 1971. Reprint. Delhi: Motilal Banarsidass Publishers.

———. 1984. "Temporary Ordination in Sri Lanka." *Journal of the International Association of Buddhist Studies* 7 (2): 41–65.

———. 1981. "A New Theravadin Liturgy." *Journal of the Pali Text Society* 9:47–73.

———. 1980. "The Significance of Former Buddhas in the Theravadin Tradition." In *Buddhist Studies in Honour of Walpola Rahula*, ed. Somaratna Balasooriya et al., 62–72. London: Gordon Fraser Gallery Ltd.

———. 1971. "'Merit Transference' in Sinhalese Buddhism: A Case Study of the Interaction between Doctrine and Practice." *History of Religions* 11 (2): 203–219.

———, and G. Obeyesekere. 1988. *Buddhism Transformed: Religious Change in Sri Lanka*. Princeton, NJ: Princeton University Press.

Gosling, D. 1980. "New Directions in Thai Buddhism." *Modern Asian Studies* 14 (3): 411–439.

Gunaratne, R.H. February 3, 2002. "From Layman to Monk in Two Weeks." *Sunday Times*, Plus section.

Gunasekara, A. 1978. "Rajakariya or the Duty to the King in the Kandyan Kingdom of Sri Lanka." In *The Concept of Duty in South Asia*, eds. Wendy Doniger O'Flaherty and J. Duncan M. Derrett, 119–143. London: School of Oriental and African Studies.

Gunasekera, T. 1994. *Hierarchy and Egalitarianism: Caste, Class and Power in Sinhalese Peasant Society*. London School of Economics Monographs on Social Anthropology, vol. 65. London and Atlantic Highlands, NJ: The Anthlone Press.

Gunatilleke, G. 1987. *Children in Sri Lanka*. Colombo, Sri Lanka: Marga Institute.
Gunawardana, R.A.L.H. 1979. *Robe and Plough: Monasticism and Economic Interest in Early Medieval Sri Lanka*. Tucson: The University of Arizona Press.
Gunawardena, D.C.R., P.H. Wickremasinghe, and D.E. Wijewardena. 1963. *Report of the Universities Commission 1962*. Sessional Paper XVI—1963. Colombo, Sri Lanka: Government Press.
Hallisey, C. 1995. "Roads Taken and Not Taken in the Study of Theravada Buddhism." In *Curators of the Buddha: The Study of Buddhism Under Colonialism*, ed. Donald Lopez Jr., 31–61. Chicago: University of Chicago Press.
———. 1990. "Apropos the Pali Vinaya As a Historical Document: A Reply to Gregory Schopen." *Journal of the Pali Text Society* 15:197–208.
———. 1988. Devotion in the Buddhist Literature of Medieval Sri Lanka. PhD diss., University of Chicago.
Hanifan, L.J. September 1916. "The Rural School Community Center." *Annals of the American Academy of Political and Social Science* 67:130–138.
Hardman, C.E. 2000. *Other Worlds: Notions of Self and Emotion Among the Lohorung Rai*. Oxford and New York: Berg.
Harvey, P. 1990. *An Introduction to Buddhism: Teachings, History, and Practices*. Cambridge: Cambridge University Press.
Hayashi, Y. 2003. *Practical Buddhism Among the Thai-Lao: Religion in the Making of a Region*. Kyoto and Melbourne: Kyoto University Press and Trans Pacific Press.
Heim, M. 2008. "Buddhism." In *The Oxford Handbook of Religion and Emotion*, ed. John Corrigan, 17–34. Oxford: Oxford University Press.
———. 2003. "The Aesthetics of Excess." *Journal of the American Academy of Religion* 71 (3): 531–554.
Helliwell, J.F., and Robert D. Putnam. September 2004. "The Social Context of Well-Being." *Philosophical Transactions of the Royal Society of London, Series B* 359 (1449): 1435–1446.
Hēmakumāra, Sisira. July 25, 1999. "Kusagini Vaḷandana Hāmuduruwaru [Monks who eat hunger]." *Lakbima*.
Hennayake, Shantha K. May 18, 2004. "Sri Lankan politics, 2004 election and JHU." *The Island*, Features.
Hettiaracci, D., ed. 1997. *Tripiṭaka Dharmaya, Pasvana Vasara* [Tripitaka dharmaya, fifth year]. Colombo, Sri Lanka: Educational Publication Department.
———. 1994a. *Tripiṭaka Dharmaya, Devana Vasara* [Tripitaka dharmaya, second year]. Colombo, Sri Lanka: Educational Publication Department.
———. 1994b. *Tripiṭaka Dharmaya, Paḷamuvana Vasara* [Tripitaka dharmaya, first year]. Colombo, Sri Lanka: Educational Publication Department.
———. 1994c. *Tripiṭaka Dharmaya, Sivvana Vasara* [Tripitaka dharmaya, fourth year]. Colombo, Sri Lanka: Educational Publication Department.
———. 1994d. *Tripiṭaka Dharmaya, Tevana Vasara* [Tripitaka dharmaya, third year]. Colombo, Sri Lanka: Educational Publication Department.
Holt, J.C. 1995. *Discipline: The Canonical Buddhism of the Vinayapiṭaka*. 1981. Reprint. Delhi: Motilal Banarsidass.

Hori, V. S., Richard P. Hayes, and James Mark Shields, eds. 2002. *Teaching Buddhism in the West: From the Wheel to the Web*. London: RoutledgeCurzon.

Hulugalle, H. A. J. 1975. *The Life and Times of Don Stephen Senanayake (Sri Lanka's First Prime Minister)*. Colombo, Sri Lanka: Gunasena.

Jayasuriya, J. E. 1976. *Educational Policies and Progress During British Rule in Ceylon, 1796–1948*. Colombo, Sri Lanka: Associated Educational Publishers.

Jayewardene, J. R. March 22, 1973. "D. S. Senanayake: Father of Independent Sri Lanka." *Ceylon Daily News*.

Jiggins, J. 1979. *Caste and Family in the Politics of the Sinhalese, 1947–1976*. London: Cambridge University Press.

Jinadasa, H. May 1957. "Social Service—The Achilles Heel of Buddhists." *The Buddhist: Jayanti Special:* 33–35.

Jinapriya, E. G. January 11, 2004a. "Bauddhayan Siṭina Pradēśavalaṭa Miṣanāri Madhyasthāna Ōne nā [Missionary centers are not needed in Buddhist areas]." Interview with Madovita Pannakitti. *Divayina*, Kalina.

———. January 18, 2004b. "Bhikṣun Vahansē Gamdanav Sisārā Bauddha Punarudaya Ätikaḷa Yutuyi [Monks travel to remote areas to arouse Buddhism]." Interview with Attangamane Ratanapala. *Divayina*, Kalina.

Kannangara, A. P. 1993. "The Rhetoric of Caste Status in Modern Sri Lanka." In *Society and Ideology: Essays in South Asian History*, ed. Peter Robb, 110–141. Delhi: Oxford University Press.

Karunaratna, Suvimalee. August 3, 2001. "Of Child Ordination and the Rights of Children" *Daily News*, Online Edition.

Karunaratna, W. S. 1979. "Citta." In *Encyclopaedia of Buddhism*, ed. Jotiya Dhirasekera, 169–180. Sri Lanka: Department of Government Printing.

Karunatillake, W. S. 1997. *Sinhalabhasha Vyakaranaya*. Colombo, Sri Lanka: M. D. Gunasena and Co.

———. 1979. "The Religiousness of Buddhists in Sri Lanka through Belief and Practice." In *Religiousness in Sri Lanka*, ed. John Ross Carter, 1–34. Colombo, Sri Lanka: Marga Institute.

Kearney, R. N. May 1977. "A Note on the Fate of the 1971 Insurgents in Sri Lanka." *The Journal of Asian Studies* 36 (3): 515–519.

———. September 1975. "Educational Expansion and Political Volatility in Sri Lanka: The 1971 Insurrection." *Asian Survey* 15 (9): 727–744.

———, and Janice Jiggins. 1975. "The Ceylon Insurrection of 1971." *The Journal of Commonwealth and Comparative Politics* 13 (1): 40–64.

Kemper, S. 2004. "Dharmapala's Dharmaduta and the Buddhist Ethnoscape." In *Buddhist Missionaries in the Era of Globalization*, ed. Linda Learman, 22–50. Honolulu: University of Hawai'i Press.

———. 1991. *The Presence of the Past: Chronicles, Politics, and Culture in Sinhala Life*. Ithaca, NY: Cornell University Press.

———. 1990. "Wealth and Reformation in Sinhalese Buddhist Monasticism." In *Ethics, Wealth, and Salvation: A Study in Buddhist Social Ethics*, eds. R. F. Sizemore and Donald K. Swearer, 152–169. Columbia: University of South Carolina Press.

———. 1984. "The Buddhist Monkhood, the Law, and the State in Colonial Sri Lanka." *Comparative Studies in Society and History* 26 (3): 401–427.

———. 1980. "Reform and Segmentation in Monastic Fraternities in Low Country Sri Lanka." *Journal of Asian Studies* 40 (1): 27–41.

———. 1978. "Buddhism Without Bhikkhus: The Sri Lanka Vinaya Vardena Society." In *Religion and Legitimation of Power in Sri Lanka*, ed. Bardwell L. Smith, 212–235. Chambersburg, PA: Anima Books.

———. 1973. The Social Order of the Sinhalese Buddhist Sangha. PhD diss., University of Chicago.

Keyes, C. F. 1983. "Merit-Transference in the Kammic Theory of Popular Theravada Buddhism." In *Karma: An Anthropological Inquiry*, eds. C. F. Keyes and E. V. Daniels, 261–286. Berkeley: University of California Press.

———. 1977. *The Golden Peninsula: Culture and Adaptation in Mainland Southeast Asia.* New York: Macmillan Publishing Company.

Kīrtiratna, N. H. n.d. "Mā Duṭu Anunāhimiyō [The deputy head monk was seen by me]." In in *Śrī Guṇaratana Lipi Saraṇiya* [*Sri Gunaratana: Collected papers*], ed. Teluvākandē Ñaṇānanda, 11–14. Siyambalaṅgamuvē Śrī Guṇaratana Guṇānusmaraṇa Padanama.

Knox, R. 1911. *An Historical Relation of the Island of Ceylon Together with Somewhat Concerning Severall Remarkeable Passages of My Life That Hath Hapned Since My Deliverance Out of My Captivity* [sic]. Glasgow: James MacLehose and Sons.

Kusaladhamma, V. 1994. "Aramuṇu Kondēsi Hā Pāḍamālāvē Svarupaya [Aims, terms, and the nature of the training course]." Ministry of Buddha Sasana. Unpublished letter for Samanera Training Centers.

Lave, J., and Etienne Wenger. 1991. *Situated Learning: Legitimate Peripheral Participation.* Cambridge: Cambridge University Press.

Leach, E. R. 1960. *Pul Eliya: A Village in Ceylon.* Cambridge: Cambridge University Press.

Learman, Linda, ed. 2004. *Buddhist Missionaries in the Era of Globalization.* Honolulu: University of Hawai'i Press.

Lewis, T. T. 1997. "Buddhist Communities: Historical Precedents and Ethnographic Paradigms." In *Anthropology of Religion: A Handbook*, ed. S. D. Glazier, 319–368. Westport, CT: Greenwood Press.

Lofland, J., and N. Skonovd. 1981. "Conversion Motifs." *Journal of the Scientific Study of Religion* 20:373–385.

Lopez, D. S. J. 2001. *Buddhism.* London: Penguin Books.

Lothe, E. 1986. *Mission in Theravada Buddhism.* PhD diss., Institute for the History of Religions, University of Oslo.

Lutz, C. A. 1988. *Unnatural Emotions: Everyday Sentiments on a Micronesian Atoll and Their Challenge to Western Theory.* Chicago: University of Chicago Press.

———. August 1986. "Emotion, Thought, and Estrangement: Emotion as a Cultural Category." *Cultural Anthropology* 1 (3): 287–309.

———, and Geoffrey M. White. 1986. "The Anthropology of Emotions." *Annual Review of Anthropology* 15:405–436.

Lynch, F. R. 1979. "'Occult Establishment' or 'Deviant Perspective'? The Rise and Fall of a Modern Church of Magic." *Journal for the Scientific Study of Religion* 18:281–298.

———. 1977. "Toward a Theory of Conversion and Commitment to the Occult." *American Behavioral Scientist* 20:887–907.
Lynch, O.M. 1990a. "The Mastram: Emotion and Person Among Mathura's Chaubes." In *Divine Passions: The Social Construction of Emotion in India*, ed. Owen M. Lynch, 91–115. Berkeley: University of California Press.
———. 1990b. "The Social Construction of Emotion in India." In *Divine Passions: The Social Construction of Emotion in India*, ed. Owen M. Lynch, 3–34. Berkeley: University of California Press.
Mahinda, Deegalle. 2006. *Popularizing Buddhism: Preaching as Performance in Sri Lanka*. New York: State University of New York Press.
———. 2004. "Politics of the Jathika Hela Urumaya Monks: Buddhism and Ethnicity in Contemporary Sri Lanka." *Contemporary Buddhism* 5 (2): 83–103.
———. 1995. *Baṇa*. PhD diss., University of Chicago.
Mahindu Jayanti Väda Saṭahana [Minutes of the Mahinda Jayanti work]. 1992. Colombo, Sri Lanka: Buddha Sasana Ministry.
Malalasekera, G.P. 1971. "Buddha." In *Encylopaedia of Buddhism*, ed. G.P. Malalasekera, 357–380. Colombo, Sri Lanka: Government of Ceylon.
———. 1960. *Dictionary of Pali Proper Names*. London: Luzac and Company.
Malalgoda, K. 1976. *Buddhism in Sinhalese Society 1750–1900*. Berkeley: University of California Press.
———. 1974. "Buddhism in Post-Independence Sri Lanka." *Ceylon Journal of Historical and Social Studies* n.s. 4 (1 & 2): 93–97.
Masson, J.M. 1981. *The Oceanic Feeling: The Origins of Religious Sentiment in India*. Dordrecht: D.Reidel.
Matthews, B. Winter 1988–1989. "Sinhala Cultural and Buddhist Patriotic Organizations in Contemporary Sri Lanka." *Pacific Affairs* 61 (4): 620–632.
McDaniel, J. 2008. "Hinduism." In *The Oxford Handbook of Religion and Emotion*, ed. John Corrigan, 51–72. Oxford: Oxford University Press.
———. 1995. "Emotion in Bengali Religious Thought: Substance and Metaphor." In *Emotions in Asian Thought: A Dialogue in Comparative Philosophy*, eds. Joel Marks and Roger T. Ames, 39–64. Albany: State University of New York Press.
Medhālaṅkārā, Vēväldeṇiyē. 2003. *Śrī Laṅkā Rāmañña Mahā Nikāya Katikāvata* [Monastic rules for the great Rāmañña fraternity of Sri Lanka]. Colombo, Sri Lanka: Government Press.
Mirando, A.H. 1985. *Buddhism in Sri Lanka in the 17th and 18th Centuries with Special Reference to Sinhalese Literary Sources*. Sri Lanka: Tisara Prakasakayo.
Mūlika Piriven Avasāna Vibhāgaya Hā Vibhāga Kārya Paṭipāṭiya [The final exam and examination procedures of Mulika *Pirivena*]. 1996. Colombo, Sri Lanka: The Pirivena Educational Unit of the Ministry of Education and Higher Education.
Ñaṇānanda, Teluvākandē. n.d. "Nā Himiyan Mama Duṭimi." In *Śrī guṇaratana Lipi Saraṇiya* [*Sri Gunaratana: Collected papers*], ed. Teluvākandē Ñaṇānanda, 1–4. Siyambalaṅgamuvē Śrī Guṇaratana Guṇānusmaraṇa Padanama.
Nārada, D. 1990. *Uḍunuvara Śrī Sārānanda Mahā Svamipādayāṇan Vahansē: Saṅkṣita Jīvana Caritaya* [*A brief biography of Udanuvara Sri Sarananda, the great honorable reverend*]. Colombo, Sri Lanka: Department of Cultural Affairs.

Nattier, J. 2004. "Buddha(s)." In *Encyclopedia of Buddhism*, ed. Robert E. Buswell, 71–74. New York: Macmillan Reference.
———. 1991. *Once Upon a Future Time: Studies in a Buddhist Prophecy of Decline*. Berkeley: Asian Humanities Press.
Nussbaum, M.C. 2001. *Upheavals of Thought: The Intelligence of Emotions*. Cambridge: Cambridge University Press.
———. 1990. *Love's Knowledge: Essays on Philosophy and Literature*. New York: Oxford University.
Obeyesekere, G. July 8, 2001. "Child Monks: Good or Bad?" *The Sunday Times*, Plus section.
———. 1991. "Buddhism and Conscience: An Exploratory Essay." *Daedalus* 102 (3): 219–239.
———. 1990. "Culturally Constituted Defenses and the Theory of Collective Motivation." In *Personality and the Cultural Construction of Society: Papers in Honor of Melford E. Spiro*, eds. David K. Jordan and Marc J. Swartz, 81–97. Tuscaloosa and London: University of Alabama Press.
———. 1981. *Medusa's Hair: An Essay on Personal Symbols and Religious Experience*. Chicago: Chicago University Press.
———. 1974. "Some Comments on the Social Backgrounds of the April 1971 Insurgency in Sri Lanka (Ceylon)." *The Journal of Asian Studies* 33 (3): 367–384.
———. 1968. "Theodicy, Sin and Salvation in a Sociology of Buddhism." In *Dialectic in Practical Religion*, ed. E.R. Leach, 7–40. Cambridge: Cambridge University Press.
O'Hyun Park. 2002. "Moving Beyond the 'Ism': A Critique of the Objective Approach to Teaching Buddhism." In *Teaching Buddhism in the West: From the Wheel to the Web*, eds. V.S. Hori, Richard P. Hayes, and James Mark Shields, 57–70. London: RoutledgeCurzon.
Olcott, H.S. 1928. *Old Diary Leaves: The Only Authentic History of the Theosophical Society*, Vol. II (1900). 2nd ed. Madras: Theosophical Publishing House.
Pannapadipo, P.P. 2001. *Little Angels*. Bangkok: Post Publishing.
Parish, S.M. 2004. "The Sacred Mind: Newar Cultural Representations of Mental Life and the Production of Moral Consciousness." In *Religion and Emotion: Approaches and Interpretations*, ed. John Corrigan, 149–183. Oxford: Oxford University Press.
———. 1994. *Moral Knowing in a Hindu Sacred City: An Exploration of Mind, Emotion, and Self*. New York: Columbia University Press.
Perera, Indu. January 3, 1999. "Bauddha Bhikṣunṭa Dōraval Vahanavā! Bauddhayan Sallivalaṭa Ganna Idha Denavā! [Doors are closed for Buddhist monks! Buddhists are being sold for money!]" Interview with Gangodavila Soma. *Lakbima*.
Perera, L.P.N. 1979. "The Significance of the Sangha for the Laity." In *Religiousness in Sri Lanka*, ed. John Ross Carter, 79–100. Colombo, Sri Lanka: Marga Institute.
Phadnis, U. 1976. *Religion and Politics in Sri Lanka*. London: C. Hurst & Co.
"PM Warns of Conspiracy against Buddhists." 2001. *The Island*.
Politicus. March 1972. "The April Revolt in Ceylon." *Asian Survey* 123 (3): 259–274.
Premasiri, P.D. 1990. "Emotion." In *Encyclopaedia of Buddhism*, ed. W.G. Weeraratne, 57–64. Colombo, Sri Lanka: Government of Sri Lanka.
"Profiles: The Prime Minister." January 26, 1950. *The Ceylon Fortnightly Review*.

Prothero, S. 1996. *The White Buddhist: The Asian Odyssey of Henry Steel Olcott*. Bloomington: Indiana University Press.

———. Summer 1995. "Henry Steel Olcott and "Protestant Buddhism." *Journal of the American Academy of Religion* 63 (2): 281–302.

Putnam, R. D. 2000. *Bowling Alone: The Collapse and Revival of American Community*. New York: Simon and Schuster.

Rahula, W. 1993. *History of Buddhism in Ceylon: The Anuradhapura Period (3rd Century BC–10th Century AC)*. 1965. Reprint. Dehiwala, Sri Lanka: The Buddhist Cultural Centre.

———. 1974. *The Heritage of the Bhikkhu: A Short History of the Bhikkhu in Educational, Cultural, Social, and Political Life*. New York: Grove Press.

———. 1967. *What the Buddha Taught*. 2nd ed. 1959. Reprint. London: Gordon Fraser.

———. 1946. *Bhikṣuvagē Urumaya*. Colombo, Sri Lanka: Svastika Press.

Rambo, L. R. 1993. *Understanding Religious Conversion*. New Haven, CT: Yale University Press.

———. 1992. "The Psychology of Conversion." In *Handbook of Religious Conversion*, eds. H. N. Malony, and Samuel Southard, 159–177. Birmingham: Religious Education Press.

Rappaport, R. 1979. *Ecology, Meaning, and Religion*. Richmond: North Atlantic Books.

Ratanasara, H. 1979. "'Reaching Out' as an Expression of 'Going Forth'." In *Religiousness in Sri Lanka*, ed. John Ross-Carter, 101–112. Colombo, Sri Lanka: Marga Institute.

———. 1974. "Calling for a Positive Role for Bhikkhus in National Leadership." In *Religion and Development in Asian Societies*, 12–34.

Ratnapala, N. 1971. *The Katikāvatas: Laws of the Buddhist Order of Ceylon from the 12th Century to the 18th Century*. Munich: R. Kitzinger.

Reddy, W. M. 1997. "Against Constructionism: The Historical Ethnography of Emotions." *Current Anthropology* 38 (3): 327–351.

Reynolds, C. 1972. The Buddhist Monkhood in Nineteenth Century Thailand. PhD diss., Cornell University.

Reynolds, F. 2002. "Teaching Buddhism in the Postmodern University: Understanding, Critique, and Evaluation." In *Teaching Buddhism in the West: From the Wheel to the Web*, eds. V. S. Hori, Richard P. Hayes, and James Mark Shields, 3–16. London: RoutledgeCurzon.

———. 2000. "Buddhist Studies in the United States." In *The State of Buddhist Studies in the World 1972–1997*, eds. Donald K. Swearer and Somparn Promta, 110–143. Bangkok: Center for Buddhist Studies, Chulalongkorn University.

Reynolds, F. E., and Charles Hallisey. 1987. "Buddha." In *Encyclopedia of Religion*, ed. Mircea Eliade, 319–332. New York: Macmillan Publishing.

Rhys Davids, T. W., and William Stede. 1972. *Pali-English Dictionary*. London: The Pali Text Society.

Roberts, M. 1982. *Caste, Conflict and Elite Formation: The Rise of a Karāva Elite in Sri Lanka, 1500–1931*. Cambridge: Cambridge University Press.

Rogers, J. D. 2004. "Caste As a Social Category and Identity in Colonial Sri Lanka." *The Indian Economic and Social History Review* 41 (1): 51–77.

———. 1993. "Colonial Perceptions of Ethnicity and Culture in Early Nineteenth-Century Sri Lanka." In *Society and Ideology: Essays in South Asian History*, ed. Peter Robb, 97–109. Delhi: Oxford University Press.

———. 1990. "Historical Images in the British Period." In *Sri Lanka: History and the Roots of Conflict*, ed. Jonathan Spencer, 87–106. London and New York: Routledge.

Rosaldo, M. Z. 1984. "Toward an Anthropology of Self and Feeling." In *Culture Theory: Essays on Mind, Self, and Emotion*, eds. Richard A. Shweder, and Robert A. LeVine, 137–157. Cambridge: Cambridge University Press.

Rotman, A. 2003. "The Erotics of Practice: Objects and Agency in Buddhist Avadana Literature." *Journal of the American Academy of Religion* 71 (3): 555–578.

Ryan, B. 1953. *Caste in Modern Ceylon: The Sinhalese System in Transition*. New Brunswick, NJ: Rutgers University Press.

Saddhatissa, Hammalawa. 1991. "The Significance of Paritta and Its Application in the Theravāda Tradition." In *Buddhist Thought and Ritual*, ed. David J. Kalupahana, 125–137. New York: Paragon House.

Samuels, J. 2008. "Is Merit in the Milk-powder? Pursuing *Puñña* in Contemporary Sri Lanka." *Contemporary Buddhism*, 9 (1): 123–147.

———. 2007a. "Monastic Patronage and Temple Building in Contemporary Sri Lanka: Caste, Ritual Performance, and Merit." *Modern Asian Studies* 41 (4): 757–794.

———. 2007b. "When Words Are Not Enough: Eliciting Children's Experiences of Buddhist Monastic Life through Photographs." In *Visual Research Methods: Image Society, and Representation*, ed. Gregory C. Stanczak, 197–224. Thousand Oaks, CA: Sage Publications.

———. 2005. "Texts Memorized, Texts Performed: A Reconsideration of the Role of *Paritta* in Sri Lankan Monastic Education." *Journal of the International Association of Buddhist Studies* 28 (2): 339–367.

———. 2004a. "Breaking the Ethnographer's Frames: Reflections on the Use of Photo Elicitation in Understanding Sri Lankan Monastic Culture." *American Behavioral Scientist* 47 (12): 1528–1550.

———. 2004b. "Toward an Action-Oriented Pedagogy: Buddhist Texts and Monastic Education in Contemporary Sri Lanka." *Journal of the American Academy of Religion*, 72 (4): 955–972, December 2004.

———. 2003. "Establishing the Basis of the Sasana: Social Service and Ritual Performance in Contemporary Sri Lankan Monastic Training." In *Approaching the Dhamma: Buddhist Texts and Practices in South and Southeast Asia*, eds. Anne Blackburn and Jeffrey Samuels, 105–124. Seattle: BPS Pariyatti Editions.

———. 2002. Becoming Novices: Buddhist Education, Monastic Identity, and Social Service in 20th- and 21st-Century Sri Lanka. PhD diss., University of Virginia.

———. 1997. "Bodhisattva Ideal in Theravada Buddhist Theory and Practice: A Reevaluation of the Bodhisattva/Sravaka Opposition." *Philosophy East and West* 47 (3): 399–414.

Schopen, G. 1991. "Archaeology and Protestant Presuppositions in the Study of Indian Buddhism." *History of Religions* 31 (1): 1–23.

Schwartz, S. L. 2004. *Rasa: Performing the Divine in India*. New York: Columbia University Press.

Senadhira, G. 2000. *Bahu Jana Hitāya* [For the sake of all]. Colombo, Sri Lanka: Samayavardha.

Senanayaka, Palita. January 25, 2004. "Raṭa Kristiyānikaraṇaya Karannē Āṇḍuvē Anugrahaya Ätivayi [Christian conversion is done with government assistance]." Interview with Kamburugamuve Vajira. *Divayina*, Kalina.

Senaratne, J. P. 1997. *Political Violence in Sri Lanka, 1977–1990: Riots, Insurrections, Counter-Insurgencies, Foreign Intervention*. Amsterdam: VU University Press.

Seneviratne, H. L. 1999. *The Work of Kings: The New Buddhism in Sri Lanka*. Chicago: University of Chicago Press.

———, and Swarna Wickremeratne. 1980. "Bodhipuja: Collective Representations of Sri Lankan Youth." *American Ethnologist* 7 (4): 734–743.

Sesonske, A. 1965. "Performatives." *The Journal of Philosophy* 62:459–468.

Silber, I. F. 1995. *Virtuosity, Charisma, and Social Order: A Comparative Sociological Study of Monasticism in Theravada Buddhism and Medieval Catholicism*. Cambridge: Cambridge University Press.

———.1981. "Dissent Through Holiness: The Case of the Radical Renouncer in Theravada Buddhist Countries." *Numen* 28 (2): 164–193.

Smith, D. E. 1966. "The Political Monks and Monastic Reform." In *South Asian Politics and Religion*, ed. D. E. Smith, 489–509. Princeton, NJ: Princeton University Press.

Smith, W. R. 1927. *Lectures on the Religion of the Semites*. 3rd ed. 1889. Reprint. London: A & C Black.

Solomon, R. C. 2003. *Not Passion's Slave*. Oxford: Oxford University Press.

———. 1995. "The Cross-Cultural Comparison of Emotion." In *Emotions in Asian Thought: A Dialogue in Comparative Philosophy*, eds. Joel Marks and Roger T. Ames, 253–294. Albany: State University of New York Press.

Sorata Nayaka Thera, ed. 1998. *Śrī Sumaṅgala Śabdakoṣaya* [The blessed and auspicious dictionary]. 3rd ed. Colombo, Sri Lanka: S. Godage and Brothers.

Southwold, M. 1983. *Buddhism in Life: The Anthropological Study of Religion and the Sinhalese Practice of Buddhism*. Dover, NH: Manchester University Press.

———. 1982. "True Buddhism and Village Buddhism in Sri Lanka." In *Religious Organization and Religious Experience*, ed. J. Davis, 137–152. London: Academic Press.

Spencer, J. 1990a. *A Sinhalese Village in a Time of Trouble: Politics and Change in Rural Sri Lanka*. Oxford: Oxford University Press.

———. 1990b. "Collective Violence and Everyday Practice in Sri Lanka." *Modern Asian Studies* 24 (3): 603–623.

———. 1990c. "Tradition and Transformation: Recent Writing on the Anthropology of Buddhism in Sri Lanka." *Journal of the Anthropological Society of Oxford* 21 (2): 129–140.

Spiro, M. E. 1982. *Buddhism and Society: A Great Tradition and Its Burmese Vicissitudes*. 2nd ed. 1970. Reprint. Berkeley: University of California Press.

Sri Lanka Census of Population and Housing, 1981. Vol. 1, Pt. 5, District Report. Matale. 1984. Colombo, Sri Lanka: Ministry of Plan Implementation, Department of Census and Statistics.

Stark, R., and William Sims Bainbridge. 1985. "Networks of Faith: Interpersonal Bonds and Recruitment to Cults and Sects." In *The Future of Religion: Secularization, Revival and Cult Formation*, eds. R. Stark and William Sims Bainbridge, 307–324. Berkeley: University of California Press.

Stark, R., and Roger Finke. 2000. "Catholic Religious Vocations: Decline and Revival." *Review of Religious Research* 42 (2): 125–145.

Strenski, I. 1983. "On Generalized Exchange and the Domestication of the Sangha." *Man, New Series* 18 (3): 463–477.

Sugathadasa, P.H. 1985. *Population Profile of the Ampara District*. Colombo, Sri Lanka: Department of Government Printing.

Sumana, Daṅketiyē. February 6, 2000. "Sivuru Harinnē Prēmaya Nisā Novē [Disrobing is not because of love]." *Divayina*.

Sumanatissa, M. 1995. *1979 Aṅka 64 Daraṇa Piriven Adhyāpana Panataṭa Hā Niyōgamālavaṭa Saṅśōdhana Nirdēśa Kirima Sandahā Pat Karanalada Kamiṭuvē Vārtāva* [The report of the committee appointed to evaluate Act 64 of 1979]. Colombo, Sri Lanka: Ministry of Education and Higher Education.

Suravīra, E.V. April 8, 2003. "Rāmañña Mahā Nikāyē Kēndrasthānayak Vana Siyavas Samarana Balagallē Sarasvatī Pirivena [100 year anniversary of Balagalle Sarasvati Pirivena, one of the centers for Rāmañña Nikāya]." *Divayina*.

Swearer, D.K. 1970. "Lay Buddhism and the Buddhist Revival in Ceylon." *Journal of the American Academy of Religion* 38 (3): 255–275.

Tambiah, H.W. 1962. "Buddhist Ecclesiastical Law." *Journal of the Ceylon Branch of the Royal Asiatic Society* n.s., 8:71–107.

Tambiah, S.J. 1992. *Buddhism Betrayed? Religion, Politics, and Violence in Sri Lanka*. Chicago: Chicago University Press.

———. 1976. *World Conqueror and World Renouncer: A Study of Buddhism and Polity in Thailand against a Historical Background*. Cambridge: Cambridge University Press.

———. 1973. "Buddhism and This-Worldly Activity." *Modern Asian Studies* 7 (1): 1–20.

———. 1968. "The Magical Power of Words." *Man* n.s., 3 (2): 175–208.

Terwiel, B.J. 1975. *Monks and Magic: An Analysis of Religious Ceremonies in Central Thailand*. Scandinavian Institute of Asian Studies Monograph Series, vol. 24.

Thangavelu, V. n. d. "Sinhalese have Cause to Celebrate the Golden Jubilee of Gal Oya Colonization Scheme" *TamilCanadian* (available at http://www.tamilcanadian.com/page.php?cat=74&id=442)

Trainor, K. 2003. "Seeing, Feeling, Doing: Ethics and Emotions in South Asian Buddhism." *Journal of the American Academy of Religion* 71 (3): 523–530.

———. 1997. *Relics, Ritual, and Representation in Buddhism: Rematerializing the Sri Lankan Theravada Tradition*. Cambridge: Cambridge University Press.

Trawick, M. 1990a. *Notes on Love in a Tamil Family*. Berkeley: University of California Press.

———. 1990b. "The Ideology of Love in a Tamil Family." In *Divine Passions: The Social Construction of Emotion in India*, ed. Owen M. Lynch, 37–63. Berkeley: University of California Press.

Udagama, P. 1999. *Rhetoric and Reality: Education in Sri Lanka after Independence*. Colombo, Sri Lanka: Amal Publishing Company.

University Grants Commission. 1998. *Statistical Handbook 1997: Statistics on University Education in Sri Lanka*. Colombo, Sri Lanka: Division of Research and Statistics.

Uphoff, N.T. 1996. *Learning From Gal Oya: Possibilities for Participatory Development and Post-Newtonian Social Science*. 2nd ed. Ithaca, NY: Cornell University Press, 1992. Reprint. London: IT Publications.

Vākaḍa Hadrā Bhikṣhuṇi. 2001. *Bāratiya Saha Laṅkā Sāsana Itihāsaya* [*The history of the sangha in India and Sri Lanka*]. Dehivala, Colombo, Sri Lanka: Shridevi Publishers.

Vanaratna, P.R., ed. 1990. *Theravāda Sāmaṇera Baṇadaham Pota*. Colombo, Sri Lanka: Samayavardhana Pot Hala.
Vanigasinha, T. April 25, 2004. "Gihigeya Häragiya Ayyālā Mallīlā [Older brothers and younger brothers who left lay life]" *Divayina*.
van Lochem, M.J. 2004. "Children of Sera Je: The Life of Children in a Tibetan Buddhist Monastery and Their Opinion about That Life." Masters Thesis, Leiden University.
Vimalavaṇśa, Baddēgama. March 8, 1992. "Kula Daruvan 2300 Pävidi Karavīma Utum Śāsanika Kaṭayuttaki [The ordination of 2300 boys is a noble religious activity]." *Silumina*.
Walters, J.S. Forthcoming. "Gods' Play and the Buddha's Way: Varieties of Levity in Contemporary Sinhala Practice." In *Ritual Levity in South Asian Religions*, eds. Selva Raj and Corinne Dempsey. Albany: State University of New York.
———. 1992. *Rethinking Buddhist Missions*. PhD diss., University of Chicago.
Wanigaratne, R.D. 1975. *The Study of Communication Flow in Selected Villages in Sri Lanka; Case Study 2, Uhuana Colony Unit-14, Gal Oya Colonisation Scheme*. Colombo, Sri Lanka: Ministry of Information and Broadcasting.
Welch, H. 1967. *The Practice of Chinese Buddhism: 1900–1950*. Harvard East Asian Studies, vol. 26. Cambridge: Harvard University Press.
Wickramasinghe, N. 2006. *Sri Lanka in the Modern Age: A History of Contested Identities*. Honolulu: University of Hawai'i Press.
Wickramasinghe, W. 2000. Review of *Studies in Sri Lankan Tamil Linguistics and Culture: Select Papers of Professor Suseendirarajah*, by K. Balasubramanian, K. Ranamalar, and R. Subathini. *Sambhāṣā: Vidyālaṅkāra 125 Vana Samaru Uḷela Venuven Paḷakerena Śāstrīya Saṅgrahaya*, 11:973–984.
Wickremegamage, Candra. December 27, 1999. "Tavakalika Paevidda Ratata Yahapatak [Temporary ordination is better for the country]." *Laṅkadīpa*.
Wijayaratna, M. 1990. *Buddhist Monastic Life: According to the Texts of the Theravada Tradition*, trans. Claude Grangier and Steven Collins. Originally published as *Le Moine Bouddhiste*. Cambridge: Cambridge University Press.
Winslow, D. 2004. "Introduction." In *Economy, Culture, and Civil War in Sri Lanka*, eds. D. Winslow, and Michael D. Woost, 31–39. Bloomington and Indianapolis: Indiana University Press.
Witanachchi, L.K. 1999. *Customs and Rituals of Sinhala Buddhists*. Dehiwala, Sri Lanka: Sri Devi.
Wittberg, P. 1996. "'Real' Religious Communities: A Study of Authentication in New Roman Catholic Religious Orders." *Religion and the Social Order* 6:149–174.
Wyatt, D.K. 1996. *Studies in Thai History: Collected Articles*. Chiang Mai: Silkworm Books.
———. 1966. "The Buddhist Monkhood as an Avenue of Social Mobility in Traditional Thai Society." *Sinlapakon* 10 (1): 41–52.
Yalman, N. 1967. *Under the Bo Tree: Studies in Caste, Kinship, and Marriage, in the Interior of Ceylon*. Berkeley and Los Angeles: University of California Press.
Yayasena, Äsala. March 31, 1992. "Kula Daruvan 2300 Denā Ataraṭa Draviḍa Daruvan 100 Ätulu Karanna [Please ordain 100 Tamils with the 2300 boys]." *Laṅkadīpa*.

Index

Abeysekara, Ananda, xxix, 8, 113n20
abhidharma, 68
action-oriented pedagogy, 72–73, 74
aesthetics: locally determined, 53; and rituals, 50; shared, xxii; and social bonds, 42
aesthetics of emotion, xxii, 8–9, 29, 32, 42, 85, 105–106, 108; and confidence, 108; and social bonds, 106
aesthetic standard, xxiii, xxiv, 23, 29; and the Buddha, 23; contextualized, 42; effects of social bonds on, 29; indeterminate nature of, 29; learned through ritual performance, 76, 78–79; locally determined, 53, 72, 90, 105–106, 107; and morality, 29; shaped by the past, xxiii, 14, 94–95, 105–106; and the *Vinaya*, 20, 29; ways of communicating, 75
affection: role of in shaping human relationships, xxii; signs of, xxi; and sustaining Buddhist communities, 81
agrarian revolution, 26, 125n12; and ethnic implications, 125n13
agricultural colonies, 26–27, 56–57, 88
ākalpa (behavior and deportment), 25, 71–72, 125n8, 136n20
alcoholism, 27, 33–34, 133n25, 140n14
Almond, Philip, xxvi
alms-giving *(dāna)* ritual: xxiii–xxiv, 18–19, 39–40, 90, 120n41, 125n11; and caste, 141n32; and concern for the laity, 133n28; and shortage of monastics, 86–87, 102, 108, 138n5
Ampāra District, 56–57, 125n13; social and economic problems in, 56–57
Ānanda, 68
Anāthapiṇḍaka, 68
Anurādhapura District, 26–27; census data, 27, 125n13, 126n15, 139n7; educational levels, 126n15
appearance, monastic, 3, 72; effects of, 27; and hair length, 23, 33, 72, 78, 137n32; influenced by the past, xxiii, 14, 105–106; learned through ritual performance, 78; locally determined, 28, 29–30, 42, 105–106; and social bonds, 3, 29. See also *ākalpa*
Ariyadhamma, Pānadurē, 127n29
Asoka, King, 68
attracting the heart, xxv, 31, 34, 35, 40, 42, 49, 52, 54, 76, 78, 79, 104, 108, 133n28; and monastic appearance, 137n32; role in protecting Buddhism, 41, 83; and speech, 45
Austin, J. L., 75, 113n17

Bainbridge, William, 48, 49, 61–62
Baṇdhāra, R. Amaravaṇśa, 141n26
Batgama (palanquin bearer) caste, 98, 116n21, 121n52
behavior, monastic, xxiii, 3, 72; and canonical norms, 29; changing nature of, 13; exhibited through speech, 52, 60; learned through ritual performance, 78; locally determined, xxviii, 29, 42, 85, 105–106; negotiating, 13; shaped by the past, xxiii, 14, 24, 105–106; and social bonds, 3, 12–13, 29, 107, 108; and temple activities, 73–74. See also *Vinaya; ākalpa*)
Bell, Catherine, 74, 79
Beravā (drummer) caste, 6–8, 116n21, 117n22
Berkwitz, Stephen, xxvi, 41
Betrayal of Buddhism, 134n4
Blackburn, Anne M., xxiii, 111n2; 113n18
bodhipūjā rituals, 70, 127n28
Bond, George D., 119n32
bonds, social: and normative behavior, 12–13
Bourdieu, Pierre, 74, 76

About the Author

Jeffrey Samuels is an associate professor in the Department of Philosophy and Religion at Western Kentucky University. He received a PhD in history of religions from the University of Virginia in 2002. Along with co-editing a book (with Anne M. Blackburn) on Buddhist texts and practices in South and Southeast Asia, he has published more than a dozen articles on monastic education, Buddhist rituals, and temple patronage in books and journals such as *Contemporary Buddhism*, *Journal of the American Academy of Religion*, *Journal of the International Association of Buddhist Studies*, and *Modern Asian Studies*. He has also received generous support for research and writing from the Fulbright Commission, Metanexus Institute, and National Endowment for the Humanities. He is currently writing a social history of Theravada Buddhism in Malaysia.

Production Notes for Samuels / *Attracting the Heart*

Jacket design by Julie Matsuo-Chun

Text design by University of Hawai'i Press Production Staff with text in Goudy Hawn and display in Hiroshige Hawn

Composition by Lucille C. Aono

Printing and binding by Edwards Brothers, Inc.

Printed on 55# EB Natural, 360 ppi